AbacusLaw
Complete Law Office Software

A Hands-On Tutorial and Guide

THOMAS F. GOLDMAN, JD

Attorney at Law
Professor Emeritus
Bucks County Community College

WORKING SMARTER SERIES

Prentice Hall

Boston   Columbus   Indianapolis   New York   San Francisco   Upper Saddle River
Amsterdam   Cape Town   Dubai   London   Madrid   Milan   Munich   Paris   Montreal   Toronto
Delhi   Mezico City   Sao Paolo   Sydney   Hong Kong   Seoul   Singapore   Taipei   Tokyo

Editorial Director: Vernon Anthony
Senior Acquisitions Editor: Gary Bauer
Editorial Assistant: Megan Heintz
Director of Marketing: David Gesell
Marketing Manager: Thomas Hayward
Senior Marketing Assistant: Les Roberts
Project Manager: Christina Taylor

Senior Operations Supervisor: Pat Tonneman
Senior Art Director: Jayne Conte
Composition: Naomi Sysak
Printer/Binder: Bind-Rite Graphics/Robbinsville
Cover Printer: Lehigh-Phoenix Color/Hagerstown
Text Font: Meridien

10 9 8 7 6 5 4 3 2

Prentice Hall
is an imprint of

www.pearsonhighered.com

ISBN-10: 0-13-139172-0
ISBN-13: 978-0-13-139172-7

Contents

SECTION 5 ▪ The Basics: Creating Reports (Hardcopy or Electronic)   128

SECTION 6 ▪ Customizing AbacusLaw   144

SECTION 10 ▪ Forms, Templates, and More Stuff   224

From the Author

If you have ever worked in a law office without a program like AbacusLaw where everything had to be done manually with paper records (now called hard copy), you know the total frustration: Tasks like checking a name for a conflict of interest using card files and lists, and not being sure if someone had removed one of the cards and caused you to miss a conflict. In large firms, physically circulating paper lists of names can take days before a conflict check can be resolved. With AbacusLaw, anyone with computer access can instantly check a name against a database of every person, company, and party that has had any contact with the firm, with the file information instantly popping up on the computer screen.

Without an integrated program like AbacusLaw, keeping track of paper time slips, phone calls, and activities may result in calls from the billing clerk to justify your lost time. With AbacusLaw, every activity can be automatically recorded. It makes you wonder how much revenue firms could be losing when staff forget to write a time slip, phone record message, or similar activity.

Academically, its greatest use has been having students treat me as a client and the course as a case or matter, tracking their time in class, reading, taking tests, meeting with other students in study groups, in court observing procedures, and even commuting to class. When grades are issued and questions asked, taking out the "bill for their time" has resulted in a quick, "I guess I really did not put the time in," or "I put in more time, it is just not on the bill," inevitably starting a discussion about the "real world" obligation to keep accurate records. Occasionally, it starts an ethical discussion of the obligation to keep accurate records. It is also a wonderful opportunity to discuss study habits for success.

For paralegal students, this is a great starting point for entry into the real world of the practice of law, learning the discipline of accurate record keeping—especially time records. For law students, this inculcates the habit of accurate timekeeping so they will not lose revenue. It is also a good introduction to developing the critical skills for successful law office management.

For any law firm, the use of the accounting program in AbacusLaw will provide the tools for avoiding ethical issues like commingling of funds, and provide an ethical safety device, because the program will not permit overdrawing trust accounts.

If you did not get an access code for the full version of the program, you may download a free 30-day version of AbacusLaw at www.abacuslaw.com to use with this tutorial and guide to see the real value of the software.

Thomas F. Goldman

Message to Students

Employers are increasingly looking to hire people with real-world experience. For the student, this is hard to accomplish while in school. In the area of technology, students can acquire real-world experience by using the actual programs used in the law offices in which they wish to work. AbacusLaw is provided for use with this guide, the actual program currently in use in law firms and government offices around the world. With the academic version of this tutorial and guide, an access code is provided that gives you a three-year unlimited license to use all of the features of the program.

At a recent conference of one of the national paralegal organizations, a question about learning one program and then going to work in an office where they used another was asked. The consensus of the paralegal managers was that it was more important that the person they hire be familiar with a program similar to what they would use, because they all offered specific in-office instruction and training.

AbacusLaw offers you the opportunity to learn how to use a practice management and law office accounting program. Transferring skills in using contact, case, and calendar management databases is a simple matter, taking at most hours and not days of training, making you a preferred person to hire.

Employers also want to see some evidence of what is called soft skills, like a good work ethic. How does one do that? You can do that by showing prospective employers a comprehensive portfolio of quality work you produced in your courses. Portfolios demonstrate that you have mastered some of the skills necessary to complete tasks successfully. Keeping a comprehensive, detailed listing of the time spent in your course demonstrates your discipline and understanding of keeping time records, which are at the heart of the financial success of any law office. Using AbacusLaw timekeeping functions over a number of courses will show you have mastered the discipline of timekeeping. Only a person with discipline and perseverance will maintain a complete and comprehensive log that can be shown to a prospective employer.

For the student concerned with grades, keeping track of the time spent is a good way to master the discipline of devoting time in the most productive way. It does take a little soul searching, at least initially, to look at your time records and admit you did or did not spend enough time reading in the library or working in a study group. Which activity was the most beneficial?

Among the features you may find useful are the contact manager and the calendar function. The contact manager keeps track of contact information for family and friends, classmates, and prospective employers. In the real world, having a list of people whom you can call for help is one of the most valuable assets you can have. In the contact manager, you can record areas of expertise to help you find the information when you need to find a person with that knowledge.

The calendar function allows you to develop time-management skills by recording future events and making a to-do list that automatically pops up on your desktop each day.

Message to Instructors

It is rare that a software company is so committed to educating future lawyers and paralegals that it makes available a multiyear license of the full version of its top-of-the-line program. In these days it is equally rare when the publisher and the software company come together to provide the software and a tutorial at an affordable price. As an educator, I am pleased to be a part of this joint venture between AbacusLaw and Pearson.

Faculty and program directors asked if they could have a program that could be introduced in an introductory course and used throughout a student's academic career, or introduced in civil litigation, technology, or other courses. Criteria for the program were that it be a full version of the software that did not expire after a semester, and that a system be provided to eliminate CDs that have time-limit expiration. Additionally, students would need their own copy that could be used on their personal portable or desktop computer with the software transferable from one computer to another. Perhaps more importantly, the instructor should not have to spend more than one hour to introduce the software in the classroom, and detailed instructions needed to be provided to allow the nontechnology-trained students to learn on their own, not on class time. Finally, it needed to be affordable.

The academic version of this tutorial and guide meets these criteria. Yes, there is a time limit—*three years*. Students have full use of the program for three years from the time they register the software, not some arbitrary year-end date on a CD.

Students can begin using the program almost immediately, learning the discipline of accurate timekeeping. Each course in the curriculum can be set up as a separate matter and each instructor as the client to whom bills are regularly issued. Review of these "bills" can be the basis of study skills discussions, helping the students to be more effective and successful in their academic career.

Reviewing "bills" is also an opportunity to discuss the ethical issues of accurate timekeeping and the use of time records in proving the value when a bill is questioned in the real world. As a starting point for a discussion of timekeeping, videos are available on my companion Web site (www.pearson highered.com/goldman).

Tutorial exercises are provided to enable quick installation and setup of AbacusLaw. Further lessons are provided to allow students to personalize the appearance of the program, including adding a daily organizer to their desktop on which they can add events and deadlines. Additionally, students can enter time tickets and bill for events, such as telephone calls to other students discussing the class. More advanced tutorials introduce the concepts of calendar rules, form filling, and use of mail merge.

Background explanations of the technology, law office management concepts, and the ethical rules are discussed throughout the tutorial lessons.

LECTURE OUTLINE—INITIAL SOFTWARE INTRODUCTION

TOPICS IN THE TUTORIAL AND GUIDE

- What is an integrated software program?
- How can I learn to use AbacusLaw?
- How can I use the tutorial and guide to learn AbacusLaw?

USING ABACUSLAW IN THIS COURSE

- Set up course as a matter (case)
- Set up instructor as the client
- Obligation to record time
  - In class
  - Reading assignments
  - In the library
  - In study groups
  - Preparing assignments
  - Meeting with instructor
- Calendar
  - Enter all class times in calendar
  - Enter all exam dates and times
  - Enter all assignment deadlines
- Contacts
  - Enter all members of study group

ASSIGNMENTS

Week 1

Manually record time spent in class activity.
Read Introduction.

Week 2

Manually record time spent in class activity.
Read Section 1.
    Install software.
Read Section 2.
    Set up personal copy of AbacusLaw.
    Enter course calendar information.

Week 3

Manually record time spent in class activity.
Read Section 3.

> Add instructor as a client.

> Add course as a matter.

Read Section 4.

> Enter student as a timekeeper.

> Manually enter kept time slips as time tickets.

Week 4

Read Section 5.

> Enter study group members as contacts.

> Prepare contacts report.

> Prepare a billing report for course to instructor.

> Prepare a productivity report for student as a timekeeper.

LECTURE OUTLINE—CIVIL LITIGATION

TOPICS IN THE TUTORIAL AND GUIDE

- What is an integrated software program?
- How can I learn to use AbacusLaw?
- How can I use the tutorial and guide to learn AbacusLaw?

USING ABACUSLAW IN THIS COURSE

- Set up course as a matter (case)
- Set up instructor as the client
- Obligation to record time
  - In class
  - Reading assignments
  - In the library
  - In study groups
  - Preparing assignments
  - Meeting with instructor
- Calendar
  - Enter all class times in calendar
  - Enter all exam dates and times
  - Enter all assignment deadlines
- Contacts
  - Enter all members of study group

ASSIGNMENTS

Week 1

Manually record time spent in class activity.
Read Introduction.

Week 2

Manually record time spent in class activity.
Read Section 1.
    Install software.
Read Section 2.
        Set up personal copy of AbacusLaw.
        Enter course calendar information.

Week 3

Manually record time spent in class activity.
Read Section 3.
        Add instructor as a client.
        Add course as a matter.
Read Section 4.
        Enter student as a timekeeper.
        Manually enter kept time slips as time tickets.

Week 4

Read Section 5.
        Enter study group members as contacts.
        Prepare contacts report.
        Prepare a billing report for course to instructor.
        Prepare a productivity report for student as a timekeeper.

Week 5

Read Section 9.
        Create calendar rules for litigation using local court rules.
        Create local statute of limitation deadlines.

Week 6

Read Section 10.
        Create templates for notification of deposition, hearing, and meeting.
        Create standard form pleading template.

LECTURE OUTLINE—LAW OFFICE MANAGEMENT AND ACCOUNTING

TOPICS IN THE TUTORIAL AND GUIDE

- What is an integrated software program?
- How can I learn to use AbacusLaw?
- How can I use the tutorial and guide to learn AbacusLaw?

USING ABACUSLAW IN THIS COURSE

- Set up course as a matter (case)
- Set up instructor as the client
- Obligation to record time
    - In class
    - Reading assignments
    - In the library
    - In study groups
    - Preparing assignments
    - Meeting with instructor
- Calendar
    - Enter all class times in calendar
    - Enter all exam dates and times
    - Enter all assignment deadlines
- Contacts
    - Enter all members of study group

ASSIGNMENTS

Week 1

Manually record time spent in class activity.
Read Introduction.

Week 2

Manually record time spent in class activity.
Read Section 1.
    Install software.
Read Section 2.
    Set up personal copy of AbacusLaw.
    Enter course calendar information.

Week 3

Manually record time spent in class activity.

Read Section 3.

    Add instructor as a client.

    Add course as a matter.

Read Section 4.

    Enter student as a timekeeper.

    Manually enter kept time slips as time tickets.

Week 4

Read Section 5.

    Enter study group members as contacts.

    Prepare contacts report.

    Prepare a billing report for course to instructor.

    Prepare a productivity report for student as a timekeeper.

Week 5

Read Section 7.

    Set up a trust account for a client.

    Make deposits and payments from a trust account.

    Reconcile a client trust account.

    Transfer funds from a client account to an operating account.

    Set up and use a law firm operating account.

Week 6

Read Section 8.

    Set up an employee payroll profile.

    Prepare a payroll and issue checks.

    Pay recurring firm bills.

Acknowledgments

A special thanks to everyone at Abacus Data Systems for their help, cooperation, and support.

A special thanks to Judd Kessler, president of Abacus, without whose support and encouragement there would not be an academic version. He was one of the earliest supporters of the academic community, providing free software, training, and scholarships for instructors.

Brian Hays, who is the brains behind the creation of the software, and worked hard to make it all come together.

Bob Elliott, a constant source of encouragement and a good friend—for only a good friend would allow me to use his bike and drive his Porsche—coordinated every aspect of getting the software and the programs to the academic community and never said no to any request for help or support.

Brian Blakistone, Tomas Suros, Craig Swartz, Glen Guy, Mike McMahon, and William McCartney for their help and insight into the program. They spent time patiently explaining the concepts and features of the software such as calendar rules and forms creation, reviewed material, and provided critical comments so necessary in making it useable for the average user.

The support desk at Abacus, especially Cheryl Lynn, Shannon Moxley, and Scott Heist, who endured numerous questions at all hours to help me install and reinstall, run, and test the program on multiple operating systems.

My friend and breakfast companion, John Bradley, Professor Emeritus and former director of the Learning Resources Center at Bucks County Community College, for not cancelling our weekly breakfast meetings even when he knew it would be to discuss my latest project and to review the manuscript from initial draft to final manuscript, and for testing every keystroke to be sure they really worked.

Students in my Technology in the Law Office class at Thomas Edison State College who took the class on the New York Times Knowledge Network.

Professor David Freeman and the students in his technology class at Community College of Philadelphia for beta testing the tutorial and software.

About the Author

Thomas F. Goldman, JD, is Professor Emeritus of Bucks County Community College. He was a professor of Law and Management, and former director of the Center for Legal Studies and of the Paralegal Studies Program. He developed the online Technology in the Law Office course for the New York Times Knowledge Network, which he teaches for Thomas Edison State College, and is a member and mentor of their Paralegal Studies Program Advisory Board, and developed the Advanced Litigation Support and Technology Certificate Program.

He is an author of textbooks in paralegal studies and technology, including *The Paralegal Professional*, in its third edition; *Accounting and Taxation for Paralegals*; *Technology in the Law Office*, in its second edition; *Civil Litigation: Process and Procedures*; *SmartDraw: A Hands-On Tutorial and Guide*; and *Basic Skills in Voice Recognition*. He is also the author and executive producer of the video series The Paralegal Professional, in which he is an occasional actor.

An accounting and economics graduate of Boston University and of Temple University School of Law, Professor Goldman has an active international law, technology law, and litigation practice. He has worked extensively with paralegals and received the Legal Support Staff Guild award. He was elected the Legal Secretaries Association Boss of the Year for his contribution to cooperative education by encouraging the use of paralegals and legal assistants in law offices. He also received the Bucks County Community College Alumni Association Professional Achievement Award. He has been an educational consultant on technology to educational institutions and major corporations, and is a frequent speaker and lecturer on educational, legal, and technological issues. He has served on the American Association for Paralegal Education Board and served as the founding chair of the Technology Task Force, where he initiated the Train the Trainer program.

Introduction

(How Do I Use This Tutorial and Guide?)

- Using This Tutorial and Guide
- Layout and Design of This Tutorial and Guide
- Navigating through the Tutorial Using Your Mouse
- Can I Learn Everything in AbacusLaw?
- Learning How to Use a Software Program
- Can I Do Every Tutorial in This Guide with My Version of AbacusLaw?
- History (Very Brief) of Law Office Management
- What Is an Integrated Software Program?
- What Is a Database? Electronic Database Basics
- What Do the Practice Manager and Abacus Accounting Look Like?
- Productivity
- Your Expectations

USING THIS TUTORIAL AND GUIDE

This book was designed to be both a reference guide and a series of hands-on step-by-step tutorials on specific features of AbacusLaw, or as it is more commonly called, Abacus. As a reference guide it quickly answers questions, and as a hands-on step-by-step tutorial, it helps you learn everything about AbacusLaw (well, almost everything). Each section provides answers to the most frequently asked questions users have about the program as well as examples and procedures to guide you in learning and using the features and tools in the program.

LAYOUT AND DESIGN OF THIS TUTORIAL AND GUIDE

Each tutorial answers a question by providing a brief explanation of the underlying concept and a step-by-step example of how to do it. The procedures are presented with the **GOAL**, **ACTION**, and **RESULT** in a step-by-step chart.

GOAL		

This section of the chart presents the goal of each step in the tutorial.

	ACTION	

This section specifies the action required to achieve the goal.

The action may be a mouse click, a keystroke, or a combination of both. In the step-by-step tutorials an ACTION such as **CLICK** will be in bold, and the text describing the item to be selected or text to be entered will be in *italics*. For example,

CLICK
Point mouse to an item, then
CLICK and RELEASE LEFT MOUSE BUTTON

CLICK refers to a mouse click (generally the LEFT MOUSE BUTTON unless **RIGHT CLICK** appears). Clicking the RIGHT MOUSE BUTTON generally opens a menu of options or help text related to the specific action being taken (referred to as Context Sensitive). The following chart shows the most frequently used commands, shortcuts, and specialty terminology you will use in AbacusLaw. Most actions, except for typing text, can be completed using the left mouse button and occasionally a keyboard key, such as the Control (Ctrl) or the Shift (Shift) key.

As you progress through the tutorial, the on-screen RESULT of the ACTION or a sample screen is presented for each step.

This section of the chart shows you the actual displays you should see on your computer screen. If there are alternatives or options, a representative screen will be shown.

NAVIGATING THROUGH THE TUTORIAL USING YOUR MOUSE

You will use your mouse to access the various menus. The following is a list of the most common mouse actions and the results.

GOAL	ACTION	RESULT
START PROGRAM FROM DESKTOP	**CLICK** *AbacusLaw icon* OR *Abacus Accounting* on your desktop	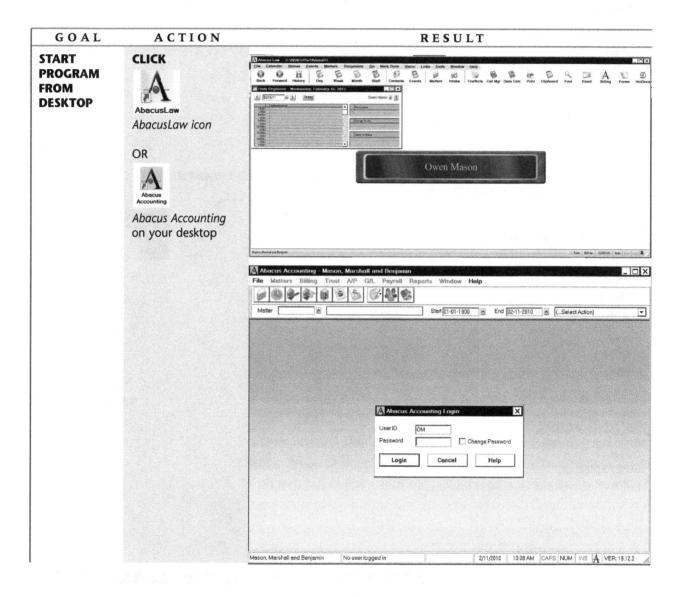

GOAL	ACTION	RESULT
START ABACUSLAW PROGRAM FROM PROGRAM LIST IF NO ICON APPEARS ON DESKTOP	**CLICK** OR start **SELECT** All Programs **CLICK** A AbacusLaw	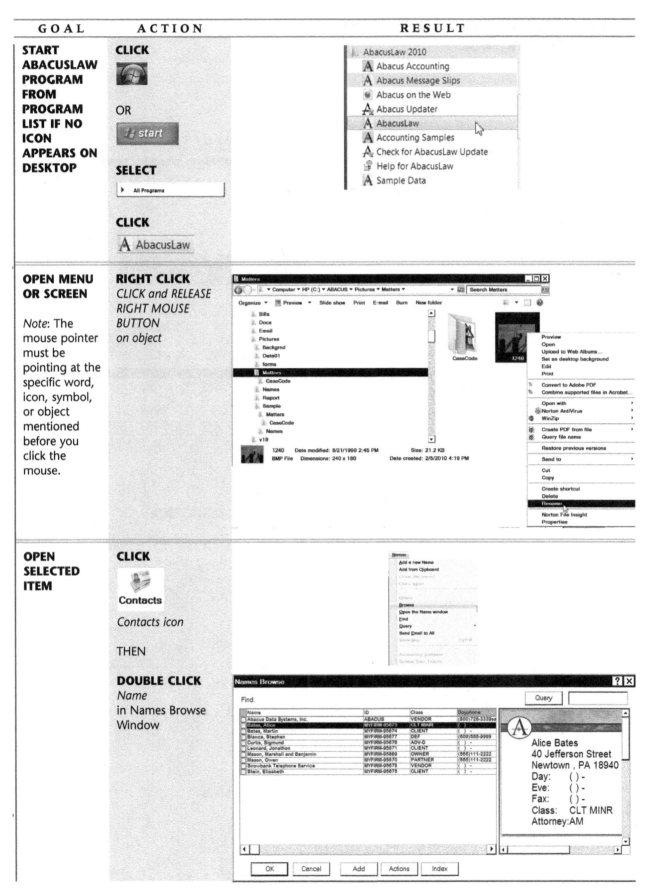
OPEN MENU OR SCREEN *Note*: The mouse pointer must be pointing at the specific word, icon, symbol, or object mentioned before you click the mouse.	**RIGHT CLICK** *CLICK and RELEASE RIGHT MOUSE BUTTON on object*	
OPEN SELECTED ITEM	**CLICK** Contacts *Contacts icon* THEN **DOUBLE CLICK** *Name* in Names Browse Window	

GOAL	ACTION	RESULT
SELECT TEXT IN A DOCUMENT	**SELECT TEXT** **PLACE** Cursor before the first letter or number **PRESS and HOLD** Left mouse button **DRAG** The mouse over the letters and numbers to be selected **RELEASE** Mouse button	IFIRM INFO FIRM INFO
SELECT AN ITEM IN A WINDOW OR LIST	**PLACE CURSOR** On item AND **DOUBLE CLICK**	
OPEN CONTEXT-SENSITIVE HELP MENU	**CLICK** *Help* OR **CLICK** *?*	
DUPLICATE THE CURRENT SCREEN OR FORM Note: *Clone* is the same terminology as *duplicate*.	**CLICK** *Clone*	

GOAL	ACTION	RESULT
ENTER INFORMATION FOR A NEW MATTER (CASE)	**ENTER** Information in blanks	*Adding a new Matter window with tabs: 1 Standard, 2 Notes, 3 Linked Names, 4 Linked Events, 5 Linked Docs, 6 Emails. Fields: Matter, File/case# (1235), Attorney, Case Code, Court, Court Case #, Opened, Closed. User-defined fields: User1, User2, User3, User4. Buttons: Save, Cancel, Add, Clone, Delete, Query, Index MATTER.*
SEARCH FOR A CASE *Note: Matter is the same terminology as case.*	**CLICK** **Matters** *Matters icon* OR **CLICK** *Browse* on Matters menu	*Matters menu: Add a new Matter, Clone this record, Clone again, Intake Forms, Delete, Browse, Open the Matter window, Find, Query, Accounting Summary, Browse Time Tickets*
MAKE A SELECTION OR CHANGE A SELECTION BY CHECKING OR UNCHECKING APPROPRIATE BOX	**CLICK** *Check or Uncheck*	*Select Components window: In the list below, select the checkboxes for the options that you want to install.* ☑ AbacusLaw — 44369 k ☐ Abacus MessageSlips — 3070 k ☐ CompanionLink — 4836 k ☑ Time, Billing & Accounting — 95466 k Disk Space Required: 139835 k Disk Space Remaining: 371455361 k Buttons: < Back, Next >, Cancel

GOAL	ACTION	RESULT
USE BACKWARD OR FORWARD ARROW TO MAKE A SELECTION OR FIND ITEM	**CLICK** *Left* or *right arrow* OR **USE** Shortcut keys Back **PRESS BOTH KEYS** *Shift Key + F7* (Forward) **PRESS BOTH KEYS**	Back Forward History
USE UP ARROW TO OPEN A SELECTION OF OPTIONS	**CLICK** *Up arrow*	Atty
USE UP OR DOWN ARROW TO SELECT A SETTING	**CLICK** *Up* or *down arrow* to select	0

Event in Rule PI SOL 2 Personal Injury 2 year Staute of Limitations

Event number   1   ☐ Allow event number editing

What   SOL

Description   2 Year Statute of Limitations   Form...

Rule Calculation   Event Details   Secondary Calculation

Interval   2   Days ▼   Relative to event#   0

Move weekend date to
  ◉ Use System Optio
  ○ Friday
  ○ Monday

Days
Court days
Weeks
Months
Quarters
Years

OK   Cancel   Help

GOAL	ACTION	RESULT
USE DOWN ARROW TO OPEN SELECTIONS OF OPTIONS	**CLICK** *Down arrow*	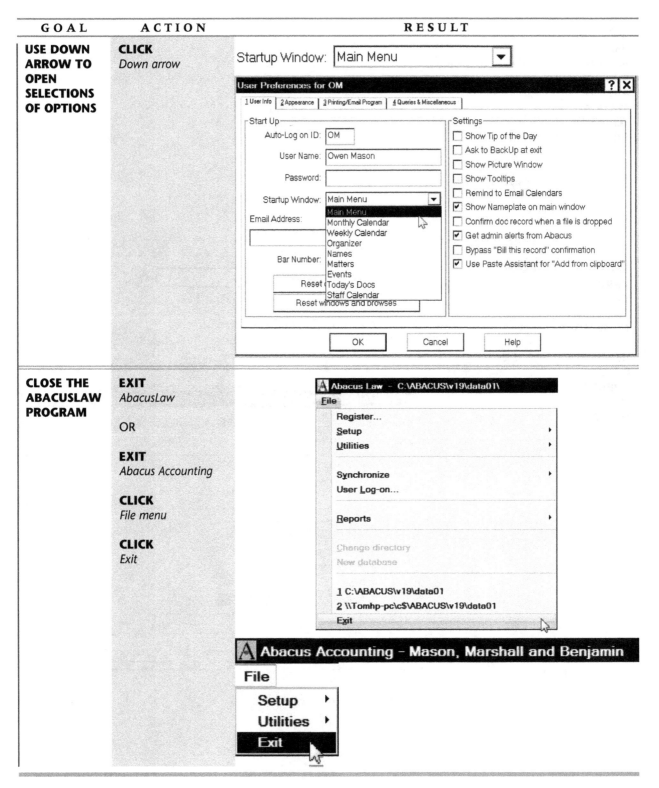
CLOSE THE ABACUSLAW PROGRAM	**EXIT** *AbacusLaw* OR **EXIT** *Abacus Accounting* **CLICK** *File menu* **CLICK** *Exit*	

The following example shows a sample tutorial including a brief explanation of a topic, in this case the use of the History buttons.

WHERE WAS I?

Ever try to find a page you were working on earlier in a session? Internet browsers allow you to back up or move forward using the arrows at the top of the screen. AbacusLaw also allows you to move backward and forward using the arrows in the menu bar and will show you the last pages or forms you were working on—your History.

TIP

You can also use the back and forward arrow buttons to move through the history list.

Back   Forward   History

History of Action: Moving Backward and Forward

GOAL	ACTION	RESULT
SEE WHAT I DID	CLICK History *History icon*	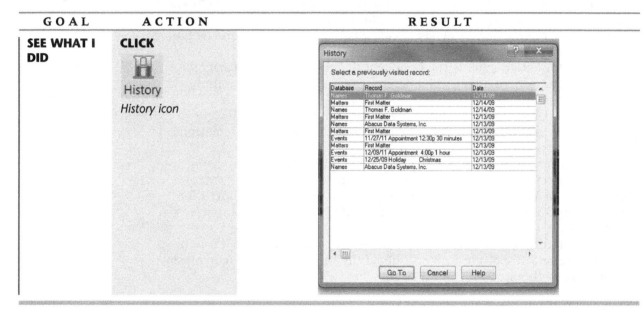

TIPS AND NOTES

Tips and **Notes** are inserted in the tutorials. These contain shortcuts, additional methods of completing the task, or other information you may find helpful.
For example:

> **TIP:** You can review your day's work to be sure you billed for everything you did by scrolling through the History for the day.

CAN I LEARN EVERYTHING IN ABACUSLAW?

With enough time you can master every aspect of AbacusLaw and modify almost every function and tool. AbacusLaw is a very powerful program that puts that power in the hands of novice users as well as power users. If you are not a computer power user, do not worry. This tutorial will get you up to speed quickly using all of the basic and some of the advanced features. As you become familiar with the functions you will be able to change, modify, and customize the program to your way of working. If you are a power user, you are probably already customizing the program, and this tutorial and guide will help you show others how to use the program.

Best advice: Complete each of the tutorials in order before changing the defaults and customizing the program. Each tutorial builds on the lessons and terminology of the prior tutorials.

LEARNING HOW TO USE A SOFTWARE PROGRAM

Learning how to use all the features in a modern integrated software program can be daunting, if not frightening. There appear to be so many options and possibilities that it can become confusing. The reality is that most of these programs have a few basic or core functions that can be customized for personal use or preference. A good example is a word processor, a program used by almost everyone. It has basic functions—entering, saving, and printing text. Word processors also have advanced features, some rarely used or even known to many users, like the ability to create tables of authorities and merge names with form letters (mail merge).

Most of the information is the same and fits into some basic categories, and can be entered in a number of different ways and looked at in a number of different formats.

In AbacusLaw, the information is stored in four categories, or as programmers like to refer to them, databases: names, events, matters, and documents.

In this tutorial and guide, you will first enter information using a simple input screen to make you familiar with the kinds of information that may be saved. Then you will be shown how to enter the same information using alternative methods, such as intake documents and specialty input forms.

Before starting we will try to explain what an integrated program and database are and dispel the mystery, hopefully eliminating the fear most people have of them.

CAN I DO EVERY TUTORIAL IN THIS GUIDE WITH MY VERSION OF ABACUSLAW?

All of the basic tutorials in this guide use the features found in AbacusLaw Gold version, which contains both the Practice Manager and Abacus Accounting. AbacusLaw, like many programs, is available in different versions: Classic and Gold. The Classic version only contains the practice management functions, such as calendars, case management, and contact lists. The Gold version adds accounting functions such as time tickets, trust accounting and check registers, payroll, and general ledger functions.

AbacusLaw may be upgraded to include add-on features such as PDF fillable forms for specific jurisdictions and courts, and specialty practice packs with specialized forms for practice areas like estates and family law. Samples of these add-ons will be shown to demonstrate how they function, but you may not be able to use these features if they are not part of your program license. As with all software, the number of users is limited by the number of user licenses purchased. A single user system is shown as well as how multiuser systems may add additional users.

COMPARISON OF FEATURES

Practice Management
(Available in Classic and Gold)

Core Features

Legal Calendaring

Rules-based Calendaring

Contact Management

Case Management

Document Management

Document Assembly

Conflict of Interest Checking

Phone Messages

Instant Messaging

Auto-fill Court Forms

Reporting

Remote Access

Additional Features

PDA and BlackBerry
    Synchronization

Laptop Synchronization

Outlook Integration

Intake Screens

Customizable Fields and Screens

Multi-Office Synchronization

Home Office Synchronization

Staff Calendar

Optional Features

AbacusLaw Specialty Versions

ELaw Integration

Federal Rules

State Rules

CA County Local Rules

CA Judicial Council Forms

Fortress—Advantage Database
    Server

Time, Billing, and Accounting
(Available only in Gold)

Core Features

Time Capture

Billing

General Ledger

Accounts Payable

Check Writing

Trust Accounting

Financial Reports

Payroll

Additional Features

Interim Statements

Past Due Notices

Credit Card Processing
    Integration

Online Bank Synchronization

Customizable Billing

Work in Process Reports

Split Billing

Financial Report Groups

1099 Reporting

Printing Deposit Slips

Budgeting

Automatic Tracking and Billing
    for Phone Calls

TalkTIMR Cell Phone Billing
    Integration

Optional Features

Cost Recovery

Electronic Billing

Real Estate Closing Package
    Integration

Multiple Company Books

HISTORY (VERY BRIEF) OF LAW OFFICE MANAGEMENT

Traditionally, law offices were managed with paper: paper forms, paper calendars, contacts lists on paper file cards, paper documents and correspondences in paper file folders and cabinets, and paper ledgers, books, and checkbooks.

The computer opened the law office to electronic creation of documents, first with word processors, then with electronic calendar programs for printing out paper calendars, programs for keeping records of names of clients, opposing attorneys, and opposing parties, and more recently, electronic checkbook programs. Slowly, preparation of all the paper stuff was being done using computers. Nonessential paper items like calendars and personal telephone directories are stored on the computer and not printed out. Of course, court filings, as well as correspondences are still printed out on paper. However, one software program performed one function and the same information had to be entered into each program separately.

Office management software has developed from the individual software applications—timekeeping, contact management, billing, accounting, and report generation—into a unified or integrated program, where information is entered once and is shared among the different specialty functions, each piece of information or data being linked to others when needed.

With the growth of computer use and desire for greater efficiency, the use of paper has decreased as courts and the government agencies accept or even require electronic copies be filed, and client and opposing attorneys accept and use e-mail and other instant messaging protocols.

WHAT IS AN INTEGRATED SOFTWARE PROGRAM?

Most of the functions of law office management include the use of the same data or information:

- Names
- Events
- Individual client matters (cases)
- Financial information

Integrated programs use the same information or data in performing a number of tasks, such as:

- Calendaring
- Contact management
- Case management
- Conflict checks
- Completion of forms
- Document management
- Timekeeping
- Billing
- Check writing
- Payroll
- Trust account reporting

Programs like AbacusLaw integrate these functions into one program shell that allows the sharing of information among the functions.

A database or sets of databases are used to save the information. This information can then be searched and sorted for the specific information desired, and assembled and reported as a response to a query, such as, what are the appointments for today?

A database is a collection of records, such as your address book or contacts list, which has a name, address, city, and phone number for each person in it, as shown below.

CLIENT	OPPOSING PARTY	CLIENT/MATTER NUMBER
Jonathan Leonard	Robert Howard	08-012

MATTER		LITIGATION ☐
Leonard vs. Howard, et.al MV Accident		NON LITIGATION ☐ MATTER FILE FOLDER

CLIENT ADDRESS	PHONE
152 Timber Ridge Road, Peidmont,IL	555 432 2098

CLIENT CONTACT	HOME PHONE	OPPOSING COUNSEL
Jonathan Leonard	555 432 2098	Teven Rich

OPPOSING COUNSEL ADDRESS	PHONE
424 Michigan Ave. Marengo, IL	555 856 4267

RESPONSIBLE LAWYER	ASSIGNED LAWYERS	FEE BASIS	TICKLER DATES
Owen Mason		Contingent	

ENGAGEMENT RECEIVED BY	ENGAGEMENT RECEIVED FROM	ENGAGEMENT DATE	FILE DISPOSITION
Owen Mason	Website Referr	Oct 3	

CLIENT	OPPOSING PARTY	CLIENT/MATTER NUMBER

TRADITIONAL INDEX CARD CONTACT AND CONFLICT SYSTEM

Fields

Field1	Field2	Field3	Field4	Field5	Field6	Field7	Field8	Field9	Field10
First Name	Last Name	Full Name	E-Mail Address	Job Title	Contact Type	Company	Salutation	Business Ph	Address

— Records

This entire group of records represents the SalesDeptContact Info table

Microsoft Access - [SalesDeptContactInfo : Table]

File   Edit   View   Insert   Format   Records   Tools   Window   Help   Type a question for help

ContactID	First Name	Last Name	CompanyName	Street Address	City	State	Business Phone
1	Susan	Scantosi	eWidgetPlus	363 Rogue Street	St. Louis	MO	(612) 444-1236
2	Thomas	Mazeman	BooksRUs	2165 Piscotti Ave	Springfield	IL	(888) 234-6983
3	Douglas	Seaver	Printing Solutions	7700 First Ave	Topeka	KS	(888) 988-2678
4	Amir	Ramiv	TechStands	1436 Riverfront Place	St. Louis	MO	(877) 867-7656
5	Franklin	Scott	WorksSuite	8789 Ploughman Drive	Tulsa	OK	(800) 864-2390
6	Ronald	Komeika	Creekside Financia	1264 Pond Hill Road	Toledo	OH	(343) 333-3333
7	Barbara	Mitchell	Market Tenders	9829 Bridge Street	LaPorte	IN	(888) 238-2123
(AutoNumber)							

The category First Name is a field

All the information for Douglas Seaver represents one record

ELECTRONIC DATABASE SYSTEM CONTACTS LAYOUT

AbacusLaw uses four main databases to store the information.

NAMES

Any persons with whom your firm has contact: clients, prospects, vendors, defendants, judges, attorneys, expert witnesses, friends, relatives, and anyone you might want on your mailing list. Notes for names are kept in a linked database so you can keep essentially unlimited notes about your contacts.

EVENTS

Any appointments, tasks, reminders, or things to do that are scheduled for specific dates. Events can be entered into AbacusLaw by many different methods. The events window is the primary data window, while the Daily Organizer and various calendar windows give you different views of your events.

MATTERS

Any matter, case, file, or project that you need to track. Once entered, matters can be attached to any number of names. Notes for matters are kept in a linked database so you can keep essentially unlimited notes about your files.

DOCUMENTS

Any previously saved word processing files, scanned images, pleadings, correspondence, or Internet Web pages. They can be files on disk or just printed documents stored in a box. AbacusLaw keeps a list of these documents in a database so you can find or edit them right from the client's Name or Matter window.

These databases can be searched individually, such as the Names databases for a list of clients presented alphabetically, or across all databases; for example, a list of all documents for a client sorted by individual matters being handled by the firm for the client, and listing important dates and deadlines.

AbacusLaw Gold version integrates the different functions using two modules: AbacusLaw Practice Manager (sometimes referred to as PM) and AbacusLaw Abacus Accounting (sometimes referred to as AM or Time, Billing, and Accounting). With both modules installed, the information is integrated and may be shared between the modules. AbacusLaw Classic integrates just the Practice Manager functions, such as contact manager, case management, and calendars or event manager, again allowing integration of the information in the different practice management functions with information like names (contacts) being shared in the calendar, case manager, electronic notekeeping, and forms.

WHAT IS A DATABASE? ELECTRONIC DATABASE BASICS

A database is just a collection of information. It may be names. Or it may be an expanded list of names with other information like addresses, dates of birth, occupation, children's names, or any other combination of information. In pre-computer days, databases frequently were a box or boxes of cards with the information about a client or important dates. These were the heart of the conflict of interest or deadline databases. The date database was checked daily and a list made up for the legal team of such things as deadlines, statutes of limitations, and appointments. Conflicts of interest were also checked in the same way, a search of the cards maintained in the boxes in alphabetical order. In some offices a card was prepared for all opposing parties. Each of these "decks of cards" was a database.

The electronic database is nothing more than a version of the cards in the boxes—except that more information can be checked more quickly, more accurately, and automatically. No more misfiled cards out of alphabetical order. It is essentially an electronic card with information that can be searched using a set of things to look for and present in a predefined manner.

The image shown on page xxxv shows a template for *input of information into a contacts management database for one record*. One of the advantages of the modern database is the ability to search across a number of different sets of information and sort the data according to a predefined set of criteria. Some have likened the World Wide Web to a big database that can be searched using a search engine.

A database is just computer talk for a collection of information. The database is the place where information is stored until a request is made for a report showing some or all of the information in a certain format or appearance. For example, a Contact Database is nothing more than a collection of information about people, names, phone numbers, addresses, and maybe birthdays or other related information.

When information about a person is needed the report showing the information is made by a question or query, asking the database program to look up the person's information and show it on the computer screen or in a printed format called a report. Any combination of information, or query, can be requested in the report about a single person or a list of all people or contacts with the same information such as zip code, or a more detailed report prepared combining specific items such as zip code and male or female with a birthday before or after a certain date.

INPUT—ENTERING INFORMATION

Most programs provide a basic set of screens for entering the different types of information. Information may be entered and stored on the law firm's computer server that includes the names, addresses, contact information, and personal data such as birth dates of every client, every opposing party, every fact witness and expert witness, and every opposing counsel with whom any member of the firm has ever had contact in litigation, contract negotiations, or counseling sessions, or met in any business or legal setting. The exhibit on the following page shows two methods of entering basic contact information using a New Names Window or an Intake Form.

OUTPUT—REPORTS

Some offices still use a manual card system to keep track of the names of clients and opposing parties. These cards are physically searched to find possible conflicts of interest before accepting new clients or matters. For the small office with few cases or clients, this system works. But for the larger office with multiple attorneys and possibly multiple offices, timely entry and searching of large amounts of information is not realistic. Computerized database software and report generator as found in AbacusLaw facilitates timely, accurate access to information by every authorized member of the legal team. Some reports of information, such as comparing the name of a potential client against all current clients' names, are preset as a standard report, like the Conflict Report Generator in AbacusLaw, shown on the following page.

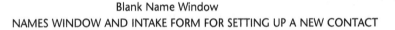

Blank Name Window   New Contact Intake Form

NAMES WINDOW AND INTAKE FORM FOR SETTING UP A NEW CONTACT

In other cases where there is no predesigned report, a search or query screen may be used to identify the information or combinations of information desired in the report, and a set of report formats for presenting the information requested. AbacusLaw provides each of these basic screens and reports and allows users to customize the input, query, and output or report screens.

With a few keystrokes, a list can be prepared by checking for conflicts of interest or a computer search can be performed with a printout of any matter or litigation where a name appears, as shown on the following page.

In addition to the obvious use in avoiding accepting a client with a potential conflict of interest, the information frequently is used in maintaining client relations. Many firms use the information to send birthday and anniversary greetings, as well as updates on specific changes in the law for which the client has consulted the firm previously.

UNDERSTANDING DATABASES

Standard terminology is used to describe the parts of a database: table, record, field, and cell, as shown below.

Databases are collections of tables.

Tables contain records.

A record is all the information about one item or person; for example:

Records contain fields of information (data)

Fields contain cells

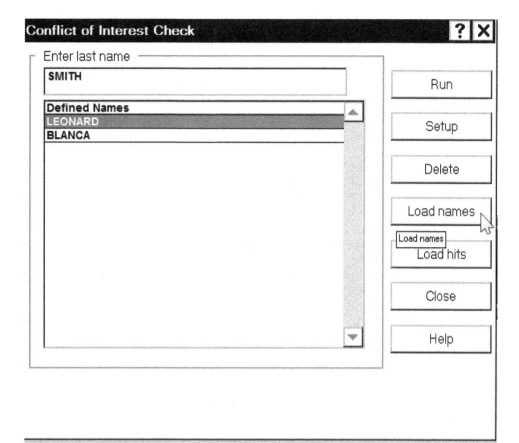

CONFLICT OF INTEREST GENERATOR WINDOW

```
CONFLICT.OM - Notepad                                                                    _ □ X
File  Edit  Format  View  Help
2:44p                    Mason, Marshall, and Benjamin          01/01/10                   ▲
                            Conflict Check Report

   Checking these names:
      LEONARD
      BLANCA
      SMITH
   ----------------------------------------------------------------
   SEARCH NAME : BLANCA

      MATCHED FIELD: MATTERS->MATTER          Record# 4
      MATCHED DATA : Jonathon Leonard v. Steven Blanca
      Jonathon Leonard v. Steven Blanca                        1235      OM PI  / /

      MATCHED FIELD: MATTERS->MATTER          Record# 6
      MATCHED DATA : Stephan Blanca v. Jonathan Leonard
      Stephan Blanca v. Jonathan Leonard                       1236      OM PI  / /
      01/01/10  1:35p DEFS     OM
        Potential Conflict of Interest

      MATCHED FIELD: MATTERS->MATTER          Record# 8
      MATCHED DATA : STEPHAN BLANCA V. JONATHAN LEONARD
      STEPHAN BLANCA V. JONATHAN LEONARD                       1237      AM PI  / /

      MATCHED FIELD: NAMES->LAST             Record# 1
      MATCHED DATA : Blanca
      Blanca, Stephan           MYFIRM-95872 CLIENT   (609)555-9999
        01/01/10  1:17p backgrnd OM
      Client was a driver involved in an accident in which he
      suffered injuries and lost time from work.

      Matters: Stephan Blanca v. Jonathan Leonard             1236
               Stephan Blanca v. Jonathan Leonard             1236
               Jonathon Leonard v. Steven Blanca              1235
               Stephan Blanca v. Jonathan Leonard             1236
   ----------------------------------------------------------------
   SEARCH NAME : LEONARD

      MATCHED FIELD: MATTERS->MATTER          Record# 3
      MATCHED DATA : Jonathon Leonard v. Steven Blanca
      Jonathon Leonard v. Steven Blanca                        1235      OM PI  / /

      MATCHED FIELD: MATTERS->MATTER          Record# 5
      MATCHED DATA : Stephan Blanca v. Jonathan Leonard
      Stephan Blanca v. Jonathan Leonard                       1236      OM PI  / /
      01/01/10  1:35p DEFS     OM
        Potential Conflict of Interest                                                   ▼
```

CONFLICT REPORT

A field is one type of information,

A cell is the box containing the individual field information, like a last name.

Think of the database as being a file cabinet; a table is a file drawer for a specific set of information like employees; the record is the individual file for each employee; and each field is the individual piece of information about the employee.

Databases can and frequently do contain two or more tables. For example, a database used in a legal office may have one table for employees of the firm, another table for clients of the firm, a third table for opposing attorneys, and a fourth table for the opposing parties in cases the firm has handled.

Reports present the data from the database in an organized presentation. A report may present just the information from one table, such as employee birthdays. Frequently, a report shows the outcome of searching multiple tables and displaying the relationships between the information and data from the different tables, such as a report of the employees that have worked for an opposing counsel in a case against a client.

WHAT DO THE PRACTICE MANAGER AND ABACUS ACCOUNTING LOOK LIKE?

The two modules are similar in appearance and have links to each other as shown below.

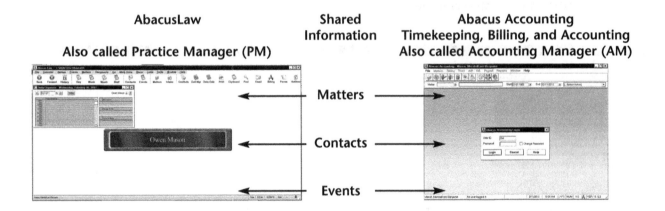

To enable you to master the features of each module with the least confusion, the Practice Manager will be discussed first, then the Abacus Accounting. For each you will be guided through the installation and registration process, personalization of user and firm information, adding or inputting information, and creating reports and using other customizing features.

After you have mastered the basics of the Practice Manager, you will be shown how to set up and integrate the information from the Practice Manager to the Abacus Accounting and create reports that combine information from both programs.

PRODUCTIVITY

A very wise man (actually, my Uncle Ralph) said "Tom, work smarter, not harder." Selecting the right tools to do the job is part of working smarter. The advantage of a program like AbacusLaw is that it does most of the work for you, so you don't have to exert as much effort. Now *that* is working smarter.

Many of the templates or forms you may need are already supplied as examples or templates in AbacusLaw. In most cases these can be used "as is," or easily modified to meet your needs. Context-sensitive help is provided.

YOUR EXPECTATIONS

What can you expect from AbacusLaw and from this guide? You *do not* have to be an accountant to keep office records and generate reports. AbacusLaw does most of the work for you. As with anything new, there is a learning curve; but with AbacusLaw, it is a very short learning curve, so you will be able to create reports the first time you use the program. With a little practice you will be able to use some of the powerful tools and features to create custom reports and manage the law office.

Before We Really Start
(So, What's It All About?)

- How Can I Learn to Use AbacusLaw?
- How Can I Use This Tutorial and Guide to Learn AbacusLaw?
- What Hardware Do I Need to Get Started?
- Will AbacusLaw Work on an Apple Computer?
- Why Do I Need an Internet Connection?
- Is There Anything I Should Do before Installing AbacusLaw?
- Installing AbacusLaw
- How Do I Install AbacusLaw?
  - ▲ *Tutorial—Installing AbacusLaw from a CD*
  - ▲ *Tutorial—Locating and Installing AbacusLaw Manually*
- How Do I Download AbacusLaw from the AbacusLaw Web Site?
  - ▲ *Tutorial—Downloading and Installing AbacusLaw from Web Site*
- How Do I Complete the Installation?
  - ▲ *Tutorial—Completing AbacusLaw Installation*
- How Do I Start AbacusLaw?
  - ▲ *Tutorial—Starting AbacusLaw*
- How Do I Register and Activate AbacusLaw?
  - ▲ *Tutorial—Activating AbacusLaw*
- Where Can I Get More Answers?
  - ▲ *Tutorial—Sources of Available Help*
  - ▲ *Tutorial—Online Tutorials*

ABACUS HELP AND LEARNING RESOURCES

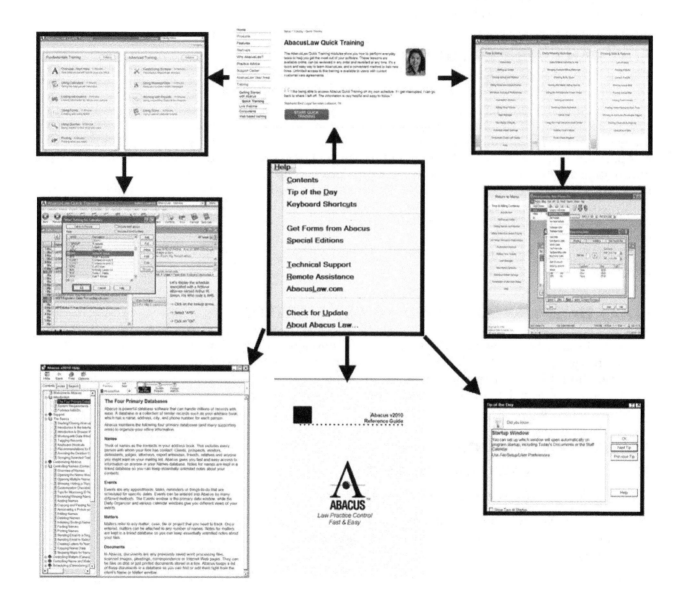

HOW CAN I LEARN TO USE ABACUSLAW?

There are many methods of learning a new software program: reading the user's manual, using the online help, or randomly trying program features and menu choices. Few users, however, will consult the manual, help screens, or detailed training course material. This text offers suggested hands-on training solutions to enable you to instantly use the program and its principal features with just a little guidance. Avoid the temptation to explore the many high-level features of AbacusLaw until you become familiar with the terminology and screens in the program.

HOW CAN I USE THIS TUTORIAL AND GUIDE TO LEARN ABACUSLAW?

Each section in this tutorial and guide introduces a new concept or function in AbacusLaw. Specific information is used to demonstrate the steps in using the features. The information used in the tutorials is based on the case study in Appendix E, a school bus and truck accident. In each section the specific information is shown in a chart. This chart provides a column for you to insert your personal information and the names and information of friends, family, and local courts. Fill out this personal information and use this as you complete the tutorial. This will set up your personal copy of AbacusLaw with your personal information.

The complete list of information with blanks for your use is also supplied in Appendix F.

WHAT HARDWARE DO I NEED TO GET STARTED?

You must install AbacusLaw on a computer that has enough hard drive space to store the program and data files, and enough memory to run the program. You also should have an Internet connection to register, download additional content and updates, and gain access to the AbacusLaw support and training information.

PC SYSTEM REQUIREMENTS

ABACUSLAW V.2010 SYSTEM REQUIREMENTS:

For a single- to 5-user network server or workstation

Windows® XP Professional, Windows Vista®*, or Windows® 7
Intel P4 or greater processor (dual core processor is preferred)
1 GB RAM
CD-ROM
4 GB of available hard disk space (install footprint is 350 MB)
*Home Premium, Business, and Ultimate are the only supported versions. Windows Vista® installs should have a minimum of 2 GB of RAM.

Networks of 6-10 users

Windows® XP Professional, Windows Vista® Business, Windows Vista® Ultimate, Windows® 7, or Windows® Server 2008

Intel P4 or greater processor

1 GB RAM for workstations, 2 GB for servers

CD-ROM

4 GB of available hard disk space

Preferred server operating system is Windows® Server 2003 and up

Networks greater than 10 users: Use a server-based operating system. We support the following operating systems: Windows® Server 2000, Windows® Server 2003, and Windows® Server 2008.

For remote access over the Internet:

Citrix or Terminal Services server

PLUS: AbacusLaw Fortress

WILL ABACUSLAW WORK ON AN APPLE COMPUTER?

AbacusLaw will work on an Apple computer in PC emulation mode. Some MAC computers can operate in a PC emulation mode with the installation of an emulation program. If you want to use AbacusLaw on a MAC you need to verify that your MAC has the minimum resources to run in emulation mode, and purchase and install the emulation program before installing AbacusLaw.

WHY DO I NEED AN INTERNET CONNECTION?

First: Unless you have a CD of the program, you will need to connect to the AbacusLaw Web site to download either the purchased or the demo version of AbacusLaw.

Second: Each copy of AbacusLaw must be activated online to be validated for use.

Third: The AbacusLaw software is initially updated when activated, as well as when new updates such as new tax tables are needed. The updates are downloaded over the Internet.

Fourth: Additional documentation and tutorials may be downloaded from the AbacusLaw Web site (http://www.AbacusLaw.com).

Fifth: You may want to add specialty forms or court calendar dates for a new jurisdiction to complete a task; for example, a case in a foreign jurisdiction.

IS THERE ANYTHING I SHOULD DO BEFORE INSTALLING ABACUSLAW?

Before installing any software, close all other programs that may be running on your computer. You should also temporarily turn off your virus protection program during installation. Any firewall on your system may need to be shut down or other steps taken to allow the program files to install.

NOTE

Windows Vista® and Windows® 7 users should change or disable the UAC setting. See Appendix B.

INSTALLING ABACUSLAW

AbacusLaw is frequently installed on office systems that have multiple work-stations and a file server. It may also be installed on a single-user workstation. In multiuser network installations, AbacusLaw allows users to communicate through the server using a program called AbacusLaw MessageSlips, a form of instant messaging. In single-user systems this is not used and should not be installed. Single-user installers should ignore the message about installing on a server.

HOW DO I INSTALL ABACUSLAW?

AbacusLaw may be installed from a CD, the AbacusLaw Web site for the demo version, or the academic version download Web site using the Web address provided with the academic version access code.

You will need the customer ID and firm name to fully install, register, and validate your copy of AbacusLaw. This information is provided with the invoice or provided to academic users when they preregister their information and access code.

Installing AbacusLaw from a CD

GOAL	ACTION	RESULT
INSTALL ABACUSLAW FROM A CD *Note:* Installation should start automatically. If it does not, perform the step below.	**INSERT** AbacusLaw CD into computer CD drive **CLOSE** Drive door **CLICK** *Run SETUP.EXE*	AutoPlay DVD RW Drive (F:) Abacus v2010 ☐ Always do this for software and games: **Install or run program from your media** Run SETUP.EXE Publisher not specified **General options** Open folder to view files using Windows Explorer View more AutoPlay options in Control Panel

Locating and Installing AbacusLaw Manually

GOAL	ACTION	RESULT

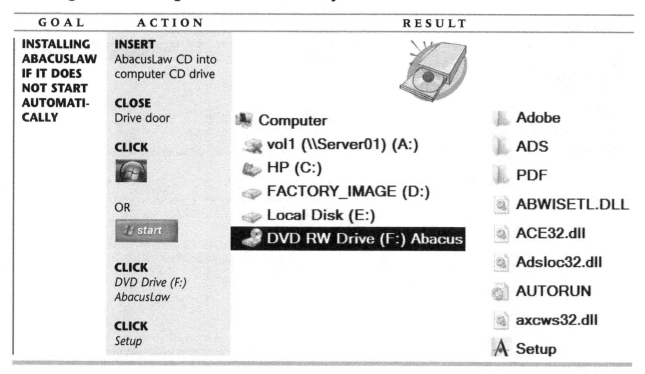

INSTALLING ABACUSLAW IF IT DOES NOT START AUTOMATI- CALLY	**INSERT** AbacusLaw CD into computer CD drive **CLOSE** Drive door **CLICK** OR *start* **CLICK** *DVD Drive (F:) AbacusLaw* **CLICK** *Setup*	

HOW DO I DOWNLOAD ABACUSLAW FROM THE ABACUSLAW WEB SITE?

Some Internet browsers may give you a choice to *Save* or to *Run*.

You may download and *save* the *installer program* or immediately *run* it on your computer. Depending on the speed of your Internet connection it may take from 1 to 10 minutes. It is recommended that you save the program and then run the program after closing your Web browser and antivirus program. When you save the program, make a note of where the program was saved so you can locate it and install it at a later time.

For example, the location where the program is saved includes

> *Drive* designation*Folder* name*File*name
> or *C:\Downloads\AbacusLaw2010ALL.exe*

The location C:\Downloads\AbacusLaw2010ALL.exe is called the *path*.

When you download the program record the path for your computer below.

Enter your Drive:_____:

Enter your download folder:_____

File name: AbacusLaw2010ALL.exe

When you run the installer program it installs the actual program files, sets up the necessary AbacusLaw folder, and adds necessary entries on your computer hard drive to allow it to run and function.

Downloading and Installing AbacusLaw from Web Site

GOAL	ACTION	RESULT
DOWNLOAD AND SAVE ABACUSLAW INSTALLER PROGRAM FROM ABACUSLAW WEB SITE	**START** Your Internet Web browser **ENTER** AbacusLaw Web address provided with the academic version or the one received from AbacusLaw OR www.abacuslaw.com for 30-day demo **CLICK** *Save* (Recommended)	**File Download – Security Warning** [X] Do you want to run or save this file? Name: **abacusgold2010ALL.exe** Type: Application, 91.1MB From: **downloads.abacuslaw.com** [Run] [Save] [Cancel] While files from the Internet can be useful, this file type can potentially harm your computer. If you do not trust the source, do not run or save this software. What's the risk?
RECORD PATH TO THE ABACUSLAW INSTALLER FILE *Note*: The Save As screen shown is from Windows® 7.	**COPY HERE** Your Drive:_____:\ Download folder: _____\ File name: AbacusLaw2010ALL.exe	**Save As** [x] ○○ ◦ Local Disk (C:) ◦ Downloads ▾ Search Organize ▾ Views ▾ New Folder Favorite Links	Name ▲	Date modified	Type	Size | abacusgold2010ALL Documents Pictures Music Recently Changed Searches Public Folders ^ File name: abacusgold2010ALL Save as type: Application Hide Folders [Save] [Cancel]

Downloading and Installing AbacusLaw from Web Site (*continued*)

GOAL	ACTION	RESULT
WAIT FOR DOWNLOAD TO FINISH AND THEN OPEN FOLDER TO INSTALL PROGRAM	**CLICK** *Open Folder*	**Download complete**　　　　　_ □ ☒ Download Complete **abacusgold2010ALL.exe from downloads.abacuslaw.com** Downloaded:　91.1MB in 1 min 48 sec Download to:　C:\downloads\abacusgold2010ALL.exe Transfer rate:　864KB/Sec ☐ Close this dialog box when download completes [Run] [Open Folder] [Close] SmartScreen Filter checked this download and did not report any threats. Report an unsafe download.
IF YOU CHOOSE TO RUN DIRECTLY FROM THE WEB SITE, ACCEPT THE SECURITY WARNING	**CLICK** *Run*	**Internet Explorer – Security Warning**　　　　☒ **The publisher could not be verified. Are you sure you want to run this software?** 　Name: abacusgold2010ALL.exe Publisher: **Unknown Publisher** [Run] [Don't Run] This file does not have a valid digital signature that verifies its publisher. You should only run software from publishers you trust. How can I decide what software to run?

Downloading and Installing AbacusLaw from Web Site (*continued*)

GOAL	ACTION	RESULT
IF YOU CHOOSE TO SAVE FIRST, OPEN FOLDER TO INSTALL AND START INSTALLATION	**DOUBLE CLICK** *abacusgold2010ALL*	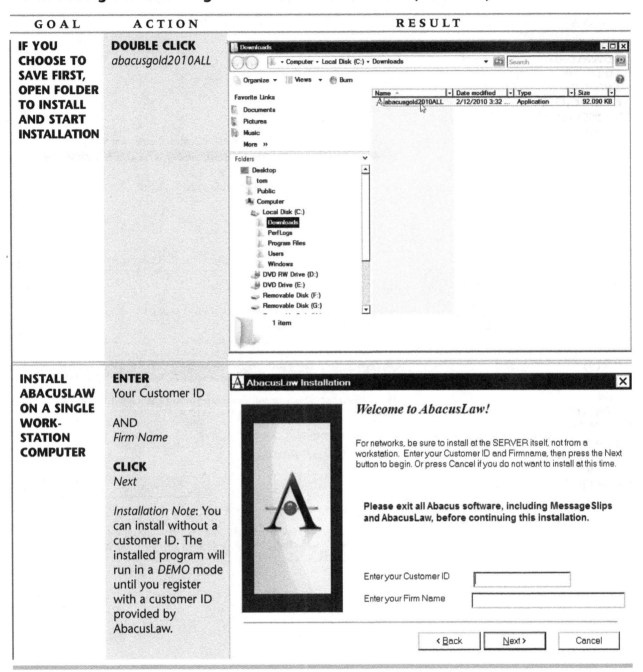
INSTALL ABACUSLAW ON A SINGLE WORK-STATION COMPUTER	**ENTER** Your Customer ID AND *Firm Name* **CLICK** *Next* *Installation Note*: You can install without a customer ID. The installed program will run in a *DEMO* mode until you register with a customer ID provided by AbacusLaw.	

HOW DO I COMPLETE THE INSTALLATION?

Installation includes deciding where the AbacusLaw files will be installed. If you are using a single-user system (one computer for one person) and not a network installation (one or more computers connected to a network server), this will normally be your main computer hard disk storage drive, usually the C:\ drive. If this is not your default location, you will be given the opportunity to change the location during the installation process.

   If you are using a single-user single PC license do not install AbacusLaw MessageSlips, which is designed for communication between users over a network.

NOTE

If you have a network license or multiuser license, you will need to install the AbacusLaw program on your server first and then on each individual workstation. Details of this process are explained in Appendix B.

Completing AbacusLaw Installation

GOAL	ACTION	RESULT
ACCEPT END USER LICENSE	**CLICK** *Accept*	
SELECT ABACUSLAW MODULES TO INSTALL *Note*: Single-user licenses should uncheck Abacus MessageSlips and CompanionLink.	**CHECK** *AbacusLaw* **CHECK** *Time, Billing & Accounting* **UNCHECK** *Abacus MessageSlips* **UNCHECK** *CompanionLink* **CLICK** *Next*	

Completing AbacusLaw Installation (*continued*)

GOAL	ACTION	RESULT

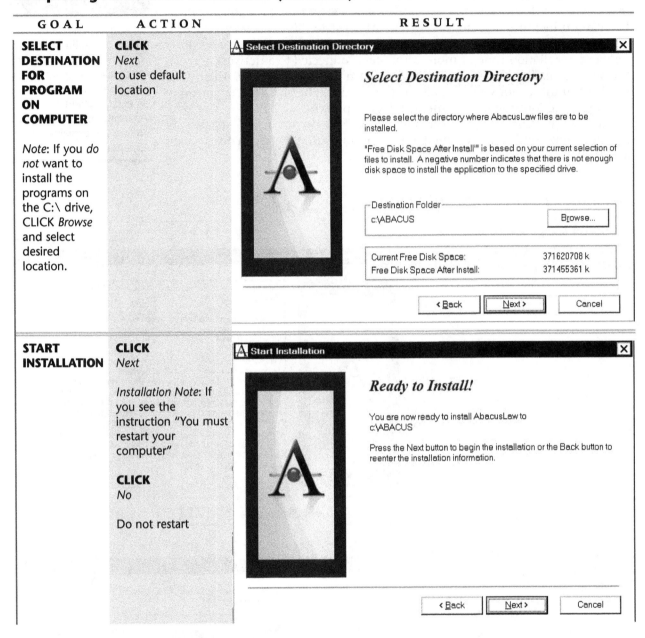

SELECT DESTINATION FOR PROGRAM ON COMPUTER

Note: If you *do not* want to install the programs on the C:\ drive, CLICK *Browse* and select desired location.

CLICK
Next
to use default location

Select Destination Directory

Please select the directory where AbacusLaw files are to be installed.

"Free Disk Space After Install'" is based on your current selection of files to install. A negative number indicates that there is not enough disk space to install the application to the specified drive.

Destination Folder
c:\ABACUS   Browse...

Current Free Disk Space: 371620708 k
Free Disk Space After Install: 371455361 k

< Back   Next >   Cancel

START INSTALLATION

CLICK
Next

Installation Note: If you see the instruction "You must restart your computer"

CLICK
No

Do not restart

Ready to Install!

You are now ready to install AbacusLaw to c:\ABACUS

Press the Next button to begin the installation or the Back button to reenter the installation information.

< Back   Next >   Cancel

Completing AbacusLaw Installation (*continued*)

GOAL	ACTION	RESULT
SET UP FIRST USER WITH INITIALS	**CLICK** *OK* **ENTER** Your initials **CLICK** *OK*	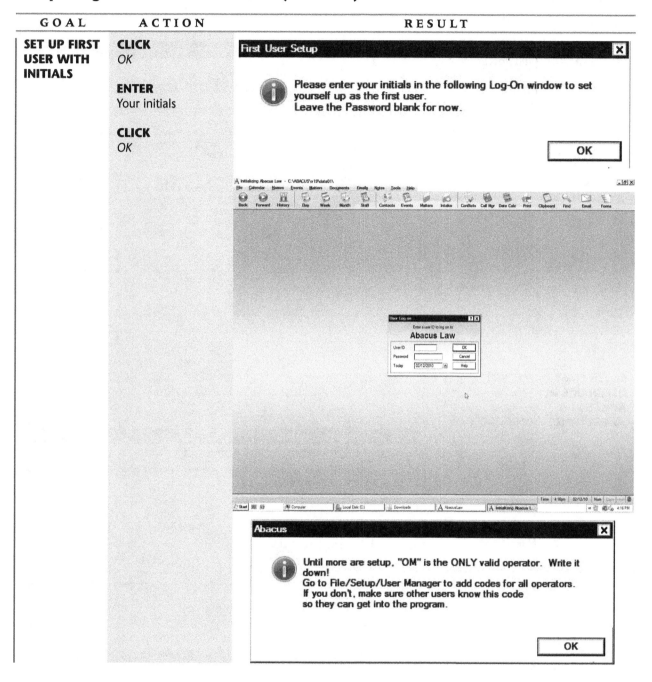

Completing AbacusLaw Installation (*continued*)

GOAL	ACTION	RESULT
FINISH INSTALLATION	**UNCHECK** *Run AbacusUpdater* **CLICK** *Finish*	**AbacusLaw Installation Complete** ✕ ***AbacusLaw Installation*** The installation of AbacusLaw has been successful. If you are installing for a Network, be sure to run C:\ABACUS\v19\Programs\Station.exe on each workstation. Note: If this server is also used as a workstation (which is not recommended) and you want Message Slips installed, run C:\ABACUS\v19\Programs\Station.exe on this server also. Click Finish to complete this installation. ☐ Run AbacusUpdater to check for purchased Rules and more. [Finish]
ENTER FIRST USERNAME IN ABACUS ACCOUNTING	**ENTER** Your name **CLICK** *Create* **CLICK** *OK*	**New Company Configuration** _ □ ✕ —Add a User and Timekeeper— Please enter you first name, middle intial, and last name, then verify your initials. Finally, enter the default hourly rate for this User/Timekeeper. First Name [Owen] Middle Initial [ ] Last Name [Mason] User Initials (Also your Logon ID) [OM] Default Rate [0.00] [Create] [Cancel] Opening Database... **Abacus Accounting** ✕ ⓘ Until more are setup, OM is the ONLY valid operator. Write it down! Go to File/Setup/User manager to Add codes for all operators. If you don't, make sure other users know this code so they can get into the program. [OK]

Completing AbacusLaw Installation (*continued*)

GOAL	ACTION	RESULT
DEMO MODE NOTICE	**CLICK** *OK* *Installation Note:* After you receive your customer ID, you may register and validate your copy of the program and it will remove the Demo mode limitation.	**Abacus Accounting** ☒ ✖ Your installation is not licensed to use Abacus Accounting. Accounting will now run in Demo mode. Please contact Abacus Sales for more information. OK Loading System Setup Parameters...

HOW DO I START ABACUSLAW?

If you installed both AbacusLaw (Practice Manager) and Abacus Accounting (Time, Billing & Accounting), two icons will be added to your computer desktop—the AbacusLaw icon and the Abacus Accounting icon. Clicking the desktop icon will start that program; you can also start the program from the list of programs on your computer.

Starting AbacusLaw

GOAL	ACTION	RESULT
START ABACUSLAW PROGRAM FROM DESKTOP	**CLICK** *AbacusLaw icon* on your desktop	
START PROGRAM FROM PROGRAM LIST IF NO ICON APPEARS ON DESKTOP	**CLICK** OR *start* **SELECT** ▸ All Programs **CLICK** A AbacusLaw	

HOW DO I REGISTER AND ACTIVATE ABACUSLAW?

If you purchased AbacusLaw directly from Abacus, you received a customer ID and firm name with your invoice.

If you purchased the academic version with this tutorial and guide, you must complete an online preregistration form to provide Abacus with the firm name you will use. Follow the instruction that came with the validation code. Abacus will e-mail you your customer ID. You may completely install the software and use it in Demo mode while you wait to receive your customer ID and activate the program.

<table>
<tr><th></th><th>N O T E</th></tr>
</table>

If you need to move your copy of AbacusLaw to another computer, you may use the same Menu option to transfer the program by unregistering the old computer and reinstalling and registering it on the new computer. Before attempting this, back up your AbacusLaw files onto a removable storage device. The data will not be transferred unless saved and reentered on the new computer.

Activating AbacusLaw

GOAL	ACTION	RESULT
ACTIVATE YOUR COPY OF ABACUSLAW	**START** *AbacusLaw* **CLICK** *File menu* **SELECT** *Register* **ENTER** Customer ID and Firm Name **CLICK** *Activate*	File Calendar Names Events Mat Register... Setup ▶ Utilities ▶ Synchronize ▶ User Log-on... Reports ▶ Change directory New database 1 c:\ABACUS\w19\data01 Exit **Registration for Abacus** ? ✕ Customer ID: 95869 Firm Name: Mason, Marshall and Benjamin License type: Registered Single user Practice Packs None Practice Packs Licensed: 0 View Report Enter your Customer ID and firm name, then click Activate to connect to the Abacus servers via the internet. You may change the firm name as long as the primary licensed names appear, e.g. "Arthur Simon, Esq." can be replaced by "Law Offices of Arthur Simon". If you have no internet access or need assistance, call Abacus Tech Support at 800-488-3334 Activate Transfer Cancel Help

Activating AbacusLaw (*continued*)

GOAL	ACTION	RESULT
RESPONSE FROM ABACUS IF SUCCESSFULLY ACTIVATED	**CLICK** *OK*	Abacus Law ☒ ⓘ License successfully activated. OK

WHERE CAN I GET MORE ANSWERS?

The AbacusLaw User's Guide may be downloaded as a PDF file from the AbacusLaw Web site (http://www.abacuslaw.com/kbase/users/kb.php?category_id=21).

A link is also provided in the AbacusLaw Practice Manager and Abacus Accounting Manager Help menus. To read a PDF file you will need to have the free Adobe Reader or another PDF reader installed on your computer. Online tutorials are also available to registered users.

> **NOTE**
>
> Additional tutorials and documentation are available at http://www.AbacusLaw.com.

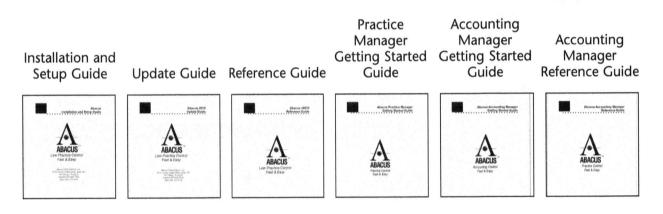

Installation and Setup Guide   Update Guide   Reference Guide   Practice Manager Getting Started Guide   Accounting Manager Getting Started Guide   Accounting Manager Reference Guide

Sources of Available Help

GOAL	ACTION	RESULT
OPEN HELP	**CLICK** *Help menu* **SELECT** *Contents*	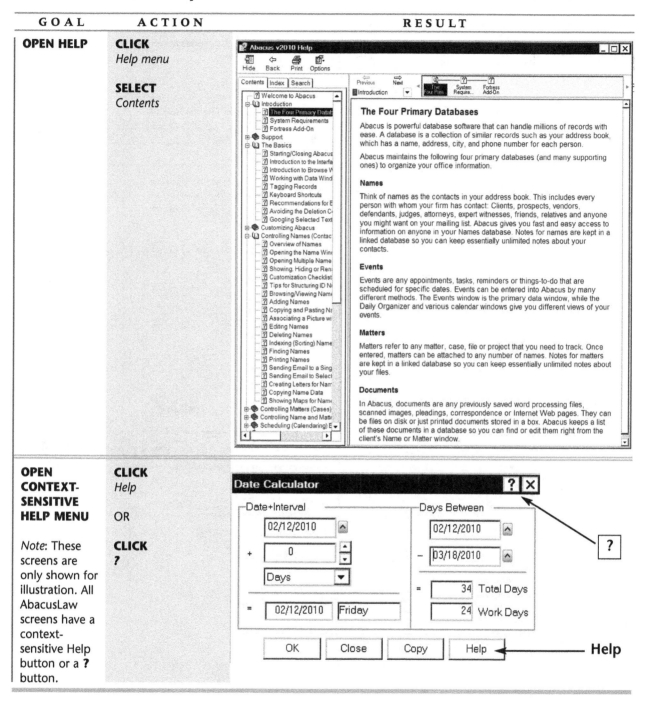
OPEN CONTEXT-SENSITIVE HELP MENU *Note*: These screens are only shown for illustration. All AbacusLaw screens have a context-sensitive Help button or a **?** button.	**CLICK** *Help* OR **CLICK** *?*	

Online Tutorials

GOAL	ACTION	RESULT
ACCESS ONLINE TUTORIALS	**OPEN** Your Web browser	
QUICK TRAINING TUTORIALS	**ENTER** http://www.abacuslaw.com/qt/index.htm AbacusLaw Quick Training Web site	

Online Tutorials (*continued*)

GOAL	ACTION	RESULT
OPEN AND SELECT AN ABACUSLAW PRACTICE MANAGER QUICK TRAINING TUTORIAL	**SELECT** *Practice Manager Training*	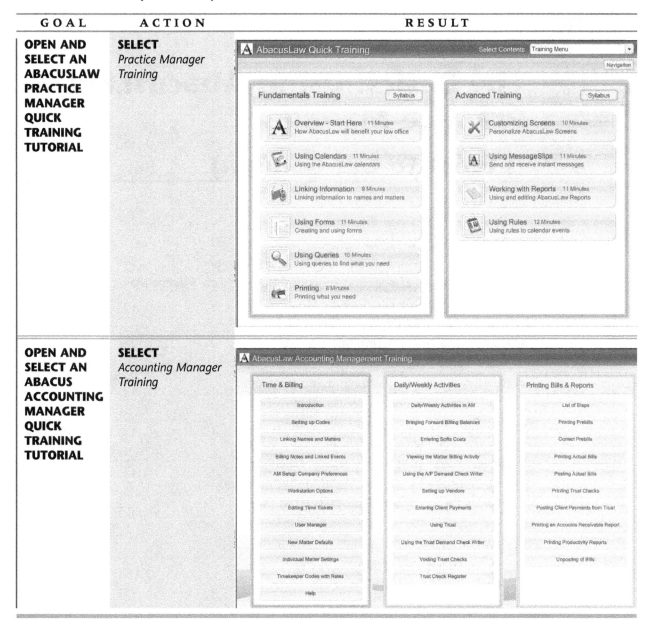
OPEN AND SELECT AN ABACUS ACCOUNTING MANAGER QUICK TRAINING TUTORIAL	**SELECT** *Accounting Manager Training*	

The Basics: Using AbacusLaw Practice Manager

(I Want to Get Going...)

- Tutorial Information Used
- What Can I Do with the AbacusLaw Practice Manager?
- How Do I Access Screens and Functions In AbacusLaw Practice Manager?
- How Do I Verify My Firm Information?
  - ▲ *Tutorial—Verifying My Firm Information*
- How Do I Change the Firm Information?
  - ▲ *Tutorial—Change Firm Information on the Names Window*
- How Do I Set Up My Personal User Information?
  - ▲ *Tutorial—Setting Up Personal Preferences*
- How Do I Add New Users to AbacusLaw?
  - ▲ *Tutorial—Setting Up New User*
- How Do I Set Up Firm and Personal Calendars?
  - ▲ *Tutorial—Adding New "WHO" to the Calendars*
- How Do I Add Appointments (Events) to Calendar?
  - ▲ *Tutorial—Add an Event to Calendar for Specific Person*
- How Can I Print My Calendar?
  - ▲ *Tutorial—Printing a Daily Organizer*
- How Do I Add Contacts (Names)?
  - ▲ *Tutorial—Adding Contacts (Names)*

AbacusLaw Practice Manager

INTEGRATED SOFTWARE

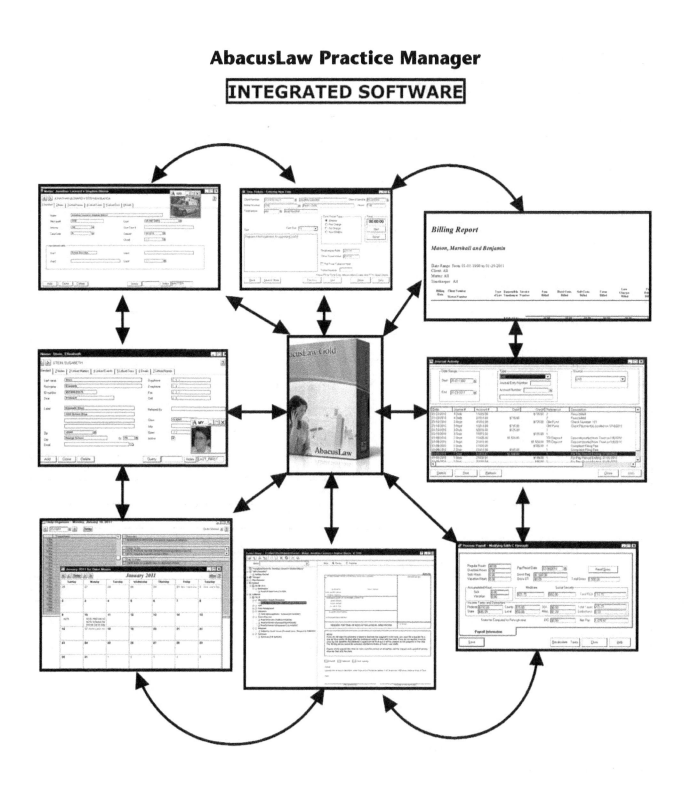

TUTORIAL INFORMATION USED

The following is the information used in the following section tutorials. You may substitute your personal information. Fill in the information *before* starting.

	TUTORIAL INFORMATION	YOUR INFORMATION
Firm Name	Mason, Marshall and Benjamin	
Attorney	Owen Mason	
ID	OM	
E-Mail	mason@masonmarshallandbenjamin.com	
Attorney	Ariel Marshall	
ID	AM	
Address	138 North Street	
City	Newtown	
State	PA	
Zip	18940	
Day Phone	555 111 2222	
Fax	555 111 3333	
Printer		
Reports	HP LASERJET 4250	
Labels	SMARTLABEL PRINTER	
Envelopes	HP LASERJET 4050	
Word Processor		
Executable	C:\programfiles\microsoft office\winword	

WHAT CAN I DO WITH THE ABACUSLAW PRACTICE MANAGER?

AbacusLaw is an integrated law office management program that can be used to track time, contacts, firm funds, and client trust accounts, and prepare many different types of time and financial reports.

CALENDARS

Maintain daily, weekly, monthly, staff, and free time calendars for each member of the legal team with reminders and links to related matters and events.

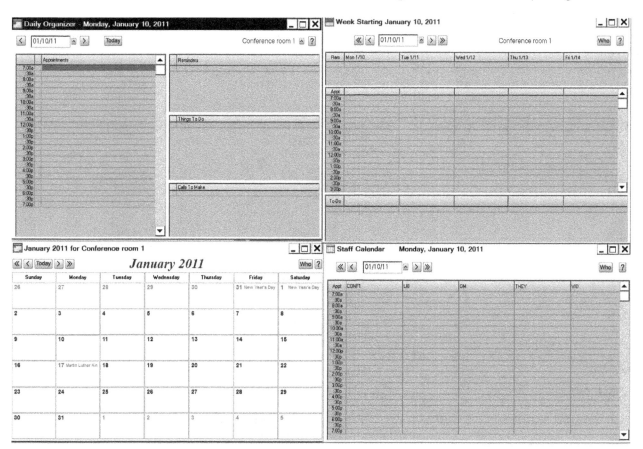

CONTACT MANAGEMENT

Create and maintain a listing of contacts, clients, potential clients, opposing parties, other attorneys, and judges in a comprehensive listing that may be used to prepare documents and as a basis for mail merged letters.

CONFLICT CHECKS

Avoid ethical conflicts of interest by quickly running conflicts checks. A predefined report function, conflict of interest check, allows new names to be easily checked against all other names in the contact lists.

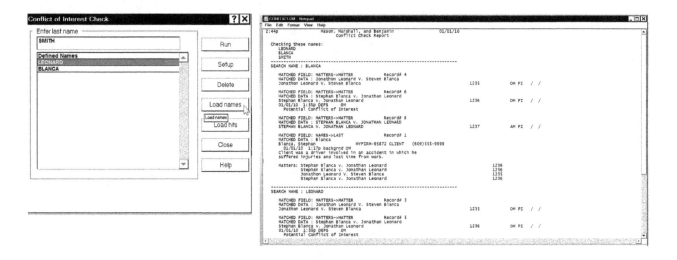

CASE MANAGEMENT

Maintain all information about each case, including all parties, events, and location of stored documents in one easily maintained location with the ability to generate and fill out documents and court forms automatically.

DOCUMENT MANAGEMENT

Create links to quickly locate and open all the documents for a matter on your computer or server.

PREPARE COURT FORMS

AbacusLaw has available many of the basic forms and documents for federal and select state courts that may be automatically filled out using the information about a matter or case.

HOW DO I ACCESS SCREENS AND FUNCTIONS IN ABACUSLAW PRACTICE MANAGER?

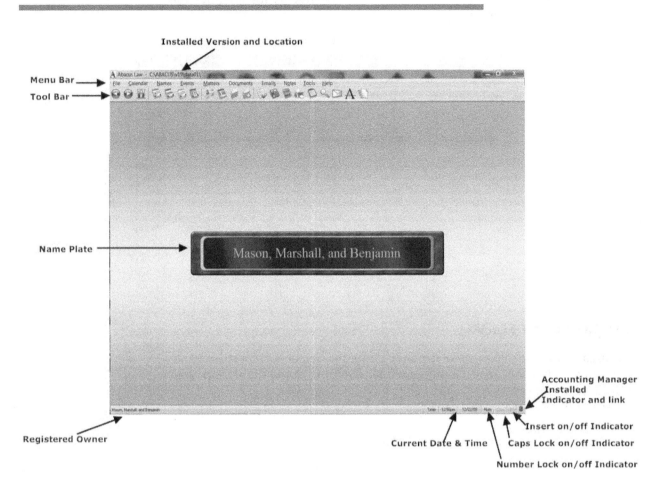

MENU BAR AND TOOLBAR

The menu bar menus and the toolbar icons are the keys to accessing the information and functions of the Practice Manager. Some of the functions and screens may be accessed from both the menu bar and a toolbar icon.

For example, the *Adding a new Matter window*, shown below, can be opened using the Add a new Matter option on the Mattters Menu on the menu bar or the Matters icon on the toolbar, or the *Names Browse window*, shown below, can be opened using the Add a new Name option in the Names menu, or the toolbar Contacts icon.

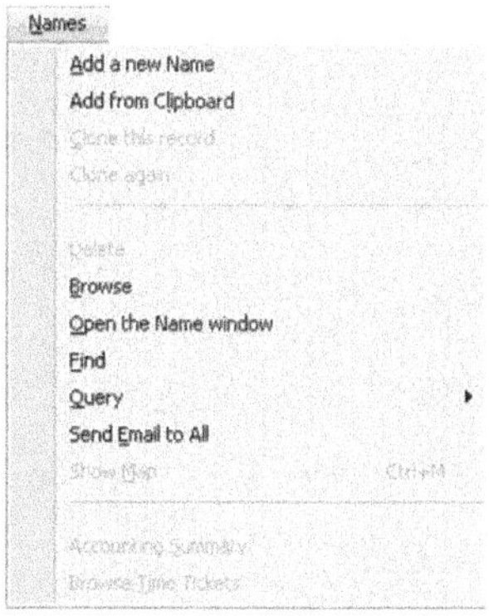

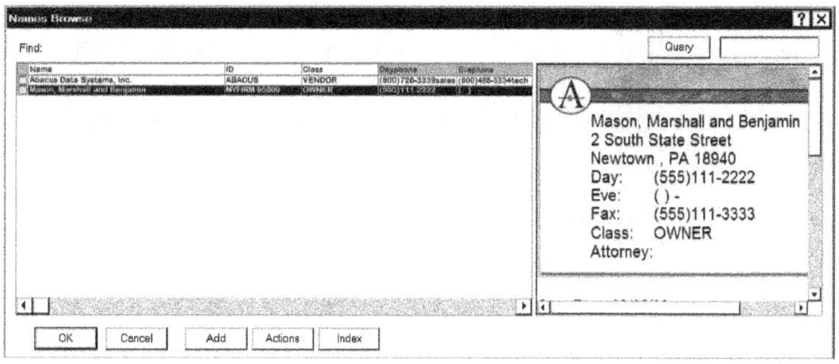

Basic functions in the Practice Manager include entering information into one of the databases:

- Names
- Events
- Matters
- Documents

Some of the windows (screens) may be used for multiple purposes. For instance, the Matter window can be used to manually input information, linking matters to other items like names, events, and documents, as well as generating reports.

All of the windows in AbacusLaw also provide a link to context-sensitve help by using the Help button or the ? button, as shown on the window above.

HOW DO I VERIFY MY FIRM INFORMATION?

Firm information is needed to use the Practice Manager. The basic firm information is entered as part of the AbacusLaw installation registration and verification process. The firm information is provided to AbacusLaw when the program is purchased, a demo version is requested, or the academic version is preregistered. It is a good idea to check the accuracy of the information and make any necessary changes or update the information. Additional information about the firm may need to be entered during the Abacus Accounting installation and setup.

Verifying My Firm Information

GOAL	ACTION	RESULT
VERIFY THE FIRM INFORMATION *Note*: The My Firm information comes from the registration information provided to AbacusLaw. You cannot change the information in this window. You will be able to change it in the next tutorial lesson.	**CLICK** *File menu* **SELECT** *Setup* **SELECT** *My Firm* **VERIFY** Firm information **CLICK** *OK*	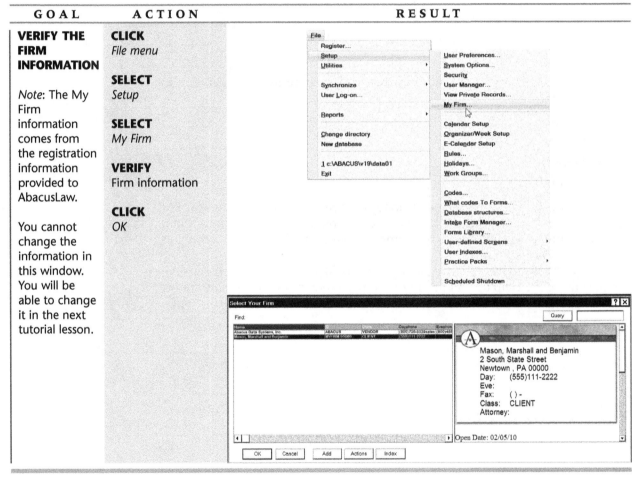

Continue with the following tutorial before exiting the program.

HOW DO I CHANGE THE FIRM INFORMATION?

Firm information like all contacts and names, including clients, vendors, opposing counsel, and parties is shown in a Names window. The Names window can be accessed using the Names menu, the Browse command, or the Names Browse window.

Substitute your personal information. Fill in the information before starting.

	TUTORIAL INFORMATION	YOUR INFORMATION
Firm Name	Mason, Marshall and Benjamin	
Attorney	Owen Mason	
ID	OM	
E-Mail	mason@masonmarshallandbenjamin.com	
Attorney		
ID		
Address	138 North Street	
City	Newtown	
State	PA	
Zip	18940	
Day Phone	555 111 2222	
Fax	555 111 3333	
Printer		
Reports	HP LASERJET 4250	
Labels	SMARTLABEL PRINTER	
Envelopes	HP LASERJET 4050	
Word Processor		
Executable	C:\programfiles\microsoft office\winword	

Change Firm Information on the Names Window

GOAL	ACTION	RESULT
START ABACUSLAW	**CLICK** AbacusLaw icon OR **CLICK** start **SELECT** All Programs **CLICK** AbacusLaw	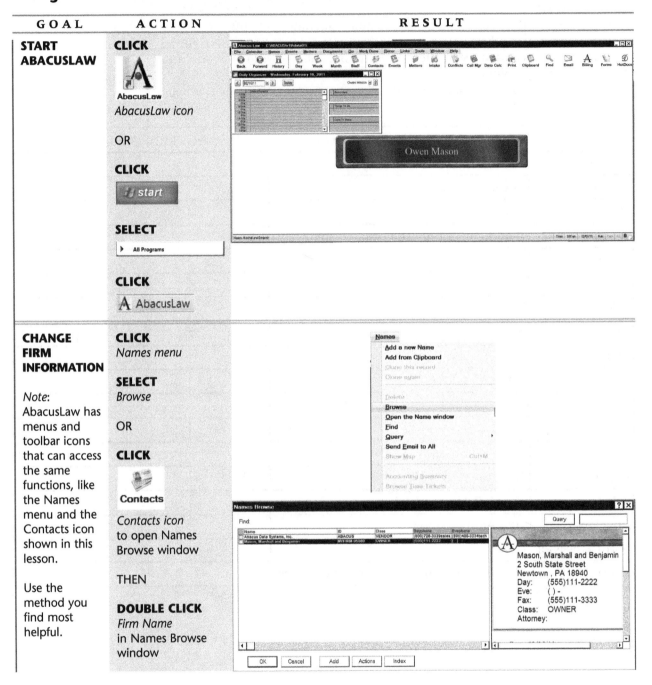
CHANGE FIRM INFORMATION *Note:* AbacusLaw has menus and toolbar icons that can access the same functions, like the Names menu and the Contacts icon shown in this lesson. Use the method you find most helpful.	**CLICK** *Names menu* **SELECT** *Browse* OR **CLICK** Contacts *Contacts icon* to open Names Browse window THEN **DOUBLE CLICK** *Firm Name* in Names Browse window	

Change Firm Information on the Names Window (*continued*)

GOAL	ACTION	RESULT
VERIFY INFORMATION FOR FIRM	**VERIFY** Information	
ENTER NEW INFORMATION OR CHANGE EXISTING INFORMATION AND SAVE RECORD *Note*: The Save button appears *after* new information is entered; in this case a new fax number and change of class from client to owner.	**ENTER** Your information OR fax number 555 111 3333 **CLICK** Class [ ] *Up arrow* **SELECT** *Owner* from Valid Class Entries **CLICK** *OK* **CLICK** *Save* on Names window for Mason, Marshall & Benjamin **CLICK** *X* (close open window)	

Continue with the following lesson before exiting the program.

HOW DO I SET UP MY PERSONAL USER INFORMATION?

Each AbacusLaw user may enter their personal information, including ID initials used to log on to AbacusLaw, personal e-mail address, and how the program will appear on the desktop when AbacusLaw is started (such as with or without a nameplate). Each user may have a different printer or word processor; these may also be customized for individual users' workstations. In some cases there may be different printers used for documents, labels, and envelopes.

The User Preference window has four tabbed screens for entering preferences: User Info, Appearance, Printing/Email Program, and Queries & Miscellaneous.

USER PREFERENCES

User Info Tab	Appearance Tab	Printing/ Email Program Tab	Queries & Miscellaneous Tab

Setting Up Personal Preferences

GOAL	ACTION	RESULT
SET UP YOUR PERSONAL USER PREFERENCES	**CLICK** *File menu* **SELECT** *Setup* **SELECT** *User Preferences*	

Setting Up Personal Preferences (*continued*)

GOAL	ACTION	RESULT
ENTER YOUR PERSONAL INFORMATION *Note*: You can change the settings at any time by checking or unchecking the settings boxes. *Note*: You may personalize the look of the desktop by selecting one of the calendar options, such as the organizer selected in this lesson.	**ENTER** Your personal information OR *OM* in Auto-Log on ID **ENTER** *Owen Mason* in User Name **CLICK** *Down arrow* by Startup Window field **SELECT** *Organizer* **CHECK** *Show Nameplate* on main window **CHECK** *Ask to backup at exit*	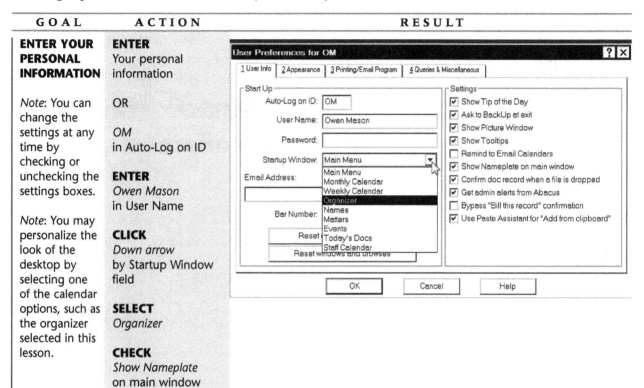

Setting Up Personal Preferences (*continued*)

G O A L	A C T I O N	R E S U L T
SELECT OR ENTER THE NAME OF THE PRINTER YOU USE TO PRINT DOCUMENTS AND REPORTS *Note:* Your *default printer* will appear as the Name on the *Print Setup* window (HP LaserJet 4250PCL6 is shown only as an example). You must enter *your* printer to be able to print AbacusLaw reports. Change this by selecting your printer in the Printing Setup window and clicking on the down arrow at the end of the Name. If you use a different printer for labels or envelopes, repeat the process of selecting the printer.	**CLICK** *Printing/Email Program tab* **CLICK** *Reports tab* in Printers **SELECT** *Your printer for reports* from the Print Setup window **CLICK** *OK* in the Print Setup window	

Setting Up Personal Preferences (*continued*)

GOAL	ACTION	RESULT
SELECT YOUR WORD PROCESSOR FROM YOUR COMPUTER PROGRAM FILES	**CLICK** *Executable button* in Word Processor option on Printing/Email Program tab **FIND** Path to your word processor using Windows Explorer window **SELECT** Your word processor **CLICK** *Open* **CLICK** *OK*	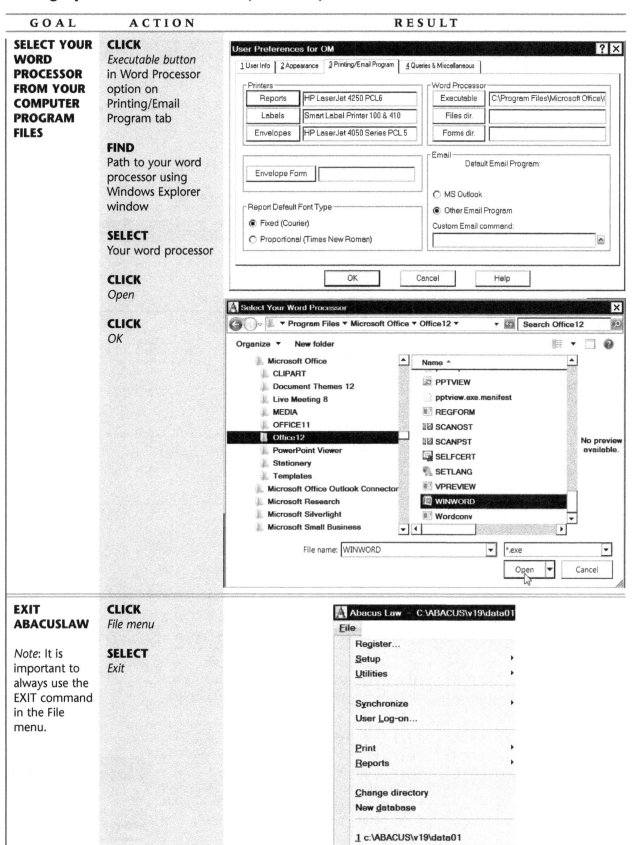
EXIT ABACUSLAW *Note:* It is important to always use the EXIT command in the File menu.	**CLICK** *File menu* **SELECT** *Exit*	

Setting Up Personal Preferences (*continued*)

G O A L	A C T I O N	R E S U L T
BACK UP FILES	**CLICK** *Yes*	**Select an option** ☒ ❓ Do you want to back up Abacus data files now? [Yes] [No]
SELECT THE DESTINATION FOR THE BACKUP *Note*: You should back up to a removable storage device by indicating that device as the Destination in the backup options window. To locate other storage devices connected to your computer, click the Destination button.	**ENTER** Path to your removable backup device OR *C:\Abacus* as destination **CLICK** *Start Backup*	**Backup Abacus Files** ❓☒ Directories Destination: `C:\` Source: `C:\ABACUS\v19\data01\` Number of backup files to retain: `7` ▾ Include along with main data ☐ Abacus MessageSlips ☐ Forms .AF files (only recommended if you design forms) ☐ Accounting data ☐ Saved PDF bills (may be huge!) Current file: File Compression ▢ Overall Progress ▢ [Cancel] [Start Backup] ☐ Send in email

When you restart AbacusLaw the changes in user preferences, including the nameplate and daily organizer calendar, will appear on your personal desktop.

HOW DO I ADD NEW USERS TO ABACUSLAW?

Single-user, demo, and trial versions are limited to one user. If you have a multiuser license, you may add additional users using the User Manager menu. The same type of information that you entered for yourself is entered for each licensed user, logon initials, name, printers, word processor, and appearance items.

TIP

Use the same initials for each user that will be used as timekeeper initials.

Setting Up New User

GOAL	ACTION	RESULT
START ABACUSLAW	**CLICK** *AbacusLaw icon* OR **CLICK** start **SELECT** ▸ All Programs **CLICK** A AbacusLaw	Owen Mason
SET UP NEW USERS	**CLICK** *File menu* **CLICK** *Setup* **CLICK** *User Manager*	File Register... Setup Utilities ▸ Synchronize ▸ User Log-on... Reports ▸ Change directory New database 1 C:\ABACUS\v19\data01 2 \\Tomhp-pc\c$\ABACUS\v19\data01 Exit User Preferences... System Options... Security User Manager... View Private Records... My Firm... Calendar Setup Organizer/Week Setup E-Calendar Setup Rules... Holidays... Work Groups... Codes... What codes To Forms... Database structures... Intake Form Manager... Forms Library... User-defined Screens ▸ User Indexes... Practice Packs ▸ Scheduled Shutdown

Setting Up New User (*continued*)

GOAL	ACTION	RESULT
ADD NEW USER INFORMATION	**CLICK** *Add*	

User Manager — ? X

Find:

User	Name	Security profile	Remind to Email Calendars
DM		Administrator	No

Add

Clone

Edit

Delete

◄ | ►

Close | Logged off | Shutdown | Security profile | Print | Help

Complete user preferences as shown in prior tutorial.

HOW DO I SET UP FIRM AND PERSONAL CALENDARS?

TIPS

As shown below, there are four primary types of calendars:

- Day (Daily Organizer)
- Week
- Month
- Staff

If room usage or use of audio-visual equipment is billed to client, add these items as timekeepers.

To be able to show more items, limit initials to three letters.

There is also a fifth calendar, the Free Time Calendar. Free time shows any periods of time when staff members or places and equipment are not scheduled. It is compiled from all of the calendars that are set up and maintained. It can be of great value in trying to schedule a meeting or the use of a room.

Each style of calendar can show any one person, thing, place (WHO code), or any combination of people or places, as shown in the staff calendar on the following page, which includes the conference room, library, video conferencing equipment, and attorney.

Calendars can be created and displayed for individuals, rooms, and equipment. Individual calendars are obvious; everyone on the legal team will want to have their own personal calendar with important professional deadlines, appointments, and personal items like anniversaries, birthdays, and other personal dates.

In the firm, conference rooms and the library may need to be scheduled to avoid conflict of use. In some offices, high-tech equipments like video conferencing, projectors, and other audio-visual equipment used in trials or presentations may also need to be scheduled to avoid conflicts.

People, places, and things in the calendar are referred to as a WHO code. WHO codes or valid entries are shortcuts for the program to locate the related information. Codes are visible to everyone using the program and provide a convenient set of abbreviations to save keystrokes. It is important for everyone in the firm to use the same set of codes to avoid confusion.

AbacusLaw provides a basic set of abbreviations for the different categories, but individual members of the legal team will need to have their initials and description set up as valid entries or WHO codes. Only those items entered on the list can be used (valid entries). This is done to prevent confusion since all these codes are shown to all users when they try to enter the appropriate codes. They can choose from the valid entries that already exist or add those that are needed if the desired code does not exist.

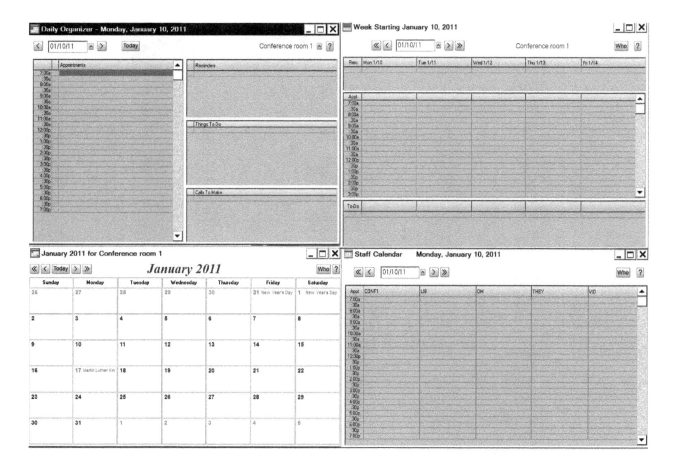

Adding New "WHO" to the Calendars

GOAL	ACTION	RESULT
START ABACUSLAW	**CLICK** AbacusLaw icon OR **CLICK** start **SELECT** All Programs **CLICK** AbacusLaw	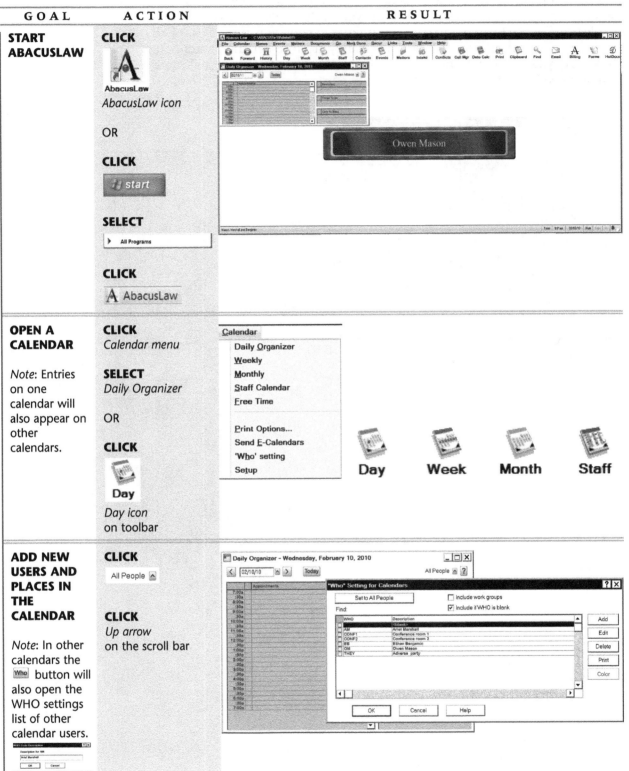
OPEN A CALENDAR *Note*: Entries on one calendar will also appear on other calendars.	**CLICK** *Calendar menu* **SELECT** *Daily Organizer* OR **CLICK** Day *Day icon* on toolbar	
ADD NEW USERS AND PLACES IN THE CALENDAR *Note*: In other calendars the Who button will also open the WHO settings list of other calendar users.	**CLICK** All People **CLICK** *Up arrow* on the scroll bar	

Adding New "WHO" to the Calendars (*continued*)

GOAL	ACTION	RESULT
ENTER NEW PERSON OR ITEMS "WHO" CODE (INITIALS)	**CLICK** *Add* **ENTER** Initials *AM* in the New "WHO" Code window **CLICK** *OK*	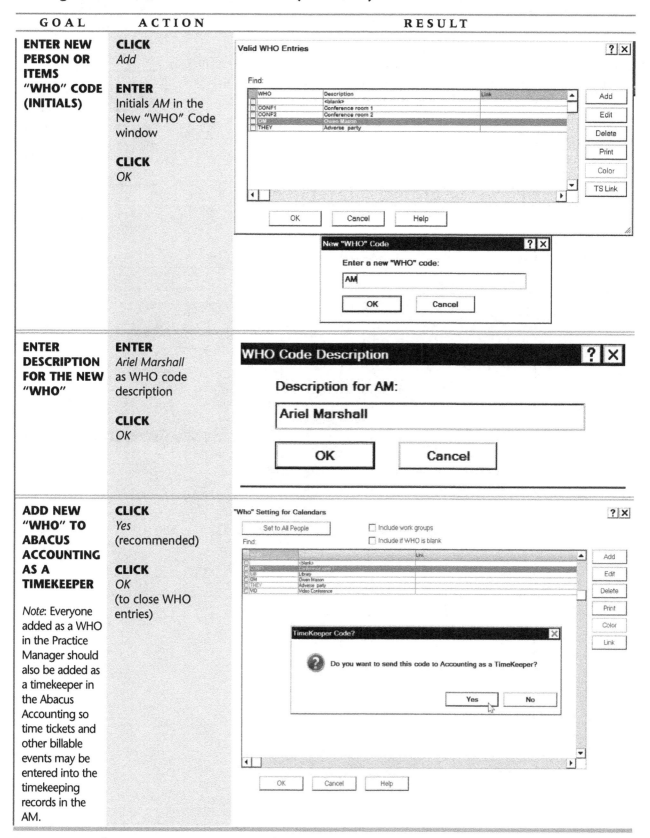
ENTER DESCRIPTION FOR THE NEW "WHO"	**ENTER** *Ariel Marshall* as WHO code description **CLICK** *OK*	
ADD NEW "WHO" TO ABACUS ACCOUNTING AS A TIMEKEEPER *Note*: Everyone added as a WHO in the Practice Manager should also be added as a timekeeper in the Abacus Accounting so time tickets and other billable events may be entered into the timekeeping records in the AM.	**CLICK** *Yes* (recommended) **CLICK** *OK* (to close WHO entries)	

You may exit the program or continue to the next tutorial.

HOW DO I ADD APPOINTMENTS (EVENTS) TO CALENDAR?

Appointments or events may be added for each person or item listed on a calendar. Items added to one calendar view, such as daily calendar, will also be added and shown on the other calendar views. Events may be entered for any person, place, or thing with a WHO code.

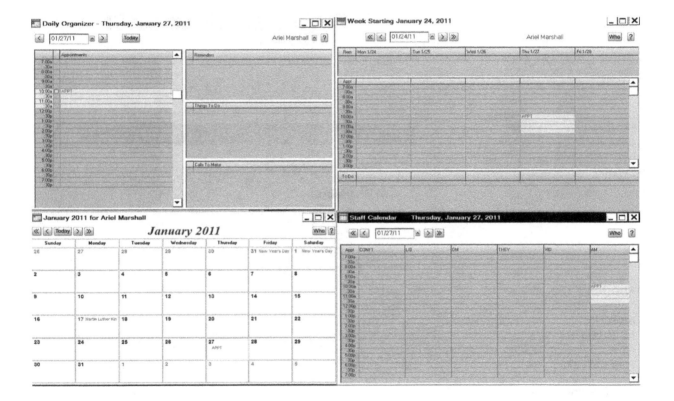

Add an Event to Calendar for Specific Person

GOAL	ACTION	RESULT
ADD NEW APPOINTMENT	**CLICK** *Events menu* **SELECT** *Add a new Event*	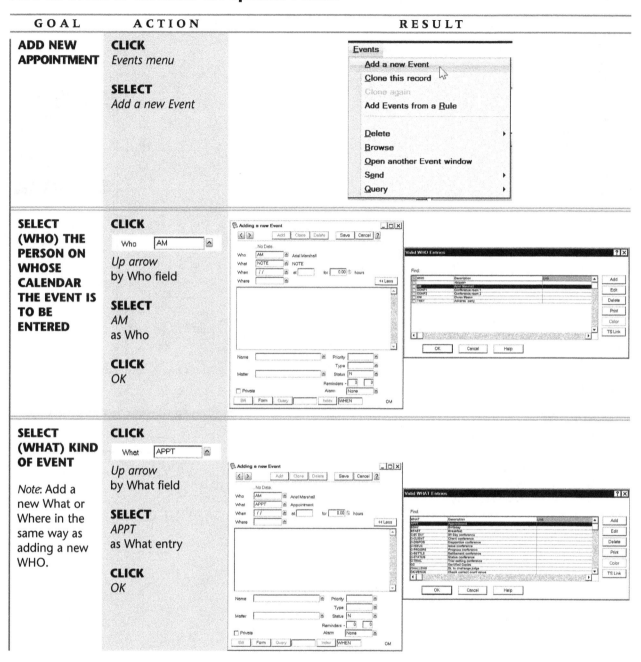
SELECT (WHO) THE PERSON ON WHOSE CALENDAR THE EVENT IS TO BE ENTERED	**CLICK** Who: AM *Up arrow* by Who field **SELECT** *AM* as Who **CLICK** *OK*	
SELECT (WHAT) KIND OF EVENT *Note*: Add a new What or Where in the same way as adding a new WHO.	**CLICK** What: APPT *Up arrow* by What field **SELECT** *APPT* as What entry **CLICK** *OK*	

Add an Event to Calendar for Specific Person (*continued*)

GOAL	ACTION	RESULT
SELECT (WHEN) DATE OF EVENT *Note*: The default date in WHEN is the current date. Select the desired date, if different, from the calendar.	**CLICK** When 01/27/11 *Up arrow* by When field **CLICK** *Date*	
SELECT (WHERE) THE LOCATION OF EVENT	**CLICK** Where HERE *Up arrow* by Where field **SELECT** *Here* as Where entry **CLICK** *OK*	

Add an Event to Calendar for Specific Person (*continued*)

GOAL	ACTION	RESULT
ENTER TIME AND DURATION OF EVENT AND SAVE THE EVENT DETAILS *Note:* The appointment on 1/27/2011 at 10:00 am for 2 hours will appear on all calendars as shown on the previous page.	**ENTER** *10:00a* **AND** *2.00* (time and how long) **CLICK** *Save* **CLICK** *X* to close event window **CLICK** *Yes* (confirm save new data)	*Adding a new Event* [< >] [Add] [Clone] [Delete] [Save] [Cancel] [?] Thursday, January 27, 2011. 355 days to go Who AM Ariel Marshall What APPT Appointment When 01/27/11 at 10:00a for 2.00 hours Where HERE Office [More >>] *Event: 01/27/11 Appointment* [< >] [Add] [Clone] [Delete] [?]

You may exit the program or continue to the next tutorial.

HOW CAN I PRINT MY CALENDAR?

Calendars can be printed in many different formats to suit personal preferences. In some offices the daily or weekly calendars are printed out for each member of the legal staff as a reminder of scheduled activity and as a *to do* list for the day or week.

Printing a Daily Organizer

GOAL	ACTION	RESULT
PRINT THE DAILY ORGANIZER	**CLICK** *Calendar menu* **CLICK** *Print Options*	Calendar Daily Organizer Weekly Monthly Staff Calendar Free Time Print Options... Send E-Calendars 'Who' setting Setup
SELECT DATE FOR DAILY ORGANIZER	**CLICK** 01/27/11 *Up arrow by date* **CLICK** On desired date **CLICK** *OK* in Calendar Print Options	Calendar Print Options Thursday, January 27, 2011 What to print Organizer · Week(s) · Month · Year · Days report · Month report · To-Do list · Other Report 01/27/11 OK · Close · Setup · Help January 27, 2011 December, 2010 January, 2011 Today: 2/6/2010 Thursday January 27, 2011

Printing a Daily Organizer (*continued*)

GOAL	ACTION	RESULT
SELECT WHO FOR CALENDAR *Note*: You may also print other calendars for yourself or others by changing the options on the different printing screens shown in this tutorial. For example, you can select another person by clicking on WHO in the Events Report Control and selecting someone else.	**CLICK** *WHO* in Events Report Control **CLICK** *Up Arrow* in "Who" Setup for Calendars window **DOUBLE CLICK** *AM* **CLICK** *Output to* **DOUBLE CLICK** *Screen* **CLICK** *Print* in Events Report Control	
PRINT DAILY ORGANIZER	**CLICK** *Print* in Report Viewer **CLICK** *OK* in Print Screen Option **CLICK** *Exit* in Report Viewer	

Close any open printing option screens and exit the Abacus program.

HOW DO I ADD CONTACTS (NAMES)?

A contact (person, firm, client, or counsel) is any name in your address book, e-mail list, or anyone whose information you want to record for future use. It may be information that has been kept in the firm's or personal address book on individual index cards or in a paper conflicts file or note cards. It may be current clients, prospective clients, other attorneys and paralegals, or other professionals or friends. All of the contacts' names and information when entered into the AbacusLaw program are saved and stored in the names database. You can add new names and contacts at any time or during the new matter setup.

T I P

You can use the shortcut CTRL + S to save the contact information entered.

Adding Contacts (Names)

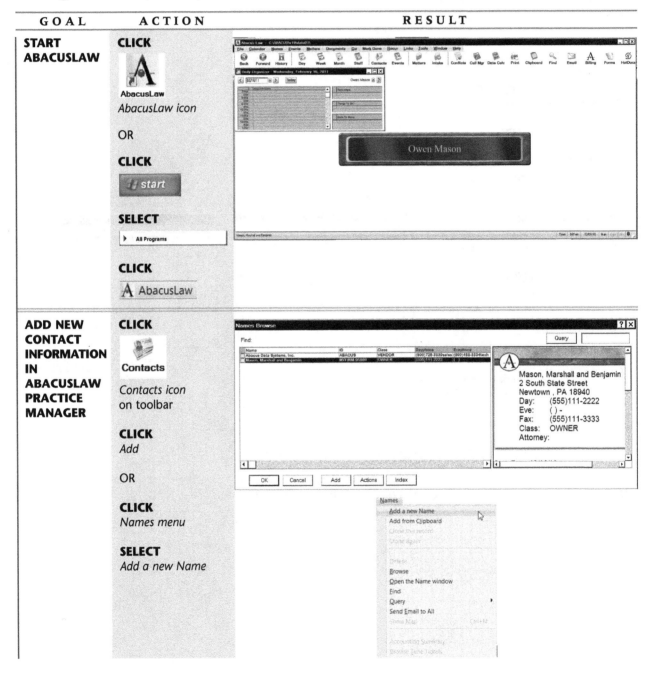

GOAL	ACTION	RESULT
START ABACUSLAW	**CLICK** AbacusLaw icon OR **CLICK** start **SELECT** All Programs **CLICK** AbacusLaw	
ADD NEW CONTACT INFORMATION IN ABACUSLAW PRACTICE MANAGER	**CLICK** Contacts icon on toolbar **CLICK** Add OR **CLICK** Names menu **SELECT** Add a new Name	

Adding Contacts (Names) (*continued*)

GOAL	ACTION	RESULT
ENTER NEW CONTACT INFORMATION AND ADD NEW CLASS CODE	**ENTER** Your information OR *Contact information for OWEN MASON from tutorial information at beginning of section* **CLICK** Class *Up arrow*	 **Adding a new Name** 1 Standard / 2 Notes / 3 Linked Matters / 4 Linked Events / 5 Linked Docs / 6 Emails / 7 Linked Names Last name: Mason — Dayphone: (555)111-2222 First name: Owen — Evephone: ( ) - ID number: MYFIRM-95870 — Fax: (555)111-3333 Dear: Owen — Cell: ( ) - Label: Owen Mason / 138 North State Street — Referred By: Class: PARTNER Atty: OM Zip: 18940 — Open: / / City: Newtown — St. PA — Active: ☑ Email: mason@masonmarshallbenjamin.com Add / Clone / Delete — Query — Index LAST_FIRST
ADD NEW CLASS CODE	**CLICK** *Add* in Valid CLASS Entries window **ENTER** *PARTNER* as new "CLASS" code **CLICK** *OK* **ENTER** *Partner* as CLASS Code Description **CLICK** *OK* **CLICK** *OK* (to add to class)	**Valid CLASS Entries** Find: CLASS — Description ADJUSTOR — Insurance adjustor ADV-D — Adversary - Defendant ADV-P — Adversary - Plaintiff ATTORNEY — Attorney CLIENT — Client EXPERT — Expert EXPNEURO — Expert neurologist EXPORTHO — Expert orthopod JUDGE — Judge OWNER — Owner PRESS — Press/media VENDOR — Vendor Add / Edit / Delete / Print OK / Cancel / Help **New "CLASS" Code** Enter a new "CLASS" code: PARTNER OK / Cancel **CLASS Code Description** Description for PARTNER: Partner OK / Cancel

Adding Contacts (Names) (*continued*)

GOAL	ACTION	RESULT
SELECT RESPONSIBLE ATTORNEY, DATE ENTERED, AND SAVE	**CLICK** Atty [ ] *Up arrow* **DOUBLE CLICK** *Owen Mason* OR *your Attorney ID from list* **CLICK** *Save*	**Valid WHO Entries** Find: | WHO	Description	Link	
	\<blank\>		Add
CONF1	Conference room 1		Edit
CONF2	Conference room 2		Delete
OM	Owen Mason		Print
THEY	Adverse party		Color
			TS Link	 OK Cancel Help **Name: Mason, Owen** < > MASON, OWEN 1 Standard 2 Notes 3 Linked Matters 4 Linked Events 5 Linked Docs 6 Emails 7 Linked Names Last name: Mason Dayphone: (555)111-2222 First name: Owen Evephone: ( ) - ID number: MYFIRM-95870 Fax: (555)111-3333 Dear: Owen Cell: ( ) - Label: Owen Mason Referred By: 138 North State Street Class: PARTNER Atty: OM Zip: 18940 Open: / / City: Newtown St. PA Active: ☑ Email: mason@masonmarshallbenjamin.com Add Clone Delete Query [ ] Index LAST_FIRST
EXIT ABACUSLAW	**CLICK** *File menu* **SELECT** *Exit*	**Abacus Law — C:\ABACUS\v19\data01** File Register... Setup ▸ Utilities ▸ Synchronize ▸ User Log-on... Print ▸ Reports ▸ Change directory New database 1 c:\ABACUS\v19\data01 Exit

The Basics: Using AbacusLaw Practice Manager

(Adding Clients and New Cases...)

- Tutorial Information Used
- Codes? (What Do I Call Them?)
- How Can I Customize Codes for My Firm?
  - ▲ *Tutorial—Adding WHO Codes*
  - ▲ *Tutorial—Adding Local Court Codes from AbacusLaw Master List*
  - ▲ *Tutorial—Adding Local Court Codes*
- How Do I Add Clients?
  - ▲ *Tutorial—Adding Client Contact Information*
- How Do I Set Up a New Client and a New Matter (Case)?
- Setting Up a New Matter
  - ▲ *Tutorial—Add a New Matter for an Existing Client*
- Linking to Abacus Accounting
  - ▲ *Tutorial—Create "Bill to" Link in Abacus Accounting*
- How Do I Add a New Client and Matter with a Separate "Bill to" Party?
  - ▲ *Tutorial—Add a New Client and Matter with Separate "Bill to" Party*
- How Do I Add Clients Using an Intake Form?
  - ▲ *Tutorial—Adding Clients Using PI Case Intake Form*
- How Do I Add Events to a Matter
  - ▲ *Tutorial—Add Events to a Matter*

CODES

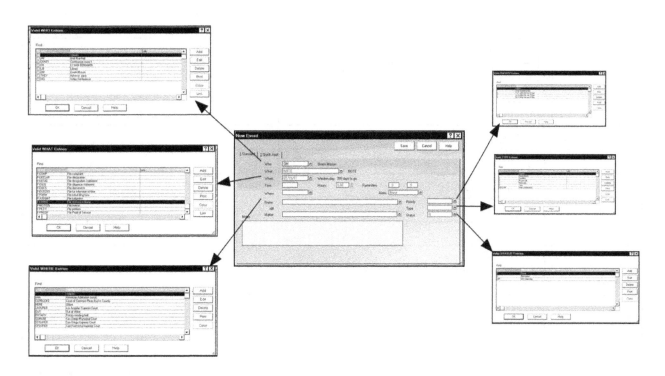

TUTORIAL INFORMATION USED

The following is the information used in the following section tutorials. You may substitute your personal information.

Fill in the information before starting.

	TUTORIAL INFORMATION	YOUR INFORMATION
Client Name	Jonathon Leonard	
Address	152 Timber Ridge Road	
City	Newtown	
State	PA	
Zip	18940	
Phone		
Matter	Jonathon Leonard vs. Stephen Blanca	
Court	Court of Common Pleas of Bucks County, Pennsylvania	
Court ID	CCP-BUCKS	
Mailing Address	Court Street	
Mailing Zip	18901	
Mailing City	DOYLESTOWN	
Mailing State	PA	
Court Phone	215 5555555	
E-Mail	www.bucks.gov/courts	
Matter	Bates v Howard	
Client	Alice Bates	
Label	40 Jefferson Court Newtown Pa 18940	
Client	Martin Bates	
Label	40 Jefferson Court Newtown Pa 18940	
Matter	Stein v Curtis	
Attorney	AM	
Last Name	Stein	
First Name	Elisabeth	
Dear	Elisabeth	
Addressee	Elisabeth Stein	

	TUTORIAL INFORMATION	YOUR INFORMATION
Street Address 1	1000 School Drive	
Zip	18940	
City	George School	
State	PA	
Responsible Attorney	AM	
Other Driver 1		
Last Name	Curtis	
First Name	Sigmund	
Dear		
Addressee	Sigmund	
Street Address 1	5 Swamp Road	
Zip	18943	
City	Penns Park	
State	PA	
Where	CCPBUCKS Court of Common Pleas Bucks County	
Court ID	US DIST_EDPA	
Jurisdiction ID	United States District Court Eastern District of Pennsylvania	
Mailing Address	601 Market Street, Room 2609	
Mailing Zip	19106-1797	
Mailing City	Philadelphia	
State	Pa	
URL	http://www.paed.uscourts.gov/	
Phone	215 597-7704	
Fax	215 597-6390	

CODES? (WHAT DO I CALL THEM?)

In Section 2, you changed a CLASS code from client to owner by selecting the code from a list of *Valid CLASS entries*, created a new CLASS code for Partner, and created a new WHO code for attorney Ariel Marshall using her initials AM.

These codes are abbreviations used in classifying information in the Matters, Names and Events windows in the AbacusLaw database. Most people use initials and abbreviations when writing notes to themselves or to others, such as phone messages in a law office, where the person taking the message will put their initials and the initials of the person called.

Each office develops, over time, its own set of abbreviations or codes to identify people, places, and things. If everyone uses the same set of codes, it can be a time saver. The key to success is having the same set of codes available to everyone, and a system to encourage their use. AbacusLaw makes available a basic set of codes for every aspect of case and office management, which may be edited or added to meet the needs of every type of practice.

HOW CAN I CUSTOMIZE CODES FOR MY FIRM?

The basic set of codes provided when you install AbacusLaw may not have specific codes you need in your practice. You will most certainly need to add all the timekeepers in the firm, rooms, and equipment that must be reserved and appear on firm calendars, local courts, and specialty areas of practice. Some of these code sets are shown below.

There are a number of different sets of codes, such as WHO codes, WHERE codes, and CLASS codes. Each of these codes is a description or abbreviation that can be used to find information and classify the information, such as insurance agent or opposing attorney, or divorce case or location such as "Here" for an activity in the office. There are a number of different code types, such as:

- Case code
- Class
- Doc_type
- Where
- Who

In a database these are also called *fields*. Remember from the introduction about databases—they are pieces of information, like a zip code or city for a person. In a database, they are one or a combination of things that can be searched for in creating a report, like all the clients who have a divorce case who are represented by a partner in your law firm. Most of the types of codes (fields) are provided with AbacusLaw. New code types (new fields) can be added if needed. In the following tutorials you will add new entries to the existing selection of Code Types. Some of the descriptions may be used in more than one place, such as the attorney initials OM (Owen Mason) as a user and as a timekeeper.

WHO codes are used to identify people, places, and things for which a calendar might be kept; for example, conference rooms or teleconference equipment. Each timekeeper also needs a WHO code, which is usually the person's initials, such as OM for Owen Mason.

The following tutorial shows how to add new a new person to the valid WHO entries.

The same method may be used to add valid entries to other codes.

Adding WHO Codes

GOAL	ACTION	RESULT
START ABACUSLAW	**CLICK** 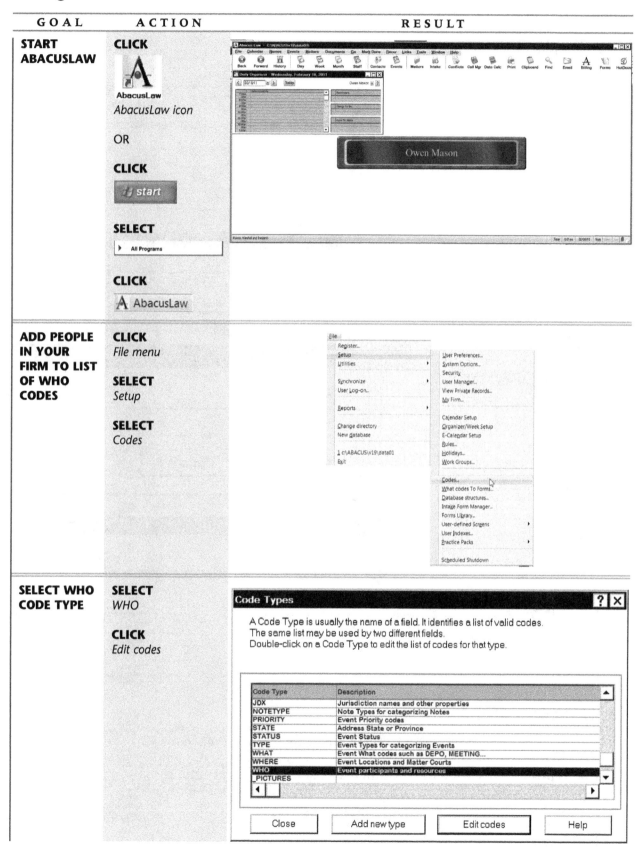 *AbacusLaw icon* OR **CLICK** start **SELECT** All Programs **CLICK** A AbacusLaw	
ADD PEOPLE IN YOUR FIRM TO LIST OF WHO CODES	**CLICK** *File menu* **SELECT** *Setup* **SELECT** *Codes*	
SELECT WHO CODE TYPE	**SELECT** *WHO* **CLICK** *Edit codes*	

Adding WHO Codes (*continued*)

GOAL	ACTION	RESULT
CREATE NEW WHO CODE	**CLICK** *Add* **ENTER** *EB* as new WHO code **CLICK** *OK*	Valid WHO Entries Find: WHO / Description / Link `<blank>` AM / Ariel Marshall CONF1 / Conference room 1 CONF2 / Conference room 2 OM / Owen Mason THEY / Adverse party Add / Edit / Delete / Print / Color / TS Link OK / Cancel / Help New "WHO" Code Enter a new "WHO" code: EB OK / Cancel
ENTER WHO CODE DESCRIPTION	**ENTER** *Ethan Benjamin* as description **CLICK** *OK*	WHO Code Description Description for EB: Ethan Benjamin OK / Cancel
ADD NEW WHO CODE TO ACCOUNTING AS A TIMEKEEPER	**CLICK** *Yes* **CLICK** *OK* **CLICK** *Close* (to close Who entries)	TimeKeeper Code? Do you want to send this code to Accounting as a TimeKeeper? Yes / No

LOCAL COURT CODES

A sample set of court codes is supplied with AbacusLaw. These include most California and New York courts. You will need to add your federal, state, and local courts or the courts in which your firm practices. The court and jurisdiction information is used to identify cases and also to fill in AbacusForms forms and templates.

TUTORIAL INFORMATION USED

The following is the information used in the following section tutorials. You may substitute your personal information.

Fill in the information before starting.

> **TIP**
>
> Use individual court Web sites to find court information such as mailing address, actual street address, telephone number, and fax number.

	TUTORIAL INFORMATION	YOUR INFORMATION
Court ID	US DIST_EDPA	
Jurisdiction ID	United States District Court Eastern District of Pennsylvania	
Mailing Address	601 Market Street , Room 2609	
Mailing Zip	19106-1797	
Mailing City	Philadelphia	
State	Pa	
URL	http://www.paed.uscourts.gov/	
Phone	215 597-7704	
Fax	215 597-6390	

Adding Local Court Codes from AbacusLaw Master List

GOAL	ACTION	RESULT
ADD LOCAL COURTS FOR YOUR PRACTICE FROM ABACUSLAW MASTER COURTS LIST	**CLICK** *File menu* **SELECT** *Setup* **SELECT** *Codes*	

Adding Local Court Codes from AbacusLaw Master List (*continued*)

GOAL	ACTION	RESULT
SELECT COURTS FROM CODE TYPES AND POPULATE COURTS LIST WITH SAMPLE COURTS FROM ABACUSLAW MASTER LIST	SELECT *COURT* from Code Type list CLICK *Edit codes* CLICK *Populate*	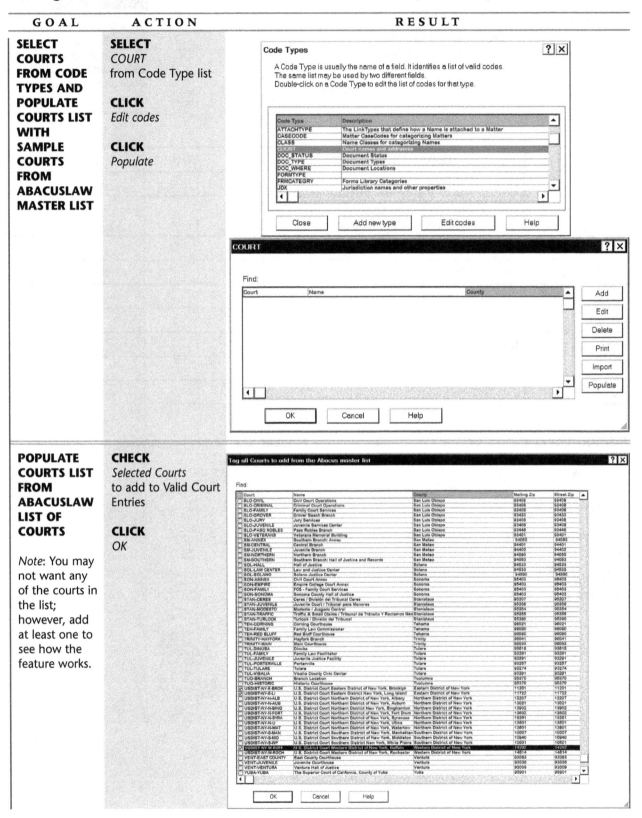
POPULATE COURTS LIST FROM ABACUSLAW LIST OF COURTS *Note*: You may not want any of the courts in the list; however, add at least one to see how the feature works.	CHECK *Selected Courts* to add to Valid Court Entries CLICK *OK*	

Adding Local Court Codes from AbacusLaw Master List (*continued*)

GOAL	ACTION	RESULT
CLOSE CODES TYPE AFTER POPULATING FROM ABACUSLAW MASTER LIST	**CLICK** *OK* **CLICK** *Close*	

COURT

Find:

Court	Name	County
USDIST-NY-E-BROK	U.S. District Court Eastern District of New York, Brooklyn	Eastern District of New York
USDIST-NY-E-LI	U.S. District Court Eastern District New York, Long Island	Eastern District of New York
USDIST-NY-W-BUFF	U.S. District Court Western District of New York, Buffalo	Western District of New York

Add
Edit
Delete
Print
Import
Populate

OK   Cancel   Help

Code Types

A Code Type is usually the name of a field. It identifies a list of valid codes.
The same list may be used by two different fields.
Double-click on a Code Type to edit the list of codes for that type.

Code Type	Description
ATTACHTYPE	The LinkTypes that define how a Name is attached to a Matter
CASECODE	Matter CaseCodes for categorizing Matters
CLASS	Name Classes for categorizing Names
COURT	Court names and addresses
DOC_STATUS	Document Status
DOC_TYPE	Document Types
DOC_WHERE	Document Locations
FORMTYPE	
FRMCATEGRY	Forms Library Categories
JDX	Jurisdiction names and other properties

Close   Add new type   Edit codes   Help

Adding Local Court Codes

GOAL	ACTION	RESULT
ADD LOCAL COURTS FOR YOUR PRACTICE	**CLICK** *File menu* **SELECT** *Setup* **SELECT** *Codes*	File Register... Setup Utilities Synchronize User Log-on... Reports Change directory New database 1 c:\ABACUS\w19\data01 Exit User Preferences... System Options... Security User Manager... View Private Records... My Firm... Calendar Setup Organizer/Week Setup E-Calendar Setup Rules... Holidays... Work Groups... Codes... What codes To Forms... Database structures... Intake Form Manager... Forms Library... User-defined Screens User Indexes... Practice Packs Scheduled Shutdown
SELECT COURTS AS CODE TYPE THAT WILL BE EDITED TO ADD ADDITIONAL COURTS TO LIST OF VALID COURT ENTRIES	**SELECT** *COURT* **CLICK** *Edit codes*	**Code Types** ? X A Code Type is usually the name of a field. It identifies a list of valid codes. The same list may be used by two different fields. Double-click on a Code Type to edit the list of codes for that type. Code Type — Description ATTACHTYPE — The LinkTypes that define how a Name is attached to a Matter CASECODE — Matter CaseCodes for categorizing Matters CLASS — Name Classes for categorizing Names COURT — Court names and addresses DOC_STATUS — Document Status DOC_TYPE — Document Types DOC_WHERE — Document Locations FORMTYPE FRMCATEGRY — Forms Library Categories JDX — Jurisdiction names and other properties Close Add new type Edit codes Help
ADD LOCAL COURT INTO VALID COURTS	**CLICK** *Add* on court list	**COURT** ? X Find: Court — Name — County USDIST-NY-E-BROK — U.S. District Court Eastern District of New York, Brooklyn — Eastern District of New York USDIST-NY-E-LI — U.S. District Court Eastern District New York, Long Island — Eastern District of New York USDIST-NY-W-BUFF — U.S. District Court Western District of New York, Buffalo — Western District of New York Add Edit Delete Print Import Populate OK Cancel Help

Adding Local Court Codes (*continued*)

GOAL	ACTION	RESULT
ENTER LOCAL COURT INFORMATON AND VALID JURISDICTION ENTRIES INFORMATION	**ENTER** Your local court OR Court ID, Name, Mailing address, Street address, and Phone numbers as shown **CLICK** *Up arrow* above the scroll bar **CLICK** *Add* on valid jurisdiction entries **ENTER** Jurisdiction ID, name (of court), URL, and State **CLICK** *OK* on Jurisdiction Properties screen **SELECT** *USDIST EDPA* **CLICK** *OK* **CLICK** *OK* on court properties	

Court Properties

Court ID:	US DIST EDPA
Name:	United States District Court Eastern District Pennsylvania
Jurisdiction ID:	USDIST EDPA	Type of Law:	

Mailing address:	601 Market Street	Street address:	601 Market Street
Mailing Zip:	19106-1797	Street Zip:	19106-1797
Mailing city:	Philadelphia St: PA	Street city:	Philadelphia St: PA
County:		Phone 1:	(215)597-7704
Branch:		Phone 2:	( ) -
Division:		Phone 3:	( ) -
Department:		Fax:	(21)559-76390
		Email:	

OK   Cancel   Help

Valid Jurisdiction Entries

Find:

Jurisdiction	Name
USDIST EDPA	U.S.District Court for Eastern District of PA
USDISTRICT-NY-E	U.S. District Court Eastern District of New York
USDISTRICT-NY-W	U.S. District Court Western District of New York

Add
Edit
Delete
Print
Populate

OK   Cancel   Help

Jurisdiction Properties

Jurisdiction ID:	USDIST EDPA
Name:	U.S.District Court for Eastern District of PA
URL:	http://www.paed.uscourts.gov/
State:	PA

OK   Cancel   Help

Adding Local Court Codes (*continued*)

GOAL	ACTION	RESULT
CLOSE CODES TYPE AFTER ADDING LOCAL COURT	**CLICK** *Close*	

Code Types   ? X

A Code Type is usually the name of a field. It identifies a list of valid codes. The same list may be used by two different fields.
Double-click on a Code Type to edit the list of codes for that type.

Code Type	Description
ATTACHTYPE	The LinkTypes that define how a Name is attached to a Matter
CASECODE	Matter CaseCodes for categorizing Matters
CLASS	Name Classes for categorizing Names
COURT	Court names and addresses
DOC_STATUS	Document Status
DOC_TYPE	Document Types
DOC_WHERE	Document Locations
FORMTYPE	
FRMCATEGRY	Forms Library Categories
JDX	Jurisdiction names and other properties

[Close] [Add new type] [Edit codes] [Help]

Continue to the next lesson or exit and restart later.

Use the methods described above to add or edit any other necessary codes. Most codes can be added or edited when the need arises from within any AbacusLaw window used to add or input information.

The following are samples included in the AbacusLaw lists provided with the program.

WHERE CODES

WHERE codes are the locations of where an event will be held. These may be businesses or other places such as restaurants regularly used, civic groups, or other locations that might appear on a calendar.

Valid WHERE Entries   ? X

Find:

WHERE	Description	
	<blank>	[Add]
AAA	American Arbitration Assoc.	
HERE	Office	[Edit]
LASUPER	Los Angeles Superior Court	
OUT	Out of office	[Delete]
ROTARY	Rotary meeting hall.	
SDMUNI	San Diego Municipal Court	[Print]
SDSUPER	San Diego Superior Court	
SFSUPER	San Francisco Superior Court	[Color]

[OK] [Cancel] [Help]

CLASS CODES

CLASS codes describe the role of the person, such as attorney, adjuster, or applicant.

Valid CLASS Entries		? X

Find:

CLASS	Description	
ADJUSTOR	Insurance adjustor	Add
ADV-D	Adversary - Defendant	
ADV-P	Adversary - Plaintiff	Edit
ATTORNEY	Attorney	
CLIENT	Client	Delete
EXPERT	Expert	
EXPNEURO	Expert neurologist	Print
EXPORTHO	Expert orthopod	
JUDGE	Judge	
OWNER	Owner	
PARTNER	Partner	
PRESS	Press/media	
VENDOR	Vendor	

OK   Cancel   Help

WHAT CODES

WHAT codes are specific activities, usually related to billing.

Valid WHAT Entries			? X

Find:

WHAT	Description	Link	
1ST.MEET	First Meeting		Add
A101	Plan and prepare for		
A102	Research		Edit
A103	Draft / revise		
A104	Review / Analyze		Delete
A105	Communicate (in firm)		
A106	Communicate (with client)		Print
A107	Communicate (other outside counsel)		
A108	Communicate (other external)		Color
A109	Appear for / attend		
A110	Manage data/files		TS Link
A111	Other		
ADM	Administrative Cost		
AN.MEET	Annual Meeting		
APPEAR	Appear		
APPT	Appointment		
BDAY	Birthday		
BFAST	Breakfast		
C-90 DAY	90 Day conference		
C-CLIENT	Client conference		
C-DISPOS	Disposition conference		
C-ISSUE	Issue conference		
C-PROGRS	Progress conference		
C-SETTLE	Settlement conference		
C-STATUS	Status conference		
C-TRIAL	Trial setting conference		
CC	Certified Copies		
CHALLENG	DL to challenge judge		
CK-VENUE	Check correct court venue		
CLOSING	Closing		
CLR	Clerk of Court		
CON	Consultation		

OK   Cancel   Help

CASE CODES

CASE codes identify the types of law practiced by your firm. In addition, these codes are used to maintain statistical data regarding different types of laws practiced. Each matter is assigned a case code.

AbacusLaw and Abacus Accounting share case codes, so any maintenance you perform in either module will be reflected in the other module.

CASECODE	Description
ADM	Administrative Law
ADR	Alt. Dispute Resolution
ANT	Antitrust
APP	Appellate
BKG	Banking
BKR	Bankruptcy
BUS	Business Law
CIV	Civil Litigation
COL	Collections
COM	Commercial
CON	Construction Defects
CONTRACT	Contract
COR	Corporate
CRI	Criminal
CVR	Civil Rights
DEATH	Wrongful death
DIVORCE	Divorce
ENT	Entertainment
ENV	Environmental
FAM	Family Law
GEN	General Practice
GOV	Government
HEA	Health
IHC	In-House Counsel
IMM	Immigration
INS	Insurance Law
INT	International Transactions
IPL	Intellectual Property Law
LAB	Labor
MA	Mergers & Acquisitions
MAL	Malpractice
MAR	Admiralty & Maritime

Valid CASECODE Entries dialog box — Find: field; buttons: Add, Edit, Delete, Print, TS Link, OK, Cancel, Help

The following are the additional base set of valid entries (codes) that come with AbacusLaw. Use the method of adding or editing to fit your special needs.

Link Type Codes		Note Type Codes		Type Codes (for events)	
Code	**Description**	**Code**	**Description**	**Code**	**Description**
ADV-P	Adversary–Plaintiff	MEETING	Meeting	A	Appointment
ADV-D	Adversary–Defendant	MEMO	Memo	D	Deadline
ADV-ATTY	Attorney for adversary	PH	Incoming phone call	R	Reminder
BILLTO	Billing party	PHONEOUT	Outgoing phone call	T	Task
CLIENT-P	Client–Plaintiff				
CLIENT-D	Client–Defendant				
EXPERT	Expert witness				
JUDGE	Judge				

Class codes		Priority codes		Status codes	
Code	**Description**	**Code**	**Description**	**Code**	**Description**
ATTORNEY	Attorney	1	Drop everything else	D	Done
CLIENT	Client	2	Do it within the next 2 days	N	Not Done
		3	Do it within the next 3 days	OFF	Off Calendar
		4	Do it within the next 4 days		

Codes may be used to find and sort information and create reports. For example, what real estate matters is attorney Marshall handling, or who has the conference room scheduled for Tuesday? In AbacusLaw, you are asked to identify the types of items when entering information into the Matter, Event, Names and Accounting records. Some of the group of codes are shown below for WHO, WHERE, WHAT, and CLASS. In the following tutorials you will use these in setting up matters and clients.

VALID ENTRIES

Before a code can be used it must be included on the list for that code group. If you try to use a new abbreviation or set of ID initials without adding it to the list you will get an invalid entry message. Choices are listed in a screen called valid entries, meaning that the code has been added so everyone will know what the code is and use the same code to avoid confusion.

HOW DO I ADD CLIENTS?

Client information can be entered either as a new name or as a new contact, as shown in the prior section. A new client's information may also be entered into AbacusLaw as part of a new case (matter) setup. Information may be entered using the new matter input menu or by using the Intake Form, which contains the basic contact information and details of the new matter.

Each contact or name can be identified by a class type. When setting up a new client, the Class Type should marked as "client" and the attorney who is handling the client's legal issues or is responsible for the client's files should be listed as the "attorney."

N O T E

Cases are referred to as MATTERS.

T I P

You can use the shortcut CTRL + S to save the contact information entered.

Adding Client Contact Information

GOAL	ACTION	RESULT
ADD NEW CLIENT CONTACT INFORMATION	**CLICK** Contacts *Contacts icon on toolbar* **CLICK** *Add* OR **CLICK** *Names menu* **SELECT** *Add a new Name*	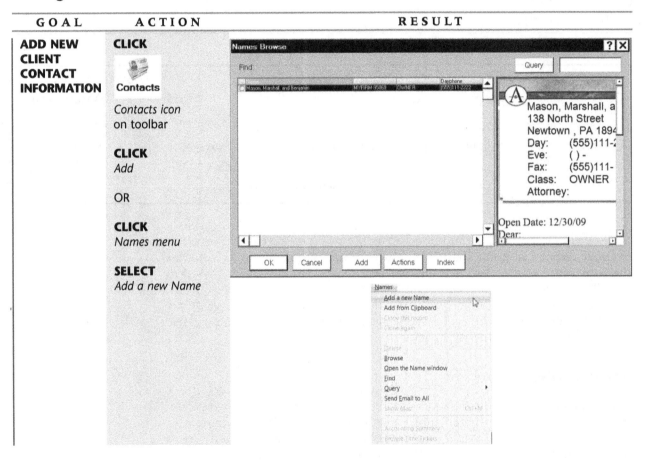

Adding Client Contact Information (*continued*)

GOAL	ACTION	RESULT
ENTER NEW CONTACT INFORMATION AND ADD NEW CLASS CODE AND SAVE	**ENTER** *Client contact information as shown* **CLICK** Class _____ *Up arrow* **SELECT (DOUBLE CLICK)** *Client* **ENTER** Atty _____ *Up arrow* **SELECT** OM **ENTER** *10/13/10* in the Date field **CLICK** *Save*	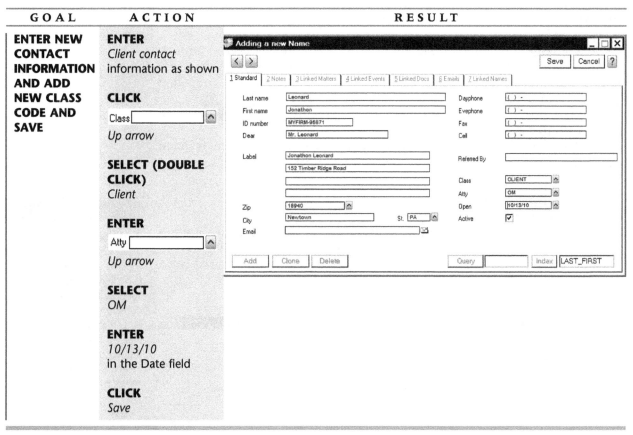

Continue to the next tutorial.

HOW DO I SET UP A NEW CLIENT AND A NEW MATTER (CASE)?

A client may be set up or entered into AbacusLaw by adding a new name using the Names window, which may be opened using the Contacts icon or the Names menu option, as shown in the previous tutorial. The client information may also be entered as part of the new case setup using the Matter window using Linked Names. As with other features in AbacusLaw, there are multiple methods of entering and accessing information. In addition to the manual entry of matter information, cases and contacts may be set up using an *intake form*. An intake form is a form with places for specific information about the person and case that will be automatically entered into a Matter or Name window. The result is the same; the information is entered into the Names and Matters databases. Each method is shown in the following tutorials.

SETTING UP A NEW MATTER

A matter is a case for a client. There may be a single client for whom you are handling a number of matters; for example, preparing a will, defending a breach of contract action, and representing the client seeking damages for a personal injury from a motor vehicle accident. You only need to input the client information once and then use the same information in each matter as it is set up.

All of the information about the case may be entered using the Matters window, including items related to the matter, like notes, people, documents, and events. These are referred to in AbacusLaw as *linked: linked notes, linked names, linked events,* and *linked documents*.

Depending on the type of matter (kind of case or area of law), you may use the generic Matter window to enter the information or use an AbacusLaw add-on product, such as the personal injury practice pack intake forms and specialty matters windows, as shown in Appendix A.

The basic information is the same, but the specialty practice screens have additional linked information.

In this tutorial you will need to enter the information about the court in which the case will be filed.

THE JURISDICTION ID

To be able to enter a code in the Jurisdiction ID, the court must be listed in the Valid Court entries. If the specific court is not listed you will need to add the court and jurisdiction information, and then add the desired court from the list of Valid Court entries.

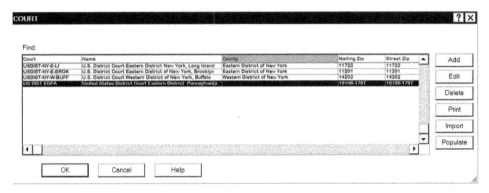

TIP

If you will be using the timekeeping functions, it is a good practice to set up the client or other party, such as the insurance company or corporation, who is paying the legal fees as the "bill to" party when setting up the individual case matter.

Add a New Matter for an Existing Client

GOAL	ACTION	RESULT
ADD A NEW MATTER	**CLICK** *Matters menu* **SELECT** *Add a new Matter* OR **CLICK** **Matters** *Matters icon* **CLICK** *Add*	
ENTER RESPONSIBLE ATTORNEY	**ENTER** *Jonathon Leonard v Stephen Blanca* as Matter name **CLICK** Atty ⌃ *Up arrow* **SELECT** *OM* **CLICK** *OK*	

Add a New Matter for an Existing Client (*continued*)

GOAL	ACTION	RESULT
ENTER CASE CODE	**CLICK** Case Code *Up arrow* **SELECT** *PI* from list **CLICK** *OK*	**Valid CASECODE Entries** Find: CASECODE / Description MAR — Admiralty & Maritime MONEY — Money complaint PATERN — Paternity PI — Personal Injury PLI — Product Liability PRB — Probate REA — Real Estate SEC — Securities TAX — Tax TEC — Technology TERMINAT — Wrongful termination TORT — Tort TRU — Trust & Estates WC — Workers Comp Add Edit Delete Print TS Link OK Cancel Help
ENTER COURT FROM EXISTING LIST *Note*: A sample list of courts is provided. You may need to add your local court as shown in prior tutorial.	**CLICK** Court *Up arrow* **DOUBLE CLICK** *US DIST EDPA*	**COURT** Find: Court / Name / County / Mailing Zip / Street Zip USDIST-NY-E-LI — U.S. District Court Eastern District New York, Long Island — Eastern District of New York — 11722 — 11722 USDIST-NY-E-BROK — U.S. District Court Eastern District of New York, Brooklyn — Eastern District of New York — 11201 — 11201 USDIST-NY-W-BUFF — U.S. District Court Western District of New York, Buffalo — Western District of New York — 14202 — 14202 US DIST EDPA — United States District Court Eastern District Pennsylvania — — 19106-1797 — 19106-1797 Add Edit Delete Print Import Populate OK Cancel Help
SAVE NEW MATTER AND ENTER IN DATABASE	**CLICK** *Save*	**Adding a new Matter** Save Cancel 1 Standard 2 Notes 3 Linked Names 4 Linked Events 5 Linked Docs 6 Emails Matter — Jonathan Leonard v Stephen Blanca File/case# — 1235 Court — US DIST EDPA Attorney — OM Court Case # — Case Code — PI Opened — 10/13/10 Closed — / / User-defined fields: User1 — School Bus Case User3 — User2 — User4 — / / Add Clone Delete Query Index MATTER

Add a New Matter for an Existing Client (*continued*)

GOAL	ACTION	RESULT
ADD CLIENT INFORMATION (LINK NAME)	**CLICK** *Linked Names tab* on Matters screen **CLICK** *Add link* **SELECT** *Leonard, Jonathon* as the client name from the Names Browse window **CLICK** *OK*	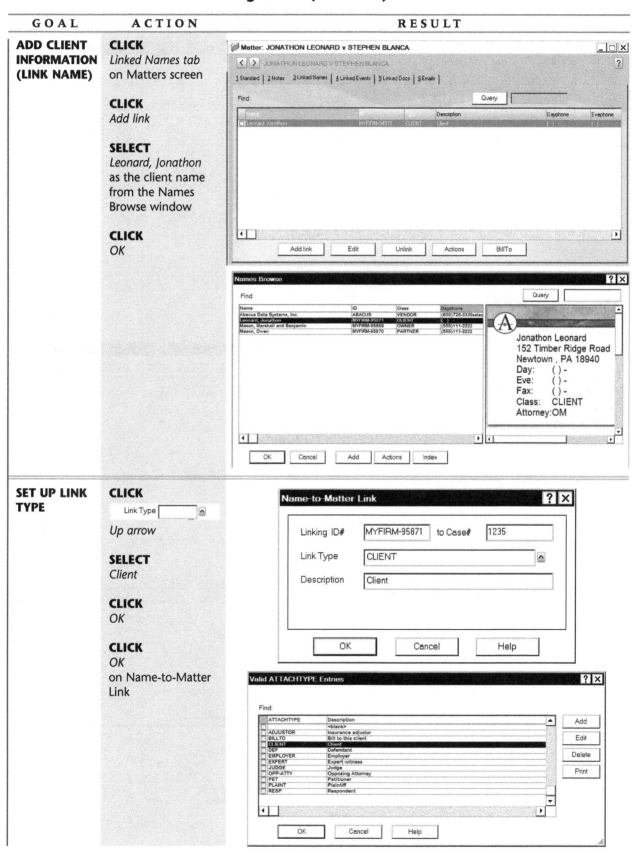
SET UP LINK TYPE	**CLICK** Link Type *Up arrow* **SELECT** *Client* **CLICK** *OK* **CLICK** *OK* on Name-to-Matter Link	

Add a New Matter for an Existing Client (*continued*)

GOAL	ACTION	RESULT
ADD NAME OF OPPOSING PARTY	**CLICK** *Contacts* *Contacts icon* **CLICK** *Add* **ENTER** Information as shown	
SAVE WITHOUT CLASS ENTRY *Note*: A warning message will appear if you try to save without a class entered.	**CLICK** *Save* **CLICK** *OK* **CLICK** *Add* in Valid CLASS Entries window	

Add a New Matter for an Existing Client (*continued*)

GOAL	ACTION	RESULT
ENTER NEW CODE AND DESCRIPTION *Note*: The Code Editor can be used to correct or change a code or description.	**ENTER** *DEF* as new "CLASS" code **CLICK** *OK* **ENTER** *Defendant* in the Description field **CLICK** *OK* **SELECT** *DEF* as class for name **CLICK** *OK*	
LINK NAME TO MATTER	**CLICK** **Matters** *Matters icon* **DOUBLE CLICK** *Leonard v Blanca* **CLICK** *Linked Names tab* **CLICK** *Add Link* **DOUBLE CLICK** *Stephen Blanca* in Names Browse window	

Add a New Matter for an Existing Client (*continued*)

GOAL	ACTION	RESULT
	CLICK Link Type *Up arrow* **DOUBLE CLICK** *DEF DEFENDANT* **CLICK** *OK*	Name-to-Matter Link Linking ID# MYFIRM-95677 to Case# 1235 Link Type DEF Description Defendant OK Cancel Help **Valid ATTACHTYPE Entries** Find: | ATTACHTYPE	Description
	<blank>
ADJUSTOR	Insurance adjustor
BILLTO	Bill to this client
CLIENT	Client
DEF	Defendant
EMPLOYER	Employer
EXPERT	Expert witness
JUDGE	Judge
OPP-ATTY	Opposing Attorney
PET	Petitioner
PLAINT	Plaintiff
RESP	Respondent	 Add Edit Delete Print OK Cancel Help
	CLOSE OPEN WINDOWS	

Exit AbacusLaw.

If you are using AbacusLaw Abacus Accounting continue to the next tutorial showing how to link a new matter to Abacus Accounting or skip to Section 4.

LINKING TO ABACUS ACCOUNTING

The Practice Manager and Abacus Accounting may be linked, permitting information to be shared when performing accounting functions like time-keeping and billing.

Each matter, except in pro bono cases, will be billed to a client or other party, such as an insurance company. Even pro bono cases have time and cost associated with them that the firm will want to track for court reporting purposes, reimbursement, or internal use.

As part of the new matter setup, a client or a third party such as an insurance company or court agency can be designated as the one to whom the matter should be billed. The party to be billed is linked to the matter as the "bill to" link.

In the following tutorial you will add a client as a "bill to" party in the Matter window.

NOTE

To use the timekeeping function in AbacusLaw there *must* be someone designated as the "bill to" party.

Create "Bill to" Link in Abacus Accounting

GOAL	ACTION	RESULT
OPEN ABACUSLAW AND SELECT MATTERS	**CLICK** *AbacusLaw icon* **CLICK** *Matters icon*	
ADD "BILL TO" PARTY *Note*: The "bill to" party is the person or company who will pay the legal fees.	**SELECT** *LEONARD V BLANCA* **CLICK** *OK* **CLICK** *Linked Names tab* **CLICK** *Add link* **SELECT** *Leonard, Jonathon* **CLICK** *OK*	

Create "Bill to" Link in Abacus Accounting (*continued*)

GOAL	ACTION	RESULT
SET UP LINK TYPE	**CLICK** Link Type CLIENT *Up arrow* by Link Type **SELECT** *Bill To* **PRESS** *the ENTER key* on keyboard **CLICK** OK in Valid ATTACHTYPE Entries window **CLICK** OK in Name-to-Matter Link window	
SET UP BILLING FORMAT	**CLICK** *Up arrow* by Billing Format Code **CLICK** C (Contingency-Settlement Statement Format) in Billing Format Codes Browse window **CLICK** OK **CLICK** OK	

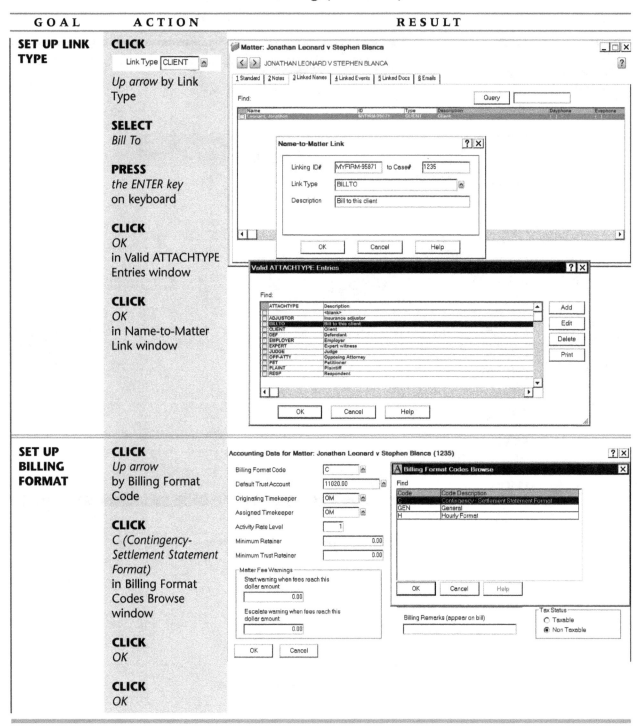

Continue to the next tutorial.

HOW DO I ADD A NEW CLIENT AND MATTER WITH SEPARATE "BILL TO" PARTY?

In the following tutorial, a new client and new matter are set up. In this case, the client is a minor and the billing will be to her father, with a reduced contingent fee required under the local court rules for cases involving minors.

Add a New Client and Matter with Separate "Bill to" Party

GOAL	ACTION	RESULT
ADD NEW MATTER	**CLICK** *Matters menu* **SELECT** *Add a new Matter* OR **CLICK** **Matters** *Matters icon* THEN **CLICK** *Add*	

Add a New Client and Matter with Separate "Bill to" Party (*continued*)

GOAL	ACTION	RESULT
ENTER BASIC MATTER INFORMATION	**ENTER** *Bates v Howard* (Matter field) *AM* (Attorney field) *PI* (Case Code field) *01/02/10* (Opened field) **CLICK** *Save*	
OPEN A NEW NAME INPUT SCREEN	**CLICK** *Linked Names tab* **CLICK** *Add link* in Matter window **CLICK** *Add* in Names Browse window	

Add a New Client and Matter with Separate "Bill to" Party (*continued*)

GOAL	ACTION	RESULT
ENTER NEW CLASS CODE FOR A MINOR CLIENT	**COMPLETE** *New Name screen* **CLICK** Class Up arrow **CLICK** *Add* in Valid CLASS Entries window **ENTER** *CLT MINR* in New "CLASS" Code **CLICK** *OK*	
ENTER NEW CODE DESCRIPTION	**ENTER** *Client Minor* in CLASS Code Description window **CLICK** *OK*	

Add a New Client and Matter with Separate "Bill to" Party (*continued*)

GOAL	ACTION	RESULT
SELECT NEW CLASS ENTRY	**SELECT** *CLT MINR* **CLICK** *OK*	
SAVE NEW NAME	**CLICK** *Save*	

Valid CLASS Entries

Find:

Class	Description
ADJUSTOR	Insurance adjustor
ADV-D	Adversary - Defendant
ADV-P	Adversary - Plaintiff
ATTORNEY	Attorney
CLIENT	Client
CLT MINR	Client Minor
EXPERT	Expert
EXPNEURO	Expert neurologist
EXPORTHO	Expert orthopod
JUDGE	Judge
OWNER	Owner
PARTNER	Partner
PRESS	Press/media
VENDOR	Vendor

Add   Edit   Delete   Print

OK   Cancel   Help

New Name

Save   Cancel   Help

1 Standard

Last name	Bates
First name	Alice
ID number	MYFIRM-95673
Dear	Alice
Label	Alice Bates
	40 Jefferson Street
Zip	18940
City	Newtown St. PA
Email	

Dayphone	( ) -
Evephone	( ) -
Fax	( ) -
Cell	( ) -
Referred By	Jonathan Leonard
Class	CLT MINR
Atty	AM
Open	01/02/10
Active	✔

Add a New Client and Matter with Separate "Bill to" Party (*continued*)

GOAL	ACTION	RESULT
ADD CLIENT AS LINKED NAME IN MATTER	**DOUBLE CLICK** *Bates, Alice* from Names Browse window	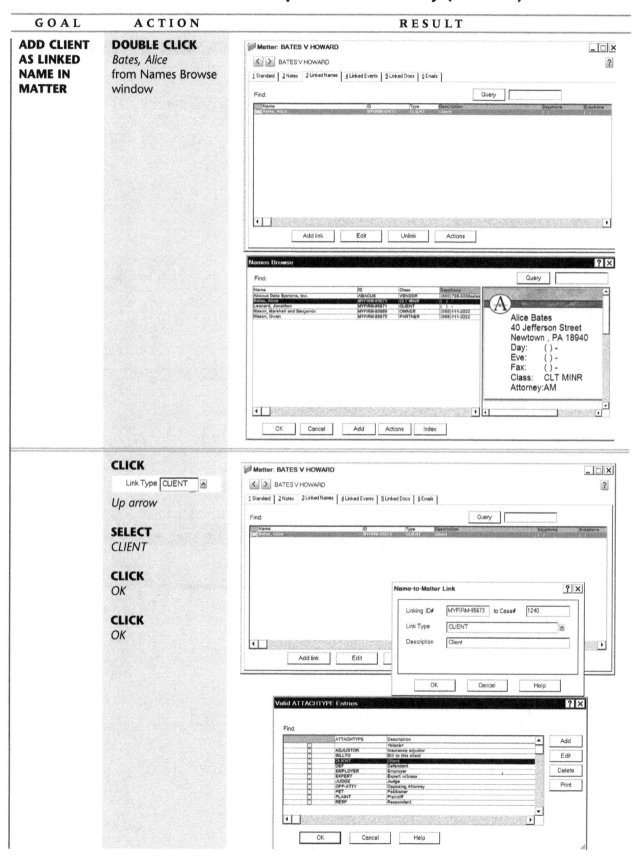
	CLICK Link Type CLIENT *Up arrow* **SELECT** *CLIENT* **CLICK** *OK* **CLICK** *OK*	

Add a New Client and Matter with Separate "Bill to" Party (*continued*)

GOAL	ACTION	RESULT
ADD NEW NAME TO NAMES	**CLICK** *Names menu* **SELECT** *Add New Name* **ENTER** Information **CLICK** *Save*	*Adding a new Name screen showing Standard tab with fields: Last name Bates, First name Martin, ID number MYFIRM-95674, Dear Mr. Bates, Label Martin Bates, 40 Jefferson, Zip 18940, City Newtown, St. PA, Dayphone, Evephone, Fax, Cell, Referred By Jonathan Leonard, Class CLIENT, Atty AM, Active checked.*
ADD A NEW BILL TO PARTY *Note*: The "bill to" party may also be set up by clicking the BILL TO button on the linked names input screen.	**CLICK** *Matters icon* **SELECT** *Bates v Howard* **CLICK** *Linked Names tab* **CLICK** *Add link* **DOUBLE CLICK** *Bates, Martin from Names Browse window*	*Matter: BATES V HOWARD screen with Linked Names tab. Names Browse window showing list including Abacus Data Systems Inc., Bates Alice, Bates Martin, Leonard Jonathan, Mason Marshall and Benjamin, Mason Owen. Detail panel shows: Martin Bates, 40 Jefferson, Newtown, PA 18940, Day: ( ) -, Eve: ( ) -, Fax: ( ) -, Class: CLIENT, Attorney: AM*

Add a New Client and Matter with Separate "Bill to" Party (*continued*)

GOAL	ACTION	RESULT
ESTABLISH THE NAME TO LINK AS THE "BILL TO" LINK	**SELECT** *BILL TO* as Link Type **CLICK** *OK* in Name-to-Matter Link window	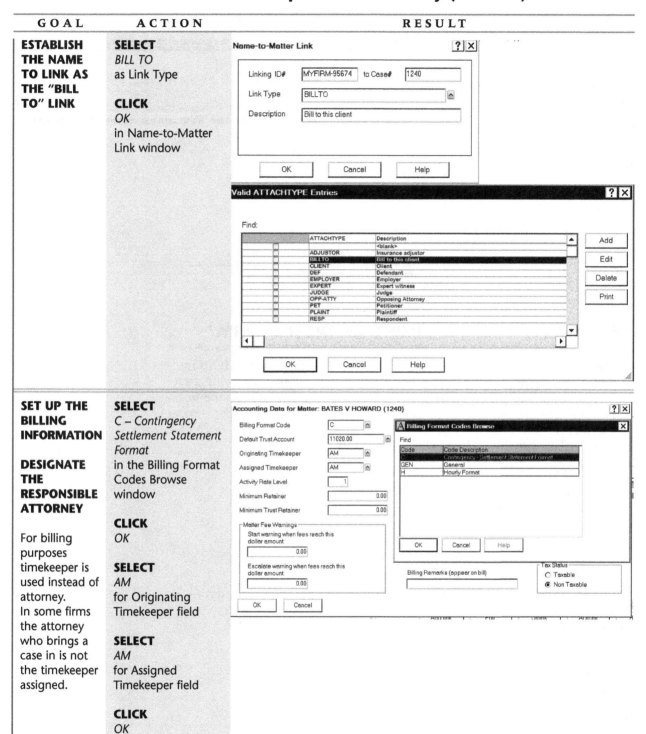
SET UP THE BILLING INFORMATION **DESIGNATE THE RESPONSIBLE ATTORNEY** For billing purposes timekeeper is used instead of attorney. In some firms the attorney who brings a case in is not the timekeeper assigned.	**SELECT** *C – Contingency Settlement Statement Format* in the Billing Format Codes Browse window **CLICK** *OK* **SELECT** *AM* for Originating Timekeeper field **SELECT** *AM* for Assigned Timekeeper field **CLICK** *OK*	

Add a New Client and Matter with Separate "Bill to" Party (*continued*)

GOAL	ACTION	RESULT
EXIT BATES V HOWARD MATTER WINDOW	CLICK *X*	

Continue or exit and restart for the next tutorial.

HOW DO I ADD CLIENTS USING AN INTAKE FORM?

Client information can be entered as contact information using the Names window or as part of a new case setup, as shown on the following page. Information may be entered using a new contact or new matter intake form, which contains the basic contact information and details of the new contact or matter.

AbacusLaw provides a basic set of intake forms for:

- Divorce case
- New case for a client—defendant
- New case for a client—plaintiff
- New case Web
- New contact
- PI case intake

Additional practice specialty packs, described in more detail in Appendix A, may also be obtained from AbacusLaw and added to the program, including:

- Adoption
- Custody
- Domestic violence
- Guardianship
- Paternity

CLIENT CONTACT INTAKE FORM AND RELATED NEW NAME INPUT SCREEN

Adding Clients Using PI Case Intake Form

GOAL	ACTION	RESULT
ADD NEW MATTER AND CLIENT INFORMATION USING PI CASE INTAKE FORM *Note*: Many forms can be accessed in different ways including the menu bar or toolbar icon, as well as from within other forms.	**CLICK** *Intake icon* **CLICK** *PI Case Intake Form* OR **CLICK** *Matters menu* **SELECT** *Intake Forms* **SELECT** *PI Case Intake Form*	Intake Divorce Case Intake Form New Case Intake Form (Client Defendant) New Case Intake Form (Client Plaintiff) New Case Web Form New Contact Form PI Case Intake Form OR **Matters** Add a new Matter Clone this record Clone again Intake Forms → Download and import web data... 　　　　　　　　　Import web data Delete　　　　　　Intake Form Manager... Browse Open the Matter window　Divorce Case Intake Form Find　　　　　　　　New Case Intake Form (Client Defendant) Query →　　　　　　New Case Intake Form (Client Plaintiff) 　　　　　　　　　　New Case Web Form Accounting Summary　New Contact Form Browse Time Tickets　PI Case Intake Form

Adding Clients Using PI Case Intake Form (*continued*)

GOAL	ACTION	RESULT
ENTER NEW CLIENT AND MATTER INFORMATION **ENTER OPPOSING PARTY INFORMATION** *Note*: The top half of the intake form is the same information entered in the New Matter screen and the New Names input screen. *Note*: After you save the intake form, a Billing Information screen will open, as shown on the following page.	**ENTER** Information as shown **CLICK** *Save*	

Intake Form: PI Case Intake Form

Please enter information about the case.

Plaintiff v. Defendant	Stein v Curtis
Court	
Court Case Number	
Opened	03/04/10
Attorney	AM
User1	
User2	
User3	
User4	/ /

Please enter the client's contact information below.

Last name	Stein
First name	Elisabeth
Dear	Elisabeth
Addressee	Elisabeth Stein
Street Address 1	1000 School Drive
Street Address 2	
Street Address 3	
Zip	18940
City	George School
State	PA
Email address	
Work Phone	( ) -
Home Phone	( ) -
Cell Phone	( ) -
Fax Number	( ) -

Select the WHO code for calendared Events.

Responsible Attorney	AM

Please enter the other driver's contact information below.

Last name	Curtis
First name	Sigmund
Dear	
Addressee	Sigmund Curtis
Address 1	5 Swamp Road
Address 2	
Address 3	
Zip	18943
City	Penns Park
State	PA
Work Phone	( ) -
Home Phone	( ) -
Email address	

If there are multiple defendants, please enter their names in the following Note field. The list you enter will be used on your forms that require specific formatting of the defendants' names.

Note	

Please review your entries carefully and then click Save to enter the Name and Matter information into Abacus, create relational links and calendar Events. Thank you.

Save   Cancel

Adding Clients Using PI Case Intake Form (*continued*)

GOAL	ACTION	RESULT
ENTER CLIENT BILLING AGREEMENT INFORMATION	**ENTER** Billing information **CLICK** *OK*	

Accounting Data for Matter: Stein v Curtis (1241)   [?][X]

Billing Format Code   H

Default Trust Account   11020.00

Originating Timekeeper   AM

Assigned Timekeeper   AM

Activity Rate Level   1

Minimum Retainer   0.00

Minimum Trust Retainer   0.00

Matter Fee Warnings
Start warning when fees reach this dollar amount:
0.00

Escalate warning when fees reach this dollar amount:
0.00

[OK]   [Cancel]

Billing Frequency
- ● Monthly
- ○ Quarterly
- ○ Special Quarterly
- ○ Semi-Annually
- ○ Annually
- ○ End of Matter
- ○ On Hold

Billing Remarks (appear on bill)

Billing Mode
- ● Hourly
- ○ Flat Fee
- ○ Monthly Fee
- ○ Minimum Fee
- ○ Contingency

Non-Hourly Billing Status
- ○ Billed
- ● Unbilled

Tax Status
- ○ Taxable
- ● Non Taxable

Billing Format Codes Browse   [X]

Find

Code	Code Description
C	Contingency - Settlement Statement Format
GEN	General
H	Hourly Format

[OK]   [Cancel]   [Help]

Adding Clients Using PI Case Intake Form (*continued*)

GOAL	ACTION	RESULT
SCHEDULE RULE-BASED CALENDAR EVENTS FOR A NEW CASE	**CLICK** *Yes* **CLICK** *OK* **CLICK** *Matters* **DOUBLE CLICK** *STEIN v CURTIS* **CLICK** *Linked events* **REVIEW** *Linked events*	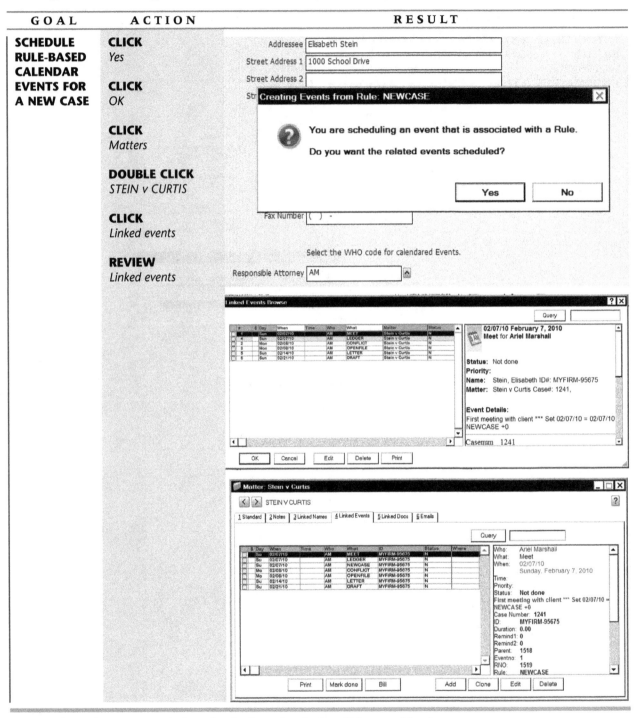

Do not close the Matter window for Stein v Curtis; it will be used in the next tutorial.

HOW DO I ADD EVENTS TO A MATTER?

An event is anything you add to a calendar. It may also be an item that is directly related to a matter. As you have seen, items may be linked to matters using the Linked tabs on the Matter screen.

Add Events to a Matter

GOAL	ACTION	RESULT
OPEN LINKED EVENTS IN MATTER AND ADD NEW LINKED EVENT	**CLICK** *Matters icon* **SELECT** *Stein v Curtis Matter* **CLICK** *Linked Events tab* **CLICK** *Add* *in Stein v Curtis Matter window*	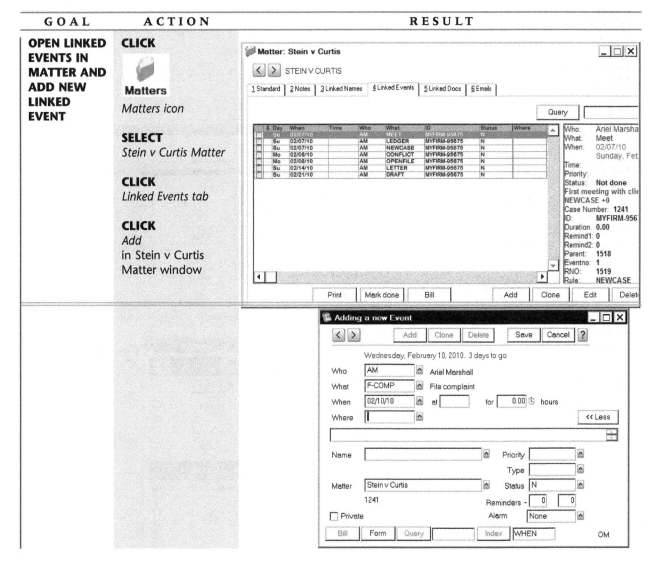

Add Events to a Matter (*continued*)

GOAL	ACTION	RESULT
ADD LINKED EVENT DETAILS OF RESPONSIBLE ATTORNEY (WHO—PERSON ON WHOSE CALENDAR EVENT WILL APPEAR, WHAT IS TO BE DONE, AND WHEN IT IS TO BE DONE APPEAR ON CALENDAR) *Note*: Valid entries are displayed by clicking the up arrows. *Note*: The up arrow by date will bring up a calendar; clicking the date in the calendar will add the date to the input.	**CLICK** Who *Up arrow* **SELECT** *AM* **CLICK** *OK* **CLICK** What *Up arrow* **SELECT** *F-COMP* **CLICK** *OK* **CLICK** When *Up arrow* **ENTER** Date	

Add Events to a Matter (*continued*)

GOAL	ACTION	RESULT
ENTER NEW WHERE CODE AND CODE DESCRIPTION	**CLICK** *Up arrow* **CLICK** *Add* in Valid WHERE Entries window **ENTER** *CCPBUCKS* **CLICK** *OK* **ENTER** *Court of Common Pleas Bucks County* **CLICK** *OK*	
SELECT THE NEW WHERE CODE THAT IS NOW IN THE VALID WHERE ENTRIES	**SELECT** *CCPBUCKS* from Valid WHERE Entries window **CLICK** *OK*	

Add Events to a Matter (*continued*)

GOAL	ACTION	RESULT
SELECT PRIORITY, EVENT TYPE, AND EVENT STATUS	**CLICK** Priority *Up arrow* **DOUBLE CLICK** *1 Drop Everything* **CLICK** Type *Up arrow* **DOUBLE CLICK** *D Deadline* **CLICK** Status *Up arrow* **DOUBLE CLICK** *N Not Done*	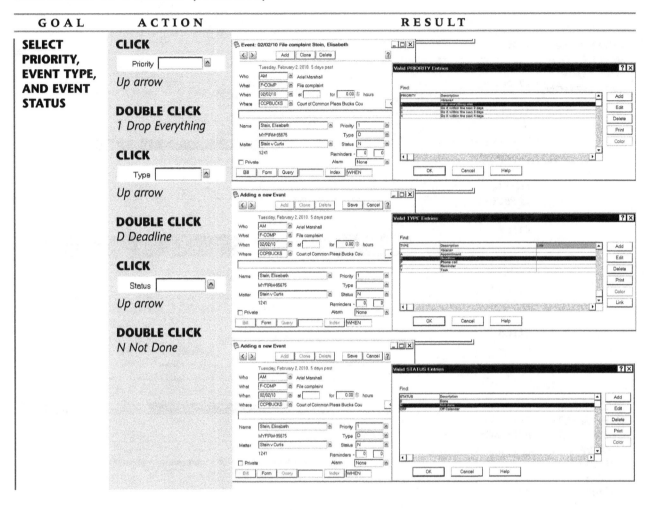

Add Events to a Matter (*continued*)

GOAL	ACTION	RESULT
SAVE EVENT INFORMATION *Note*: Saved event is automatically added to linked events in Matter window.	**CLICK** *Save*	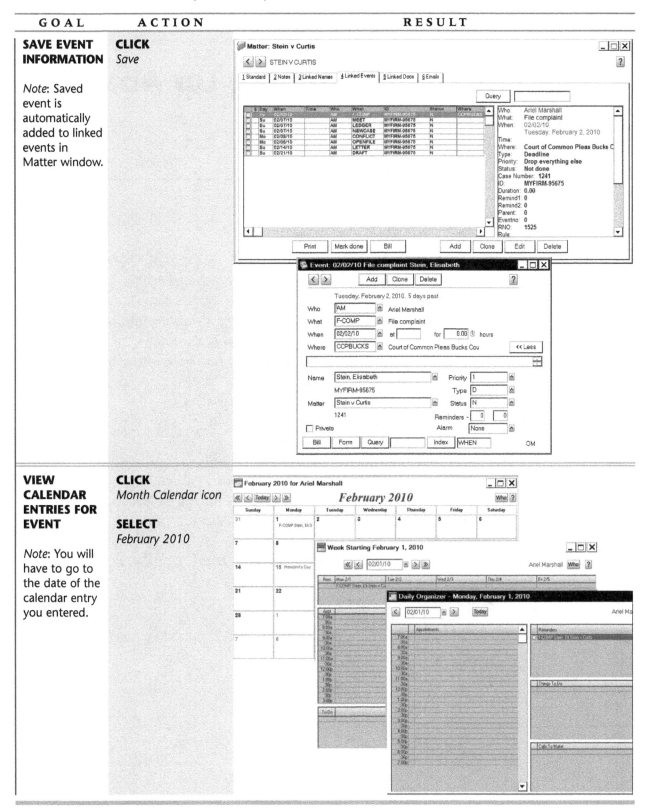
VIEW CALENDAR ENTRIES FOR EVENT *Note*: You will have to go to the date of the calendar entry you entered.	**CLICK** *Month Calendar icon* **SELECT** *February 2010*	

Exit AbacusLaw.

The Basics: Setting Up Abacus Accounting

- Tutorial Information Used
- What Can I Do with Abacus Accounting?
- How Do I Access Screens and Functions in Abacus Accounting?
- How Do I Set Up Abacus Accounting for Timekeeping and Billing?
  - ▲ *Tutorial—Installing Abacus Accounting from the AbacusLaw Practice Manager*
- How Do I Set Up My Firm's Information in Abacus Accounting?
  - ▲ *Tutorial—Entering Firm Information in Abacus Accounting (Accounting Manager)*
- How Do I Set Up Users in Abacus Accounting?
  - ▲ *Tutorial—Setting Up New Users in Abacus Accounting*
- How Do I Set Up Timekeepers in Abacus Accounting?
  - ▲ *Tutorial—Setting Up New Timekeeper Codes*
- How Do I Create Time Tickets in Abacus Accounting?
  - ▲ *Tutorial—Creating a Time Ticket in a Contingency Fee Case*
- How Do I Enter Time Charges for Events from the AbacusLaw Practice Manager?
  - ▲ *Tutorial—Enter Chargeable Event in Practice Manager*
- How Do I Prepare a Time Report?
  - ▲ *Tutorial—Prepare a Time Report—Time Ticket Diary*
- How Do I Print a Bill?
  - ▲ *Tutorial—Printing a Prebill*
  - ▲ *Tutorial—Printing a Bill*

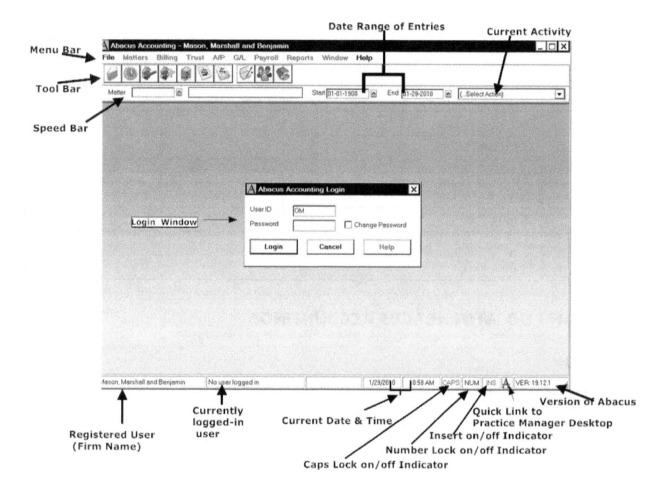

Date Range of Entries

Current Activity

Menu Bar

Tool Bar

Speed Bar

Abacus Accounting – Mason, Marshall and Benjamin

File   Matters   Billing   Trust   A/P   G/L   Payroll   Reports   Window   Help

Matter   Start 01-01-1900   End 01-29-2010   (...Select Action)

Login Window

Abacus Accounting Login

User ID   OM
Password   ☐ Change Password

Login   Cancel   Help

Mason, Marshall and Benjamin | No user logged in | 1/29/2010   10:58 AM   CAPS   NUM   INS   A   VER: 19.12.1

Registered User
(Firm Name)

Currently
logged-in
user

Current Date & Time

Caps Lock on/off Indicator

Number Lock on/off Indicator

Insert on/off Indicator

Quick Link to
Practice Manager Desktop

Version of Abacus

TUTORIAL INFORMATION USED

The following is the information used in the following section tutorials. You may substitute your personal information.

Fill in the information before starting.

	TUTORIAL INFORMATION	YOUR INFORMATION
Firm Name	Mason, Marshall and Benjamin	
Attorney	Owen Mason	
ID	OM	
Attorney	Ariel Marshall	
ID	AM	
Attorney	Ethan Benjamin	
ID	EB	
Address	138 North Street	
City	Newtown	
State	PA	
Zip	18940	
Day Phone	555 111 2222	
Fed Tax ID	23 000 0001	

WHAT CAN I DO WITH ABACUS ACCOUNTING?

TIMEKEEPING

The key to a successful practice is timekeeping and billing. The Accounting Manager allows the creation of time tickets for all matters in the Practice Manager. It also is linked with the events in the Practice Manager to permit event activities to be recorded and billed.

CHECK WRITING

Accurate record keeping of client fund disbursements is required by the ethical rules of the legal profession. Accurate recording of firm expenses is required to prepare federal, state, and local tax returns. Paying expenses and costs by check provides a useful source of proof.

MAINTAIN TRUST ACCOUNTS

Ethical guidelines and requirements require that lawyers not commingle client funds with personal or firm funds. It is essential that separate trust accounts be maintained for client advances, such as retainers and cost advances, until the firm has expended the funds or earned the fees.

Time Tickets - Modifying Existing Time

Client Number 1   Roger Adams   Date of Service 03-06-2006

Matter Number SD-2007-097   Main Street Center   Hours 1.00

Timekeeper NPB   Neil Barnes

Time Ticket Type
- ◉ Billable
- ○ Flat Charge
- ○ No Charge
- ○ Non-Billable

Timer   00:00:00   Start   Reset

Text   Font Size 10

Prepare Answer

Timekeeper Rate $375.00
Time Ticket Value $375.00

☐ Put Time Ticket on Hold

Ticket Number 24

Press F5 for Time Entry Abbreviation Codes and F7 to Spell Check

Save   Save & Clone   Delete   Previous   Next   Close   Help

Demand Check Writer

Checking Account # 11010.00   Cash - Operating Account   Acct. Balance 136,312.12

Check #: AUTO

☐ ATM/Debit Card/Bnk Chrgs Transaction

Payee $

Dollars

Address

Memo

Expense Account #   Invoice #

Description

Matter ID   Exp. Code

Print   Clear   Close   Help

General   Matters to Charge

Matter Trust Activity

Matter Number	1242	Stein v Curtis			Trust Balance Forward	$0.00
Client Name	Jonathan Leonard				Trust Ending Balance	$1,335.00
Start Date	01-01-1900	End Date	01-08-2010			

△ Date	Deposits	Withdrawals	Account #	Payee	Description
01-08-2010	$1,000.00		11020.00	Trust Deposit	Cost advance
01-08-2010	$500.00		11020.00	Trust Deposit	
01-08-2010		$165.00	11020.00	Clerk of Court	Complaint Filing Fee

| A/R Balance: | $0.00 | UnBilled Time: | $310.00 | UnBilled Costs: | $0.00 | Total Due: | $310.00 |

Details | Print | Refresh | Close | Help

PAYROLL

Except for the sole practitioner with no employees, preparing and paying payroll is one of the most important activities within the firm. Employees must be paid if they are to continue working productively.

Typically, this function is done by the in-house staff in the smaller firms, frequently by the paralegal staff.

Process Payroll - Modifying Edith C Hannaah

Regular Hours	40.00		Pay Period Date	02-08-2010		Reset Gross
Overtime Hours	0.00					
Sick Hours	0.00		Gross Reg	$1,500.00		
Vacation Hours	0.00		Gross OT	$0.00	Total Gross	1,500.00

Accumulated Hours

		Medicare	Social Security	
Sick	0.00	$21.75	$93.00	Total FICA	114.75
Vacation	0.00			

Income Taxes and Deductions

| Federal | $193.03 | County | $15.00 | SDI | $0.00 | Total Taxes | 305.28 |
| State | $46.05 | Local | $50.00 | Misc | $1.20 | Deductions | 0.00 |

State tax Computed for Pennsylvania.   EIC $0.00   Net Pay 1,079.97

Payroll Information

Save | Recalculate Taxes | Close | Help

FIRM ACCOUNTING

While beyond the scope of this tutorial and guide, AbacusLaw Abacus Accounting provides a full set of accounting tools to allow the maintenance of all the accounting records from receivables to payables, income to expense, and the preparation of all the necessary income statements and reports required to prepare tax returns from a full set of journals and ledgers.

HOW DO I ACCESS SCREENS AND FUNCTIONS IN ABACUS ACCOUNTING?

The Abacus Accounting has a menu bar and toolbar containing icons to access the various functions in the module. It also has a third bar, the *speed bar*. The speed bar allows you to select the specific matter that will be worked, the date range, and the function.

HOW DO I SET UP ABACUS ACCOUNTING FOR TIMEKEEPING AND BILLING?

Just as the AbacusLaw Practice Manager required some customization or personalization, so does the Abacus Accounting. The Abacus Accounting needs financial information including billing rates, any sales taxes assessed on services, and whose time is billed to which client.

   If you have not already installed the Time, Billing and Accounting Module, you will need to do so before continuing. See the introduction on installing AbacusLaw.

Installing Abacus Accounting from the AbacusLaw Practice Manager

GOAL	ACTION	RESULT
START PROGRAM FROM DESKTOP	**CLICK** 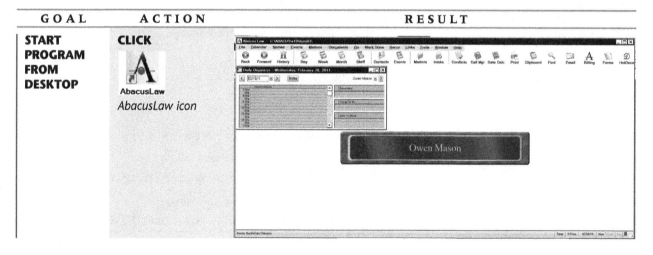 **AbacusLaw** *AbacusLaw icon*	

Installing Abacus Accounting from the AbacusLaw Practice Manager (*continued*)

GOAL	ACTION	RESULT
START PROGRAM FROM PROGRAM LIST IF NO ICON APPEARS ON DESKTOP	**CLICK** OR start **SELECT** All Programs **CLICK** A AbacusLaw	AbacusLaw 2010 A Abacus Accounting A Abacus Message Slips Abacus on the Web A Abacus Updater A AbacusLaw A Accounting Samples A Check for AbacusLaw Update Help for AbacusLaw A Sample Data
INSTALL ABACUS ACCOUNTING FROM THE PRACTICE MANAGER	**CLICK** *Tools menu* **SELECT** *Accounting Setup* **SELECT** *Setup* in AbacusLaw Practice Manager	Tools Conflict of Interest... Call Manager... Phone Dialer... Date Calculator... F6 PopUp Calendar... F4 Timer... Accounting Setup Setup HotDocs Link User Options... eLaw Bill Pending Items... Browse Time Tickets
ACCEPT DEFAULT DIRECTORY FOR ABACUS ACCOUNTING FILES	**CLICK** *OK*	**Accounting Setup** ? X Accounting data directory: C:\ABACUS\v19\data01\Accounting\ Current Abacus data directory: C:\ABACUS\v19\data01 Client Link Type = BILLTO ☐ Set Originating Timekeeper to client's attorney ☑ Use Confirmation Window when billing ☑ Use Confirmation Window when synchronizing Link Abacus codes to Accounting codes: [Case Codes] [Who Codes] [Note types] [What Codes] [OK] [Cancel]

Exit AbacusLaw.

HOW DO I SET UP MY FIRM'S INFORMATION IN ABACUS ACCOUNTING?

Firm and user preferences and information may be entered in the Abacus Accounting after the initial setup. As with the Practice Manager, the initials of the user must be set up and used to log on each time. The user will generally be the same person licensed to use the Practice Manager.

Personalize your copy of Abacus Accounting by using your personal information.

Enter your information before starting this tutorial.

	TUTORIAL INFORMATION	YOUR INFORMATION
Firm Name	Mason, Marshall and Benjamin	
Attorney	Owen Mason	
ID	OM	
Attorney	Ariel Marshall	
ID	AM	
Attorney	Ethan Benjamin	
ID	EB	
Address	138 North Street	
City	Newtown	
State	PA	
Zip	18940	
Day Phone	555 111 2222	
Fed Tax ID	23 000 0001	

Entering Firm Information in Abacus Accounting (Accounting Manager)

GOAL	ACTION	RESULT
START ABACUS ACCOUNTING	**CLICK** *Abacus Accounting icon* OR **CLICK** *Billing Link icon in AbacusLaw Practice Manager* **ENTER** ID and Password **CLICK** *Login*	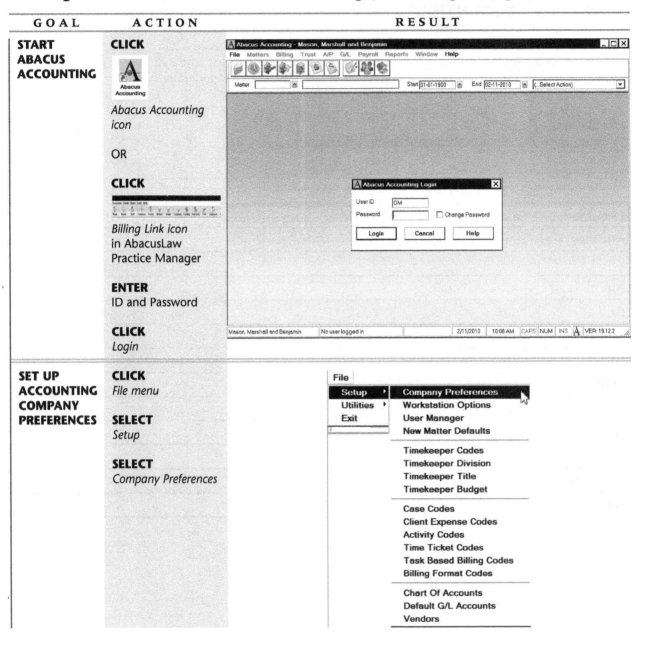
SET UP ACCOUNTING COMPANY PREFERENCES	**CLICK** *File menu* **SELECT** *Setup* **SELECT** *Company Preferences*	

Entering Firm Information in Abacus Accounting (Accounting Manager) (*continued*)

GOAL	ACTION	RESULT
ENTER FIRM INFORMATION IN ABACUS ACCOUNTING	**CLICK** *Address Info tab*	
ENTER FIRM ADDRESS INFORMATION *Note*: Company name, address, and phone are entered from registration information; make any necessary changes.	**ENTER** Your information OR 555-111-3333 (Fax Number) 18940 (Zip) 23-0000001 (Sample Fed Tax ID) **CLICK** *Save* **CLICK** *X* to close	

Do not close the program; continue to the next tutorial.

HOW DO I SET UP USERS IN ABACUS ACCOUNTING?

In AbacusLaw the terms timekeepers and users are used to define different functions. To use the program you must be a *user*. A user is a person with a license to use the program and make entries and generate reports. A *timekeeper* can be anyone for whom time is to be kept. Ideally each timekeeper is also a user and can enter his or her own time tickets and make other entries. But a user may enter time tickets and other items for timekeepers.

Valid timekeeper entries are usually the same as those listed in the WHO valid entries in the Practice Manager, but they may be different or use different initials. To avoid confusion and the potential for not properly recording billable time, use the same initials for timekeepers that identify that person in the WHO codes in the Practice Manager.

While a timekeeper traditionally is a person, in modern practices it may be equipment, such as video conferencing, which is billed to clients at an hourly or other rate.

NOTE

Clone duplicates and preserves an existing record, but allows the original to be edited. For example, in this tutorial we will use the same setup for a timekeeper as another timekeeper, but change the name and the initials, permitting each to have the same rights and privileges without manually making all the changes.

TIP

Until you have some experience with the permitted levels of access to the program, use the samples of different levels of access to the accounting records in the User ID section of the User Profile Maintenance screen.

Setting Up New Users in Abacus Accounting

GOAL	ACTION	RESULT
SELECT USER MANAGER FROM FILE SETUP MENU	**CLICK** *File menu* **SELECT** *Setup* **SELECT** *User Manager* in Abacus Accounting	Abacus Accounting – Mason, Marshall and Benjamin File Setup ▸ Company Preferences Utilities ▸ Workstation Options Exit **User Manager** New Matter Defaults Timekeeper Codes Timekeeper Division Timekeeper Title Timekeeper Budget Case Codes Client Expense Codes Activity Codes Time Ticket Codes Task Based Billing Codes Billing Format Codes Chart Of Accounts Default G/L Accounts Vendors

Setting Up New Users in Abacus Accounting (*continued*)

GOAL	ACTION	RESULT
ADD NEW USER USING CLONE FUNCTION	**CLICK** *ATTORNEY* (or other job function) **CLICK** *Clone* **ENTER** *Ariel, Marshall, AM* (First Name, Last Name, and User ID) **CLICK** *Save* **CLICK** *OK* **CLICK** *Close*	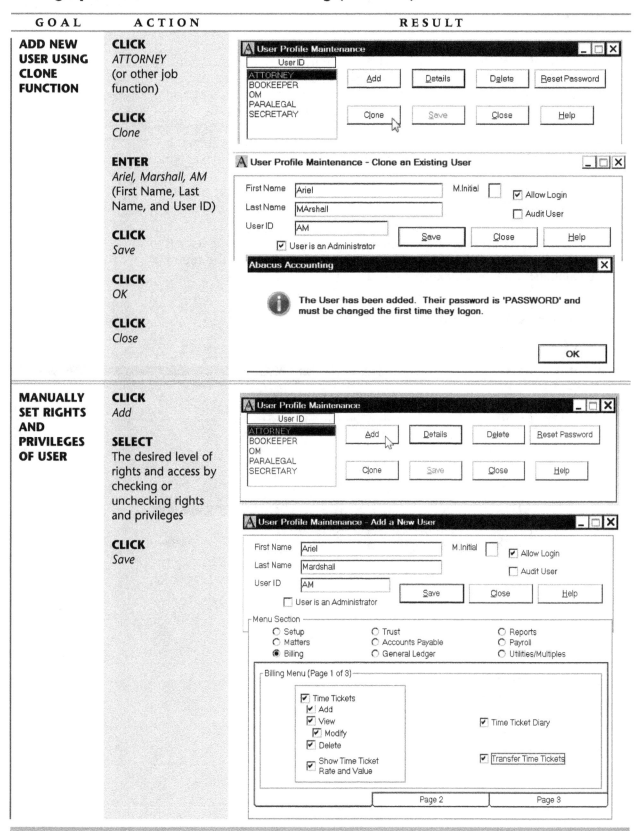
MANUALLY SET RIGHTS AND PRIVILEGES OF USER	**CLICK** *Add* **SELECT** The desired level of rights and access by checking or unchecking rights and privileges **CLICK** *Save*	

Exit or continue to the next tutorial.

HOW DO I SET UP TIMEKEEPERS IN ABACUS ACCOUNTING?

Everyone—attorneys, paralegals, law clerks, and secretaries—and everything, such as video conferencing facilities for which an hourly rate is charged, must have a *timekeeper code*, an abbreviation and description identifying the person, which is usually the person's initials. The rates to be charged for each person or service can have a default hourly rate or a schedule of hourly rates. It is possible to set up a timekeeper without an hourly rate, but it is easier to set it all up initially rather than come back to complete that information when it is time to bill a client. The schedule of rates or the individual timekeeper default rate can always be changed later using the edit function.

T I P

Avoid confusion and use the same initials as the user ID.

Set the rate schedule including all rates charged by the firm and use this for all timekeepers.

SENIORITY LEVEL

The seniority level is used to sort information in reports. Seniority level 1 is first on the report. If all timekeepers are assigned seniority level 1, the report is sorted alphabetically by timekeeper code.

Setting Up New Timekeeper Codes

GOAL	ACTION	RESULT
START AND LOGIN TO ABACUS ACCOUNTING	**CLICK** *Abacus Accounting icon* OR **CLICK** *Billing icon in AbacusLaw Practice Manager* **ENTER** ID and Password **CLICK** *Login*	

Setting Up New Timekeeper Codes (*continued*)

GOAL	ACTION	RESULT
SELECT USER MANAGER FROM FILE SETUP MENU	**CLICK** *File menu* **SELECT** *Setup* **SELECT** *Timekeeper Codes*	File Setup ▶ Company Preferences Utilities ▶ Workstation Options Exit User Manager New Matter Defaults **Timekeeper Codes** Timekeeper Division Timekeeper Title Timekeeper Budget Case Codes Client Expense Codes Activity Codes Time Ticket Codes Task Based Billing Codes Billing Format Codes Chart Of Accounts Default G/L Accounts Vendors
ADD NEW TIMEKEEPER CODE *Note*: Timekeeper initials may already be in the list.	**CLICK** *Add* **ENTER** *EB* OR Your Initials as timekeeper initials AND *Ethan Benjamin* OR Your Name and default rate per hour **ENTER** *1* as Seniority Level **ENTER** *1* as Division	

Setting Up New Timekeeper Codes (*continued*)

GOAL	ACTION	RESULT
SET UP DIVISION	**CLICK** *Up arrow* by Division **CLICK** *Add* **ENTER** *1* as Code **ENTER** *Legal Staff* as Description **CLICK** *Save* **CLICK** *Cancel* **CLICK** *OK*	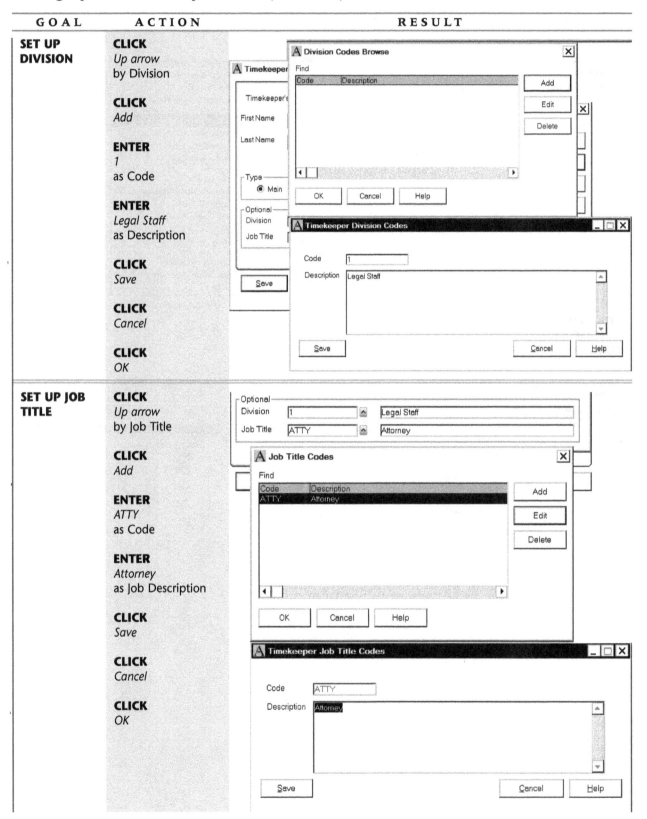
SET UP JOB TITLE	**CLICK** *Up arrow* by Job Title **CLICK** *Add* **ENTER** *ATTY* as Code **ENTER** *Attorney* as Job Description **CLICK** *Save* **CLICK** *Cancel* **CLICK** *OK*	

Setting Up New Timekeeper Codes (*continued*)

GOAL	ACTION	RESULT
SET UP A RATE SCHEDULE *Note*: Many firms charge different rates for different types of cases or clients, such as reduced rates for low income clients. The rate levels can be set here.	**CLICK** *Rates tab* **ENTER** Rate schedule as shown **CLICK** *Save* in Timekeeper Manager **CLICK** *Cancel* in Timekeepers Browse window	

Continue to the following tutorial or exit and restart Abacus Accounting.

HOW DO I CREATE TIME TICKETS IN ABACUS ACCOUNTING?

Time is billed to clients and to matters (cases) for events (things that happen). The linked events in matters are usually billable activities and can be set to be billed to that matter. A separate time ticket may also be created for each activity on each matter. This may be a result of entering paper time records or a record of time spent on a matter while out of the office and away from a computer.

N O T E S

To enter a time ticket you must identify the matter.

Task-based billing codes were established by the American Bar Association (ABA) and are used to organize time entries by category to meet the ABA billing standards. Abacus Accounting is preloaded with the ABA task-based billing codes. You do not need to modify or delete these codes unless the ABA changes its code set.

Creating a Time Ticket in a Contingency Fee Case

GOAL	ACTION	RESULT
OPEN BLANK TIME TICKET IN ABACUS ACCOUNTING	**CLICK** Matter *Up arrow* **SELECT** *Bates v Howard* **CLICK** OK **CLICK** *Time Tickets icon*	

Creating a Time Ticket in a Contingency Fee Case (*continued*)

GOAL	ACTION	RESULT
LOCATE AND ENTER RELATED MATTER TO POPULATE TIME TICKET	OR **CLICK** *Time Tickets icon* **CLICK** Matter Number *Up arrow* **SELECT** *Bates v Howard* (case handled on contingency fee)	
IDENTIFY NATURE OF CHARGE USING TIME TICKET CODES *Note:* Activity code will only appear if you have Task Based Billing selected as the billing format for the selected matter or client, or if you have the firm preferences set to Force Activity Code on Time Tickets.	**CLICK** Timekeeper *Up arrow* **SELECT** *EB* as Timekeeper **CLICK** *OK* in Timekeeper Browse window **ENTER** *12-07-2010* (Date of Service field) *1.00* (Hours field) **CHECK** *No Charge* **CLICK CURSOR** In Text box **CLICK** *F5 key* **SELECT** *Legal Research* **CLICK** *OK* **CLICK** *Save*	

Creating a Time Ticket in a Contingency Fee Case (*continued*)

GOAL	ACTION	RESULT
VERIFY INFORMATION FOR ACCURACY	**CLICK** *Close*	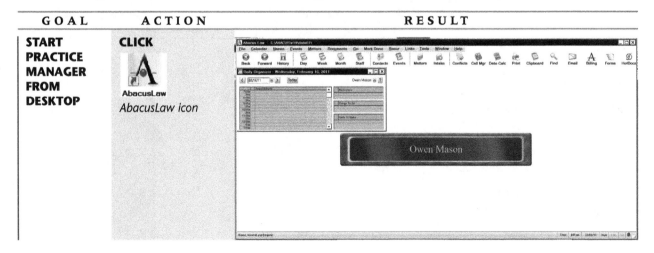

Close Abacus Accounting.

HOW DO I ENTER TIME CHARGES FOR EVENTS FROM THE ABACUSLAW PRACTICE MANAGER?

Events within a matter may be set up as time tickets within the Practice Manager. Events include time spent working with a client or on a client case, including conferences, drafting, research, and other billable time. These events may be charged as time tickets using the same method as entering an event into a calendar.

Enter Chargeable Event in Practice Manager

GOAL	ACTION	RESULT
START PRACTICE MANAGER FROM DESKTOP	**CLICK** **AbacusLaw** *AbacusLaw icon*	

Enter Chargeable Event in Practice Manager (*continued*)

GOAL	ACTION	RESULT
START PROGRAM FROM PROGRAM LIST IF NO ICON APPEARS ON DESKTOP	**CLICK** OR start **SELECT** ▶ All Programs **CLICK** A AbacusLaw	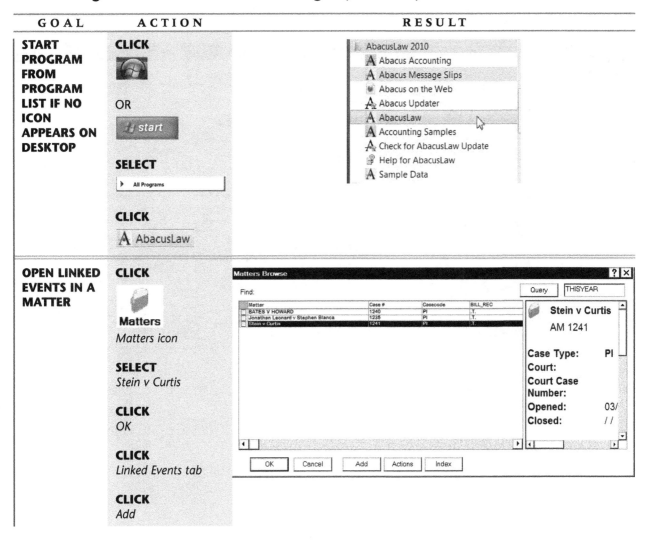
OPEN LINKED EVENTS IN A MATTER	**CLICK** **Matters** *Matters icon* **SELECT** *Stein v Curtis* **CLICK** *OK* **CLICK** *Linked Events tab* **CLICK** *Add*	

Enter Chargeable Event in Practice Manager (*continued*)

GOAL	ACTION	RESULT
CREATE AN EVENT LISTING	**CLICK** Who ☐ *Up arrow* **DOUBLE CLICK** *AM* **CLICK** What ☐ *Up arrow* **DOUBLE CLICK** *CON* **CLICK** When ☐ *Up arrow* **DOUBLE CLICK** *02/10/10* **CLICK** Where ☐ *Up arrow* **DOUBLE CLICK** *Here* **CLICK** Name ☐ *Up arrow* **DOUBLE CLICK** *Stein, Elisabeth* **ENTER** *2 hours* **CLICK** *Save*	Adding a new Event _ ☐ ✕ < > Add Clone Delete Save Cancel ? Wednesday, February 10, 2010. 3 days to go Who AM Ariel Marshall What CON Consultation When 02/10/10 at ☐ for 2.00 ☺ hours Where HERE Office << Less Name Stein, Elisabeth Priority ☐ MYFIRM-95675 Type ☐ Matter Stein v Curtis Status N 1241 Reminders - 0 0 ☐ Private Alarm None Bill Form Query Index WHEN OM

Enter Chargeable Event in Practice Manager (*continued*)

GOAL	ACTION	RESULT
ENTER A LINKED EVENT IN THE BILLING RECORDS	**SELECT** *CON* as item to bill **CLICK** *Bill* **CLICK** *Yes* in Send to Accounting window	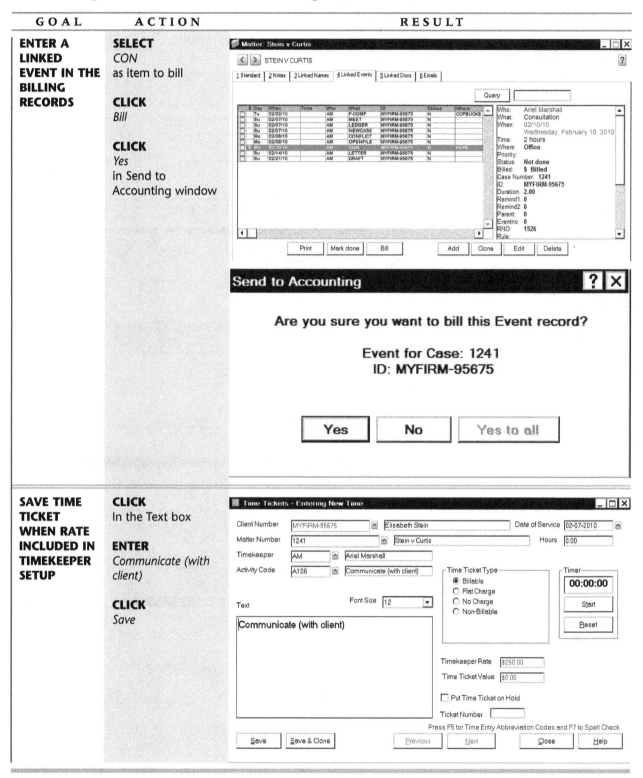
SAVE TIME TICKET WHEN RATE INCLUDED IN TIMEKEEPER SETUP	**CLICK** In the Text box **ENTER** *Communicate (with client)* **CLICK** *Save*	

Continue without closing and go on to the next tutorial.

HOW DO I PREPARE A TIME REPORT?

Time reports are a useful way of tracking activity on files and matters. In weekly or monthly legal team meetings they may be used to determine what has been done by members of the legal team and what remains to be done. Partners will frequently want to see the productivity or efforts being made by associates or others in the firm.

They are also an important source of information when a court asks what has been done on a case or to justify a billing request to the court for court assigned cases, or to request reimbursement for paralegal time spent on a case.

Prepare a Time Report—Time Ticket Diary

GOAL	ACTION	RESULT
OPEN ABACUS ACCOUNTING USING LINK FROM ABACUSLAW PRACTICE MANAGER DESKTOP	CLICK Billing *Billing icon*	

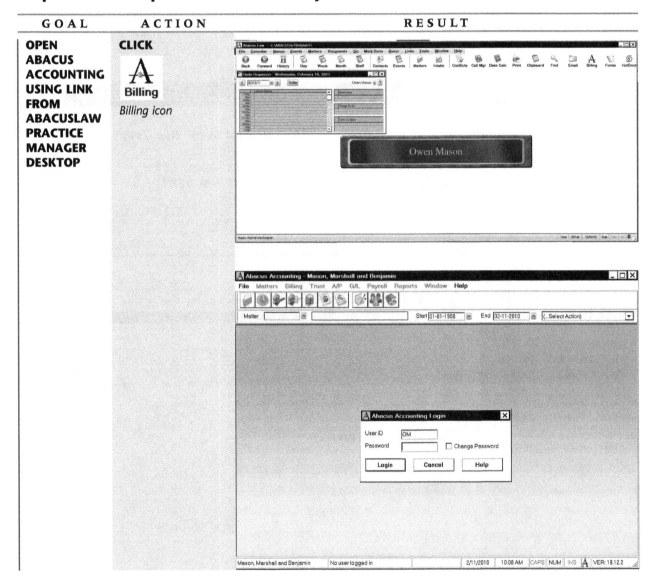

Prepare a Time Report—Time Ticket Diary (*continued*)

GOAL	ACTION	RESULT
PREPARE A TIME TICKET DIARY REPORT IN ABACUS ACCOUNTING	**CLICK** *Billing menu* in Abacus Accounting **SELECT** *Time Ticket Diary* **ENTER** *02-27-2013* in the End field in Date Range **CLICK** *Preview*	
PRINT OUT THE TIME TICKET DIARY OR REVIEW IT ON THE COMPUTER SCREEN	**VERIFY** Accuracy of report **CLICK** *Print*	

Do not exit Abacus Accounting; close all open windows.

HOW DO I PRINT A BILL?

A bill is a specialized report that merges stored information and assembles other data (information) from records (time tickets). Part of the merged information is the firm information, or letterhead information, presented in a specialized format such as a bill or invoice. The following tutorial shows the details of a matter for a client. The information may be selected by time frame, such as one month, or since the matter was first opened. It may be by specific timekeeper or all timekeepers. The starting point for any report is to create a search or query that identifies the desired information or data. In the following tutorial you will select the data for one matter. It is common practice in many firms to print or preview bills before the bills are printed and sent to clients. This allows the timekeepers to verify accuracy and modify or eliminate charges.

In AbacusLaw Accounting, the initial process is called *Prebill*.

T I P

To include all, use the asterisk (*), as shown.

Printing a Prebill

GOAL	ACTION	RESULT
SELECT ALL MATTERS FOR PREBILL REPORTS AND PREVIEW	**CLICK** *Billing menu* **SELECT** *Prebills* OR **CLICK** *Prebills icon* **CLICK** *Add* **CLICK** *Select Bills Individually tab* in the Prebill Selection window	

Printing a Prebill (*continued*)

GOAL	ACTION	RESULT
SELECT INDIVIDUAL MATTER TO PREBILL	**CLICK** *Up arrow* by Matter # **Select** *Stein v Curtis* **CLICK** OK **CLICK** *Add to Billing Run*	
SELECT AND PREVIEW	**CLICK** *Select All* **CLICK** *Preview*	

Printing a Prebill (*continued*)

G O A L	A C T I O N	R E S U L T
PREVIEW PREBILL OF SELECTED MATTER PRINT PREBILL	**REVIEW** *Prebill* **CLICK** *Print icon* on the Report Preview toolbar	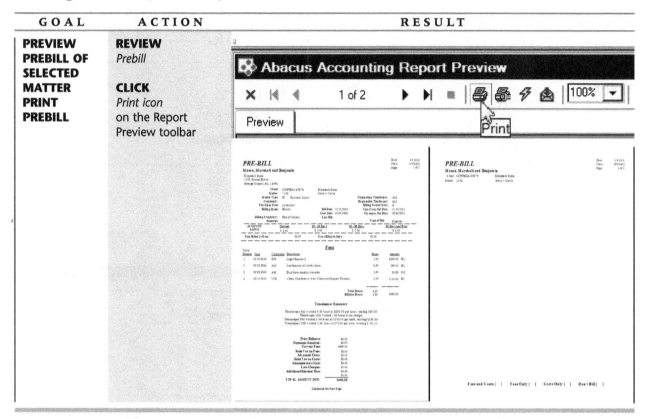

Printing a Bill

GOAL	ACTION	RESULT
SELECT SINGLE MATTER FOR BILL REPORT	**CLICK** *Billing menu* **SELECT** *Print Bills* **CLICK** *Add* OR **CLICK** *Bill icon* **CLICK** *Select Bills Individually tab*	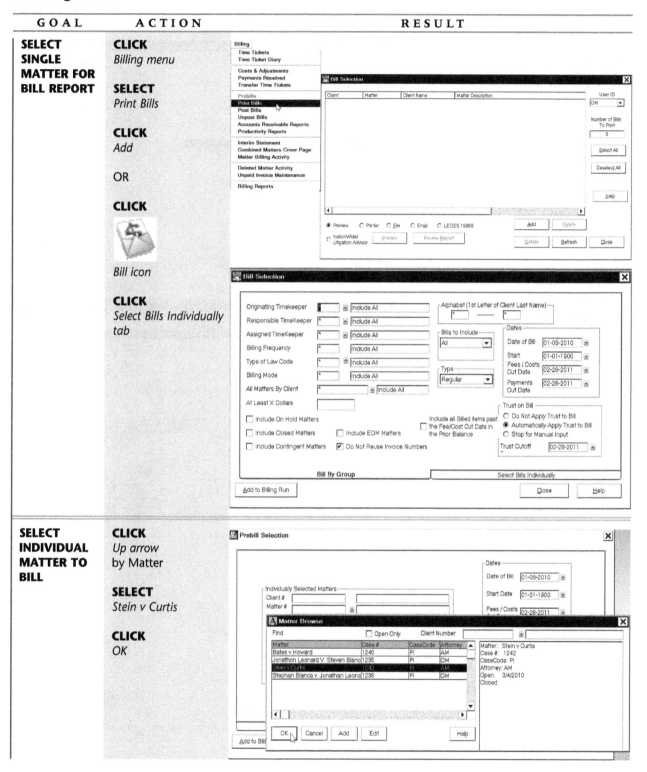
SELECT INDIVIDUAL MATTER TO BILL	**CLICK** *Up arrow* by Matter **SELECT** *Stein v Curtis* **CLICK** *OK*	

Printing a Bill (*continued*)

GOAL	ACTION	RESULT
PREVIEW BILL OF SELECTED MATTER	**CLICK** *Add to Billing Run*	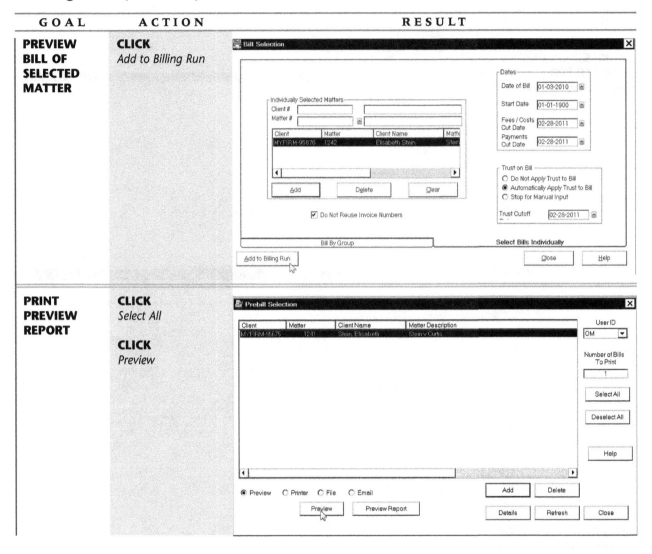
PRINT PREVIEW REPORT	**CLICK** *Select All* **CLICK** *Preview*	

Printing a Bill (*continued*)

GOAL	ACTION	RESULT
REVIEW BILL AND PRINT BILL	**REVIEW** For accuracy **CLICK** *Print icon* on the Report Preview toolbar	

Exit Abacus Accounting and exit AbacusLaw.

The Basics: Creating Reports
(Hardcopy or Electronic)

- How Do I Create Reports?
- How Do I Create a Report of Contacts?
  - ▲ *Tutorial—Creating a Names (Contacts) Report*
- How Can I Print Out Selected Contact Information?
  - ▲ *Tutorial—Create a Contact List Using a Query*
- How Do I Create a Matters Report?
  - ▲ *Tutorial—Creating a Matters Report*
  - ▲ *Tutorial—Create a Matter Query Report*
- How Do I Create a Conflict Check Report?
  - ▲ *Tutorial—Creating a Conflict Report*
- How Do I Create a Billing Report?
  - ▲ *Tutorial—Creating a Matter Summary Report in Abacus Accounting*
- How Do I Print a Productivity Report?
  - ▲ *Tutorial—Printing a Productivity Report*

REPORTS

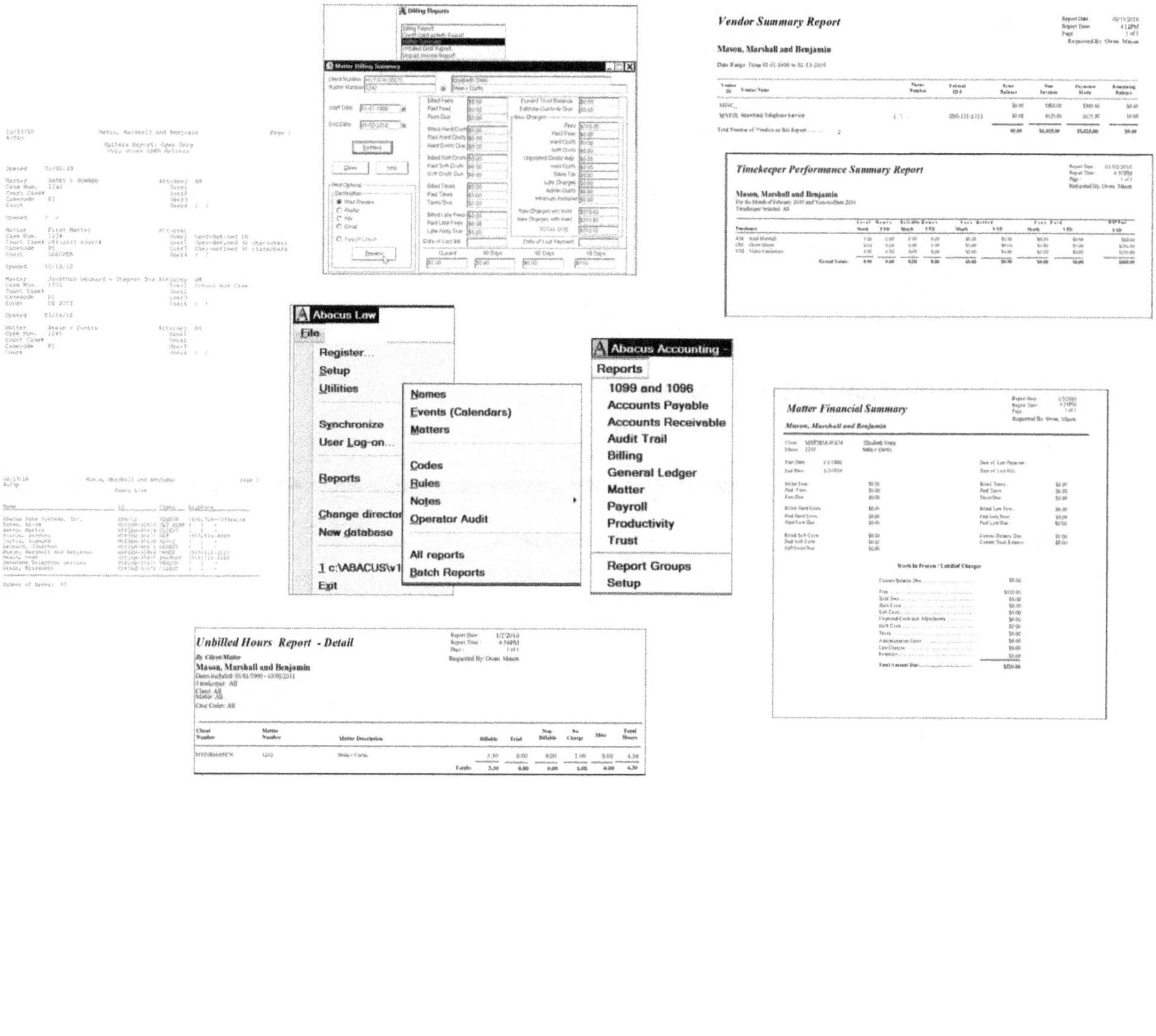
Billing Reports
Matter Billing Summary
Vendor Summary Report
Mason, Marshall and Benjamin
Timekeeper Performance Summary Report
Mason, Marshall and Benjamin
Abacus Law
File
Register...
Setup
Utilities
Synchronize
User Log-on...
Reports
Change director
New database
1 c:\ABACUS\w1
Exit
Names
Events (Calendars)
Matters
Codes
Rules
Notes
Operator Audit
All reports
Batch Reports
Abacus Accounting
Reports
1099 and 1096
Accounts Payable
Accounts Receivable
Audit Trail
Billing
General Ledger
Matter
Payroll
Productivity
Trust
Report Groups
Setup
Matter Financial Summary
Mason, Marshall and Benjamin
Unbilled Hours Report - Detail
Mason, Marshall and Benjamin

HOW DO I CREATE REPORTS?

A report is a response to some question for information in the database; the question or the terms used are called a *query* in computer talk. The response is a report. It may be as short as one item, like who is the responsible attorney on a case (matter), or as complex as a compilation of all the cases in which a particular person is involved as a party, witness, attorney, or expert.

STEPS IN CREATING A REPORT

Select the desired database, such as Calendar, Contacts, or Matters.

Sort (filter in computer talk) the information to eliminate unwanted information by making a query (another computer talk word).

Decide where you want the report to appear—on your screen, in hardcopy, or in an e-mail to someone.

HOW DO I CREATE A REPORT OF CONTACTS?

Contacts in AbacusLaw are the same as your address book. It is sometimes necessary to print out a hard copy to carry and use when away from a computer or cell phone on which the contact information is stored. Unlike the predefined calendars, which are reports of events, other reports in AbacusLaw require an extra step—creating a query.

Creating a Names (Contacts) Report

GOAL	ACTION	RESULT
START ABACUSLAW PRACTICE MANAGER	**CLICK** AbacusLaw *AbacusLaw icon* OR **CLICK** *start* **SELECT** All Programs **CLICK** A AbacusLaw	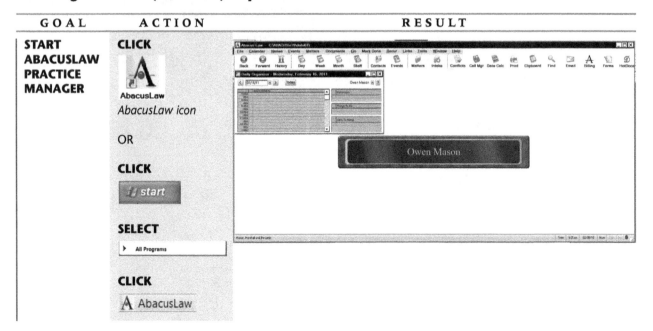

Creating a Names (Contacts) Report (*continued*)

GOAL	ACTION	RESULT
CREATE A REPORT OF ALL NAMES *Note*: The same report can be created from the Names menu.	**CLICK** *Contacts icon* **CLICK** *Actions* in Name Browse window **CLICK** *Reports* **CLICK** *All (in query)*	
SELECT REPORT FORMAT AND METHOD	**CLICK** *Report button* **DOUBLE CLICK** *Names List* **CLICK** *Output to button* **DOUBLE CLICK** *Screen* **CLICK** *Print*	
REVIEW AND PRINT	**REVIEW** **CLICK** *Print*	

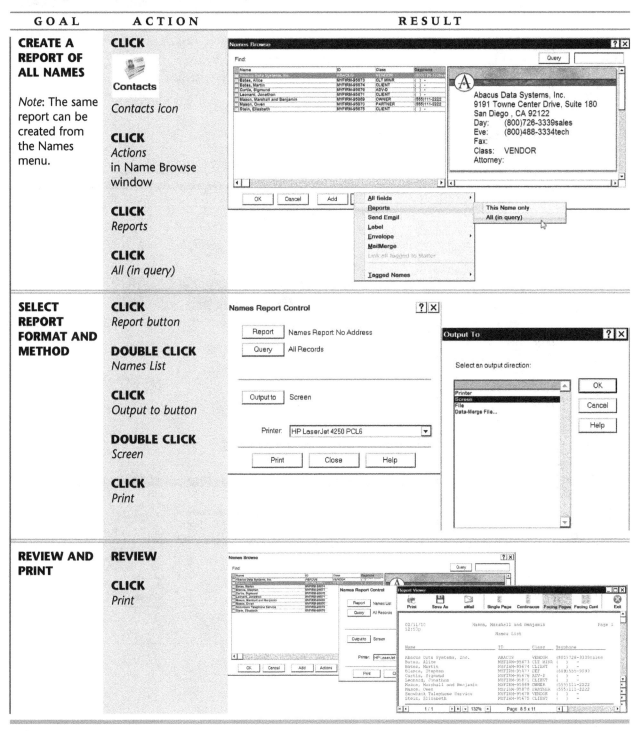

Exit program.

HOW CAN I PRINT OUT SELECTED CONTACT INFORMATION?

You may want a select contact list, such as clients or experts, or a report showing other information such as client and related matters. In this tutorial you will use the query function and select from a list of possible reports and particular group of contacts, and then create a report.

Create a Contact List Using a Query

GOAL	ACTION	RESULT
START ABACUSLAW PROGRAM MANAGER	**CLICK** AbacusLaw *AbacusLaw icon* OR **CLICK** start **SELECT** ▶ All Programs **CLICK** A AbacusLaw	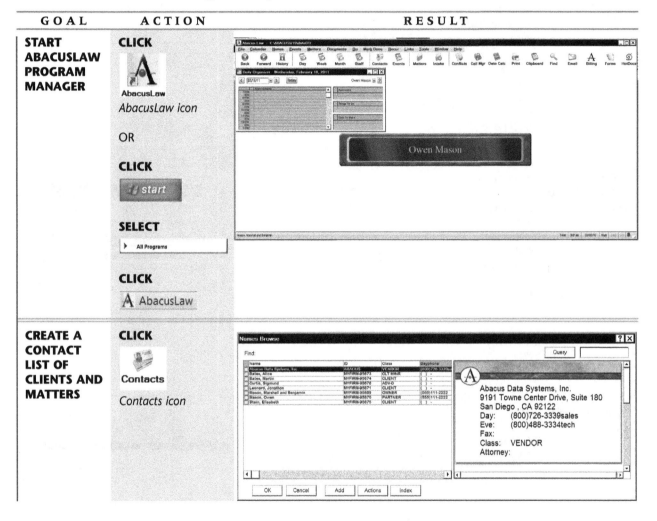
CREATE A CONTACT LIST OF CLIENTS AND MATTERS	**CLICK** Contacts *Contacts icon*	

Create a Contact List Using a Query (*continued*)

GOAL	ACTION	RESULT
CLEAR PRIOR QUERY AND SELECT NEW QUERY WITH QUERY MANAGER	**CLICK** *Query* in Names Browse window **CLICK** *Clear current query* if shown on query manager **CLICK** *Query Manager*	
SELECT NAMES GROUP DESIRED (CLIENT)	**CHECK** *Clients* in Queries for NAMES window **CLICK** *OK* **CLICK** *First* on Where to go? screen	

Create a Contact List Using a Query (*continued*)

GOAL	ACTION	RESULT
SELECT WHAT REPORT FORMAT	**CLICK** *Actions* **CLICK** *Report* **CLICK** *All (in query)* **CLICK** *Report button on Names Report Control* **DOUBLE CLICK** *Labels: Rolodex*	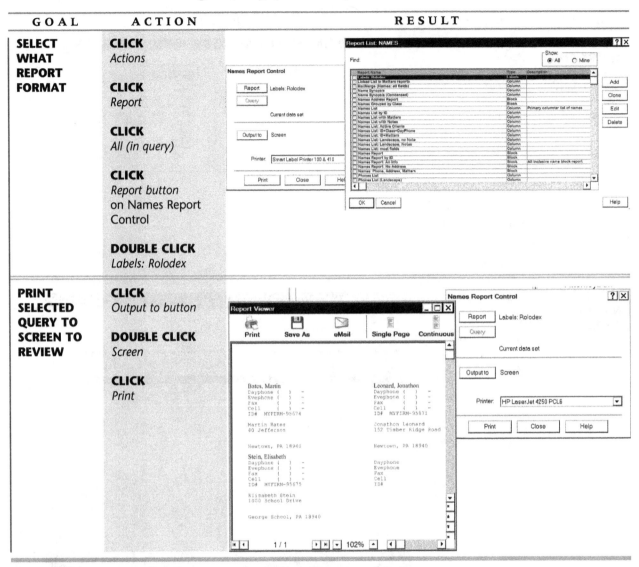
PRINT SELECTED QUERY TO SCREEN TO REVIEW	**CLICK** *Output to button* **DOUBLE CLICK** *Screen* **CLICK** *Print*	

Close all open windows and continue with the following tutorial.

HOW DO I CREATE A MATTERS REPORT?

Just as it is easy to create standard and custom contacts information reports, reports showing different information about matters may also be prepared. Queries can be used to create specialized versions and combinations of information.

Creating a Matters Report

GOAL	ACTION	RESULT
OPEN MATTERS BROWSE WINDOW IN ABACUSLAW TO START REPORT SEQUENCE	**CLICK** **Matters** *Matters icon* OR **CLICK** *Matters menu* **SELECT** *Browse* **CLICK** *Actions* **CLICK** *Reports* **CLICK** *All (in query)*	
SELECT REPORT FORMAT AND PRINT TO LOCATION	**CLICK** *Report button on Matters Report Control* **DOUBLE CLICK** *Matter List on Report List Matters* **CLICK** *Output to button* **DOUBLE CLICK** *Screen* **CLICK** *Print*	

Exit open windows and continue with the following tutorial.

Reports may also be prepared from the Query button on the Matters Browse window as demonstrated in the following tutorial. In this tutorial you will prepare a report for open files only. The query is a combination of all matters that are open.

The first step, clear current query, clears any query criteria from previous reports. The second step selects the matters that are open.

Create a Matter Query Report

GOAL	ACTION	RESULT
OPEN MATTERS BROWSE IN THE PRACTICE MANAGER TO START REPORT SEQUENCE	**CLICK** *Matters menu* **SELECT** *Browse* **CLICK** *Query* **CLICK** *Clear current query*	
	CLICK *Actions* **CLICK** *All (in query)* in Reports option	

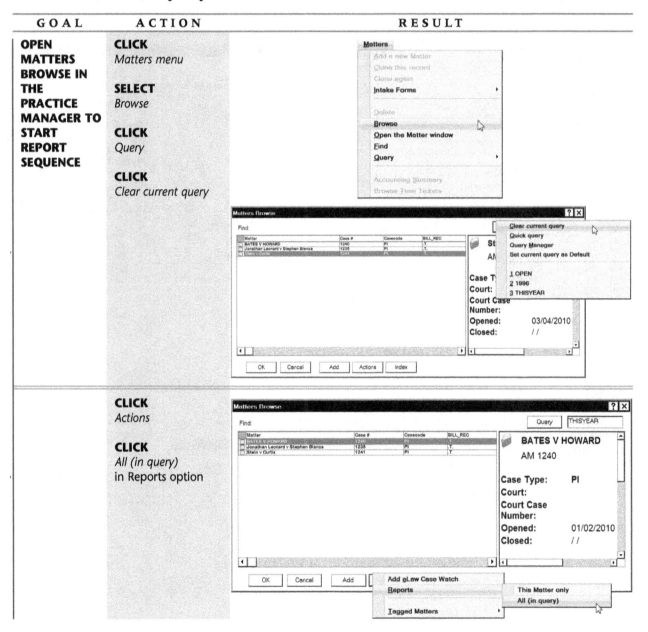

Create a Matter Query Report (*continued*)

GOAL	ACTION	RESULT
	CLICK *Query button* in Matters Report Control window **CLICK** *Query Manager* **CHECK** *Open* in Queries for MATTERS window **CLICK** *OK*	
SELECT REPORT	**CLICK** *Report button* in Matters Report Control window **CHECK** *Matters Report: Open Only* **CLICK** *OK*	
PRINT REPORT TO SCREEN	**CLICK** *Print*	

Close all windows and continue with the following tutorial.

HOW DO I CREATE A CONFLICT CHECK REPORT?

A conflict of interest check is the first thing a law firm will perform before talking with or accepting a new client or case. It is an ethical violation to represent multiple parties who have opposing interests; it is fairly easy to conduct a conflict check when all the plaintiffs and defendants are known in a small case. It is more difficult when there are multiple attorneys in a firm, particularly when the firm has multiple locations. Sometimes the conflict results from a conflict with another firm client in a different matter where there may not be a direct conflict but a situation where the old client would not be happy having the firm represent a new client who may have some adverse real or potential interest.

A fairly standard practice is to search through a list of clients and opposing parties to see if there are any obvious conflicts. Many firms circulate a list of potential names for each attorney to review to be sure they do not see a potential conflict based on a case they are working on where not all parties have been identified.

Creating a Conflict Report

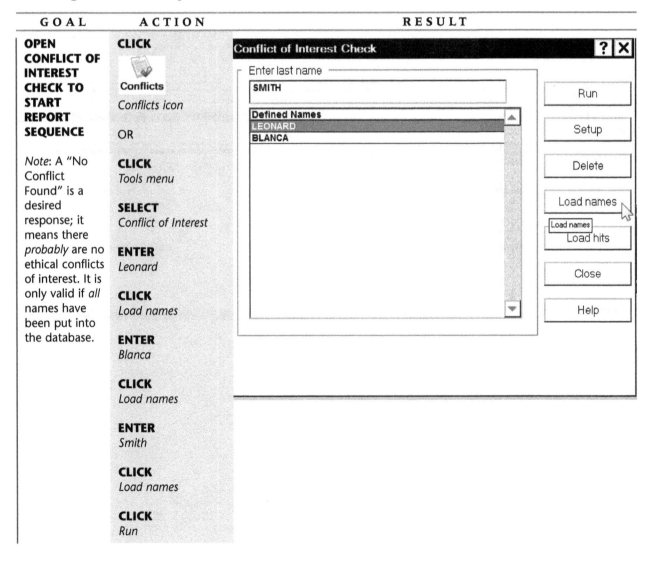

GOAL	ACTION	RESULT
OPEN CONFLICT OF INTEREST CHECK TO START REPORT SEQUENCE *Note*: A "No Conflict Found" is a desired response; it means there *probably* are no ethical conflicts of interest. It is only valid if *all* names have been put into the database.	**CLICK** Conflicts icon OR **CLICK** *Tools menu* **SELECT** *Conflict of Interest* **ENTER** *Leonard* **CLICK** *Load names* **ENTER** *Blanca* **CLICK** *Load names* **ENTER** *Smith* **CLICK** *Load names* **CLICK** *Run*	

Creating a Conflict Report (*continued*)

GOAL	ACTION	RESULT
PRINT TO SCREEN OR PRINTER	**CLICK** *Print* **CLICK** *OK*	
REVIEW CONFLICTS REPORT	**REVIEW** Conflicts	
PRINT REPORT TO PRINTER	**CLICK** *File menu* **CLICK** *Print*	

Creating a Conflict Report (*continued*)

GOAL	ACTION	RESULT
VIEW INDIVIDUAL CONFLICT ENTRY	**CLICK** Desired item to view **CLICK** *View*	

Conflict Check Hit List   ? X

Del	Name	DATA
☐	BLANCA	Jonathon Leonard V. Steven Blanca
☐	BLANCA	Stephan Blanca v. Jonathan Leonard
☐	BLANCA	STEPHAN BLANCA V. JONATHAN LEONARD
☐	BLANCA	Blanca
☐	LEONARD	Jonathon Leonard V. Steven Blanca
☐	LEONARD	Stephan Blanca v. Jonathan Leonard
☐	LEONARD	STEPHAN BLANCA V. JONATHAN LEONARD
☐	LEONARD	Leonard

Close	View	Print	Delete	Help

Hit found in Matters database   _ □ X

| Name | BLANCA | | Found in | MATTERS->MATTER | Rec# | 4 |

Data   STEPHAN **BLANCA** V. JONATHAN LEONARD

Standard Fields | User Fields | Notes

Matter	STEPHAN **BLANCA** V. JONATHAN LEONA			
Case Number	1237		Court	
Attorney	AM		Opened	/ /
Casecode	PI		Closed	/ /

Press the User Fields tab to see user-defined fields

| Close |

Exit AbacusLaw.

HOW DO I CREATE A BILLING REPORT?

A statement of all billable time and expenses may be needed to prepare a report to the court for approval of a case, such as those involving a minor, or a review to see if the case is costing more than reasonable given the potential outcome for the client and the firm. A billing report showing the time and costs can be used for these purposes.

Creating a Matter Summary Report in Abacus Accounting

GOAL	ACTION	RESULT
CREATE A MATTER SUMMARY REPORT IN ABACUS ACCOUNTING	**OPEN** Abacus Accounting **CLICK** *Reports menu* **SELECT** *Billing* **SELECT** *Matter Summary*	
SELECT AND RETRIEVE INFORMATION ON MATTER	**CLICK** *Up arrow* by Matter Number **DOUBLE CLICK** *Stein v Curtis* **CLICK** *Retrieve* **CLICK** *Preview*	

Creating a Matter Summary Report in Abacus Accounting (*continued*)

GOAL	ACTION	RESULT
REVIEW REPORT	**REVIEW** For accuracy	*(report image below)*

Matter Financial Summary

Report Date: 1/8/2010
Report Time: 3:29PM
Page: 1 of 1
Requested By: Owen Mason

Mason, Marshall and Benjamin

Client: MYFIRM-95871   Jonathan Leonard
Matter: 1242   Stein v Curtis

Start Date: 1/1/1900
End Date: 1/8/2010

Date of Last Payment:
Date of Last Bill:

Billed Fees:	$0.00	Billed Taxes:	$0.00
Paid Fees:	$0.00	Paid Taxes:	$0.00
Fees Due:	$0.00	Taxes Due:	$0.00
Billed Hard Costs:	$0.00	Billed Late Fees:	$0.00
Paid Hard Costs:	$0.00	Paid Late Fees:	$0.00
Hard Cost Due:	$0.00	Paid Late Due:	$0.00
Billed Soft Costs:	$0.00	Current Balance Due:	$0.00
Paid Soft Costs:	$0.00	Current Trust Balance:	$0.00
Soft Costs Due:	$0.00		

Work In Process / Unbilled Charges

Current Balance Due	$0.00
Fees	$310.00
Held Fees	$0.00
Hard Costs	$0.00
Soft Costs	$0.00
Unposted Costs and Adjustments	$0.00
Held Costs	$0.00
Taxes	$0.00
Administration Costs	$0.00
Late Charges	$0.00
Retainers	$0.00
Total Amount Due	$310.00

Continue with the following tutorial.

HOW DO I PRINT A PRODUCTIVITY REPORT?

Productivity reports may be produced in different forms with different uses of the information. Frequently, they are used to see how many hours were spent in a billable activity. They may also be used to show how much time was spent in pro bono activities to satisfy court-imposed pro bono work under the ethical guidelines.

Printing a Productivity Report

GOAL	ACTION	RESULT
CREATE AND PRINT A STAFF PRO-DUCTIVITY REPORT *Note:* Productivity reports can also be started from the Billing menu.	**CLICK** *Reports menu* **SELECT** *Productivity*	Reports 1099 and 1096 Accounts Payable Accounts Receivable Audit Trail Billing General Ledger Matter Payroll **Productivity** Trust Report Groups Setup
SELECT DESIRED REPORT FORMAT WITH DESIRED TIME PERIOD AND STAFF MEMBERS	**SELECT** *Timekeeper Performance Summary Report* **ENTER** Month and year **CHECK** *All*	Productivity Reports Hours & Fees Budget Comparison Hours Report, by Location & Title/Status Monthly Hours & Fees Recap Receipts Pending By Orig/Resp Referrals Report Timekeeper Cash Receipts Timekeeper Performance Summary Rep Unbilled Hours - Detail Unbilled Hours - Summary Weekly Time Ticket Value Work in Process - Aged Work in Process - Summary Write Off Report Timekeeper Performance Summary Report Criteria Month - Year Selection Month 1 Year 2010 Timekeeper ⦿ All ○ Timekeeper Initials Destination ⦿ Print Preview ○ Printer ○ File ○ Email ○ Report Group Preview Close Help
PRINT REPORT TO SCREEN (PREVIEW) **CHECK PRINTER IN DESTINATION TO PRINT HARDCOPY**	**CLICK** *Preview*	*Timekeeper Performance Summary Report* Report Date: 02/13/2010 Report Time: 4:12PM Page: 1 of 1 Requested By: Owen Mason **Mason, Marshall and Benjamin** For the Month of February 2010 and Year-to-Date 2010 Timekeeper Selected: All See table below

Timekeeper	Total Hours Month	YTD	Billable Hours Month	YTD	Fees Billed Month	YTD	Fees Paid Month	YTD	WIP Fees YTD
AM Ariel Marshall	0.00	0.00	0.00	0.00	$0.00	$0.00	$735.00	$735.00	$500.00
Grand Totals:	0.00	0.00	0.00	0.00	$0.00	$0.00	$735.00	$735.00	$500.00

Customizing AbacusLaw

- How Can I Change the Appearance of My AbacusLaw Desktop?
  - ▲ *Tutorial—Changing the Startup Desktop Look*
- How Can I Make My Calendar Appear when I Start Up?
  - ▲ *Tutorial—Changing the Calendar on Startup*
- How Do I Make Codes Stand Out in Color?
  - ▲ *Tutorial—Coloring a WHO Code*
- How Do I Set Up Folders in AbacusLaw?
  - ▲ *Tutorial—Creating Folders in the Docs Folder in AbacusLaw*
- How Can I Add a Picture to a Contact (Name)?
  - ▲ *Tutorial—Add a Picture to a Contact*
- How Can I Add a Picture to a Matter?
  - ▲ *Tutorial—Add a Picture to a Matter*

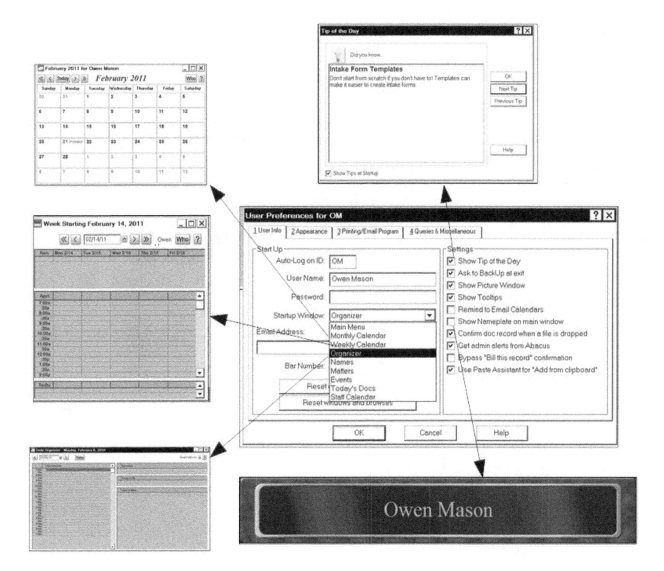

HOW CAN I CHANGE THE APPEARANCE OF MY ABACUSLAW DESKTOP?

Each user can customize the appearance of his or her personal AbacusLaw desktop. Users may choose to have a daily tip on using the features of AbacusLaw appear as part of the logon process. Each user may also choose to have a nameplate showing the user's name or the firm name. One of the most used options is the ability to show users a daily organizer calendar with a list of reminders and activities for the day.

Other customization features include the ability to change font and size to suit personal preferences or visibility needs.

Changing the Startup Desktop Look

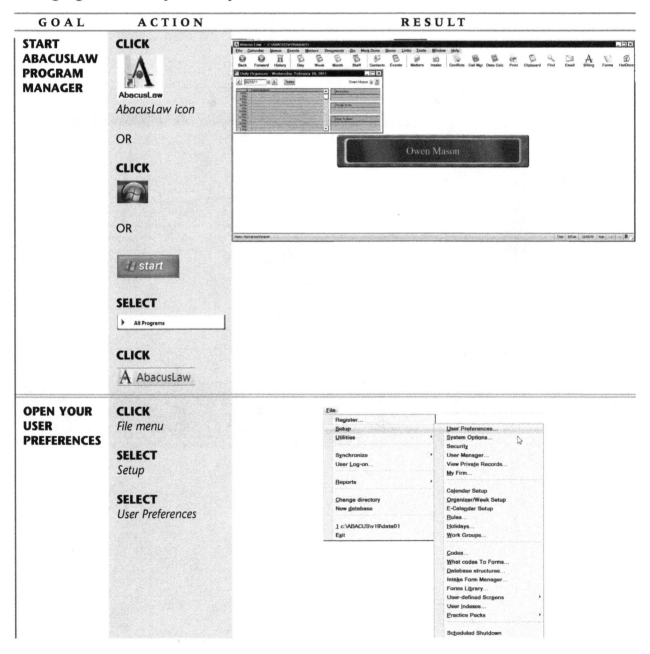

GOAL	ACTION	RESULT
START ABACUSLAW PROGRAM MANAGER	**CLICK** *AbacusLaw icon* OR **CLICK** OR **SELECT** All Programs **CLICK** AbacusLaw	
OPEN YOUR USER PREFERENCES	**CLICK** *File menu* **SELECT** *Setup* **SELECT** *User Preferences*	

Changing the Startup Desktop Look (*continued*)

GOAL	ACTION	RESULT
ENTER YOUR NAME AS YOU WANT IT TO APPEAR ON THE DESKTOP NAMEPLATE *Note*: This is your copy of AbacusLaw; use your name for nameplate.	**ENTER** Your Name OR *Owen Mason* **CHECK** *Show Nameplate on main window* **CLICK** *OK*	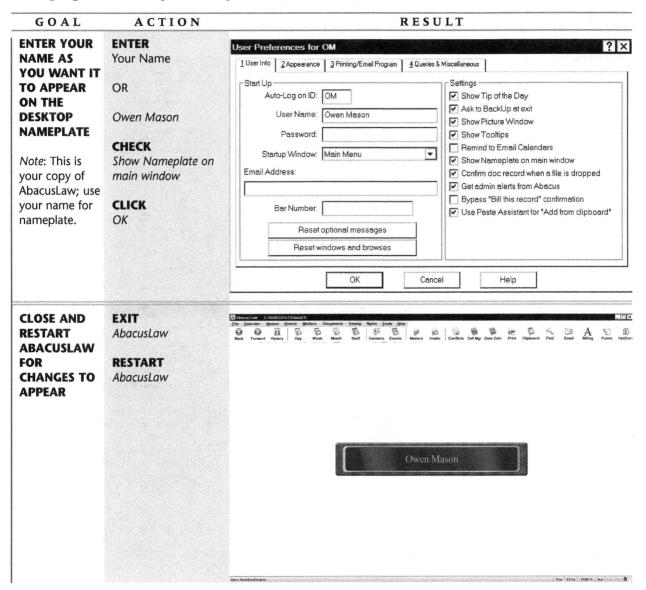
CLOSE AND RESTART ABACUSLAW FOR CHANGES TO APPEAR	**EXIT** *AbacusLaw* **RESTART** *AbacusLaw*	

Changing the Startup Desktop Look (*continued*)

GOAL	ACTION	RESULT
REMOVE THE NAMEPLATE FROM THE DESKTOP MAIN WINDOW	**CLICK** *File menu* **SELECT** *User Preferences* **UNCHECK** *Show Nameplate on main window* **CLICK** *OK*	

File

Register...
Setup
Utilities

Synchronize
User Log-on...

Reports

Change directory
New database

1 c:\ABACUS\v19\data01
Exit

User Preferences...
System Options...
Security
User Manager...
View Private Records...
My Firm...

Calendar Setup
Organizer/Week Setup
E-Calendar Setup
Rules...
Holidays...
Work Groups...

Codes...
What codes To Forms...
Database structures...
Intake Form Manager...
Forms Library...
User-defined Screens
User Indexes...
Practice Packs

Scheduled Shutdown

User Preferences for OM   ? X

1 User Info | 2 Appearance | 3 Printing/Email Program | 4 Queries & Miscellaneous

Start Up
Auto-Log on ID: OM
User Name: Owen Mason
Password:
Startup Window: Organizer
Email Address:

Bar Number:

Reset optional messages
Reset windows and browses

Settings
☑ Show Tip of the Day
☑ Ask to BackUp at exit
☑ Show Picture Window
☑ Show Tooltips
☐ Remind to Email Calendars
☐ Show Nameplate on main window
☑ Confirm doc record when a file is dropped
☑ Get admin alerts from Abacus
☐ Bypass "Bill this record" confirmation
☑ Use Paste Assistant for "Add from clipboard"

OK | Cancel | Help

HOW CAN I MAKE MY CALENDAR APPEAR WHEN I START UP?

AbacusLaw allows each user to select the type of calendar or calendar information that they want on their desktop. You may want to experiment to find the one you prefer. In addition to scheduled activity, the daily calendar, also called the Organizer, shows lists of Reminders, Things to Do, and Calls to Make.

Changing the Calendar on Startup

GOAL	ACTION	RESULT
CHOOSE A PERSONAL CALENDAR STYLE TO APPEAR ON YOUR DESKTOP	**CLICK** *File menu* **SELECT** *Setup* **SELECT** *User Preferences*	
SELECT CALENDAR TYPE TO APPEAR ON DESKTOP	**CLICK** Startup Window: Organizer ▾ *Down arrow* **SELECT** *Organizer* **CLICK** *OK*	

Changing the Calendar on Startup (*continued*)

GOAL	ACTION	RESULT
EXIT AND RESTART ABACUSLAW TO ENABLE CHANGES *Note*: Some features require a restart of the program to be activated.	**CLICK** *File menu* **CLICK** *Exit* **CLICK** **AbacusLaw** *AbacusLaw icon*	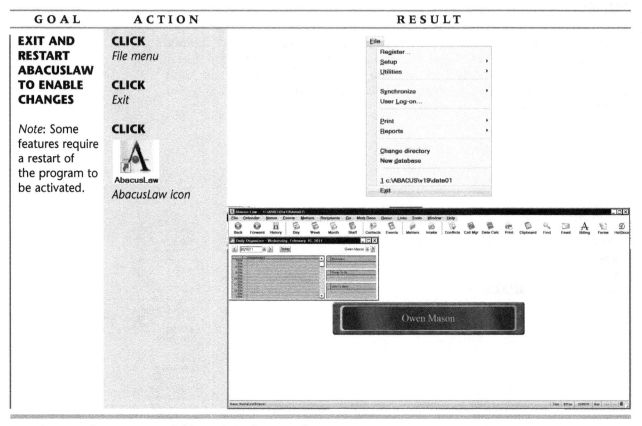

Continue to the next tutorial or exit and restart later.

HOW DO I MAKE CODES STAND OUT IN COLOR?

A frequently used code may be set to appear in color to stand out in a list. The following code types may be colored:

- Priority
- Status
- Type
- What
- Where
- Who

In this tutorial you will open the list of codes using the setup menu. The WHO code is shown as an example.

Coloring a WHO Code

GOAL	ACTION	RESULT
OPEN THE LIST OF CODES	**CLICK** *File menu* **SELECT** *Setup* **SELECT** *Codes*	
CHANGE COLOR OF A WHO CODE *Note*: You can change the color of a WHO, or other colorable codes, any time the Valid Entries screen is opened.	**DOUBLE CLICK** *WHO* **CLICK** *Your initials* OR *OM* to highlight desired WHO **CLICK** *Color button* **SELECT** A color from the color palette **CLICK** *OK* **CLICK** *OK* in Valid WHO Entries window **CLICK** *Close* in Code Types window	

HOW DO I SET UP FOLDERS IN ABACUSLAW?

Documents and other files, including photographs and graphic files, can be stored on the hard drive on a computer workstation, a server, or a removable storage device, like a memory card. In order to find the files easily, it would be helpful to establish a standard practice of how and where these items will be stored. With increased storage capacity of the storage devices, and more items being filed electronically, a computer filing system becomes very important, if not essential, to have all the members of a legal team know where to look for files.

Think of the *folders* and *files* as if they were a group of filing cabinets, each with drawers containing folders and files in each folder. Each cabinet might contain one type of information, such as client's wills and trusts, while another cabinet contains all real estate matters or corporate clients. On a computer, a main folder may replace a cabinet or cabinet drawer. A *subfolder* may be set up for a client, and additional subfolders for different matters within those folders.

FOLDERS, SUBFOLDERS, AND FILES FOR MASON, MARSHALL AND BENJAMIN

CLIENTS

Bates
    Personal Injury Case
        Pleadings
            Complaint
            Answer
        Correspondence
            Client
            Opposing Counsel
        Photographs
        Depositions
    Custody Matter
        Correspondence
        Documents
        Pleadings

Leonard
    Personal Injury Case
        Pleadings
            Complaint
            Answer
        Correspondence
            Client
            Opposing Counsel
        Photographs
        Depositions
    Will
        Correspondence
        Documents

Stein
    Personal Injury Case
        Pleadings
            Complaint
            Answer

  Correspondence
   Client
   Opposing Counsel
  Photographs
  Depositions
 Real Estate Matter
  Correspondence
  Agreement of Sale
  Finance Documents

Paperless law offices have similar type folders, usually on their network file server, so everyone has access to the files.

AbacusLaw installs an AbacusLaw main folder when the program is installed. Subfolders are set up for the program and the data (information) that is used in preparing reports and bills. The Forms folder is installed with sample AbacusLaw forms. The Docs folder under the main AbacusLaw folder, also set up automatically on installation of the AbacusLaw program, may be used to store finished case or matter documents. This is a convenient location for setting up additional subfolders for each matter.

The following expanded view shows the main and subfolders with the Forms subfolder opened in the right panel. A folder is opened in the right panel by clicking on the label in the tree view, which shows all the branches on the left.

The *main folder* in the C:\ drive is the ABACUS folder.

The *second level folder* is the v19 folder.

The *third level folder* is the data01 folder.

The *fourth level folder* is the Forms folder with the files, shown in the right window.

The destination to the final file is called a *path*. In this case the path is C:\Abacus\v19\data01\forms\ and the path to the setlet file is C:\Abacus\v19\data01\forms\setlet.

Each folder can be opened and explored using Windows Explorer. Each folder that contains other folders has a "+" in front of it that will open the folder if you click on it. The folder will also close if you click the "−". Double clicking any file, such as the Welcome file created with Microsoft Word, will open that file.

The Forms folder is a good place to save any forms or template files that will be used for more than one specific matter.

Files only related to specific matters should be stored in a folder for that matter. In the following exhibit, folders for the three matters set up previously in the tutorials have been created using the file ID numbers as the folder names.

In the following tutorial you will set up a folder for a specific matter.

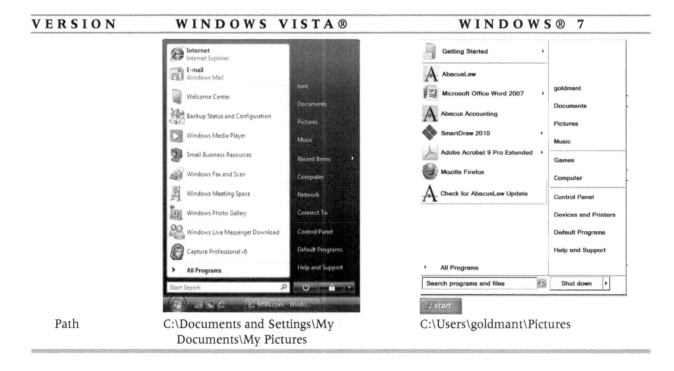

Notice the − *sign* has been clicked to close the v19 folder and the + *sign* clicked to open the Docs folder showing three folders for three matters.

Each version of the Windows® operating system—Windows® XP, Windows Vista®, and Windows® 7—has a different appearance. The same fundamental features, like opening the computer to see what drives and devices are part of the computer and find files and folders, are the same. The paths to specific items, such as My Pictures, may be different. Take a few minutes to locate the My Pictures folder on your computer.

VERSION	WINDOWS VISTA®	WINDOWS® 7
Path	C:\Documents and Settings\My Documents\My Pictures	C:\Users\goldmant\Pictures

Creating Folders in the Docs Folder in AbacusLaw

GOAL	ACTION	RESULT
OPEN COMPUTER LIST OF STORAGE DEVICES *Note:* The operating system used in this example is Windows® 7.	**CLICK** OR **CLICK** All Programs	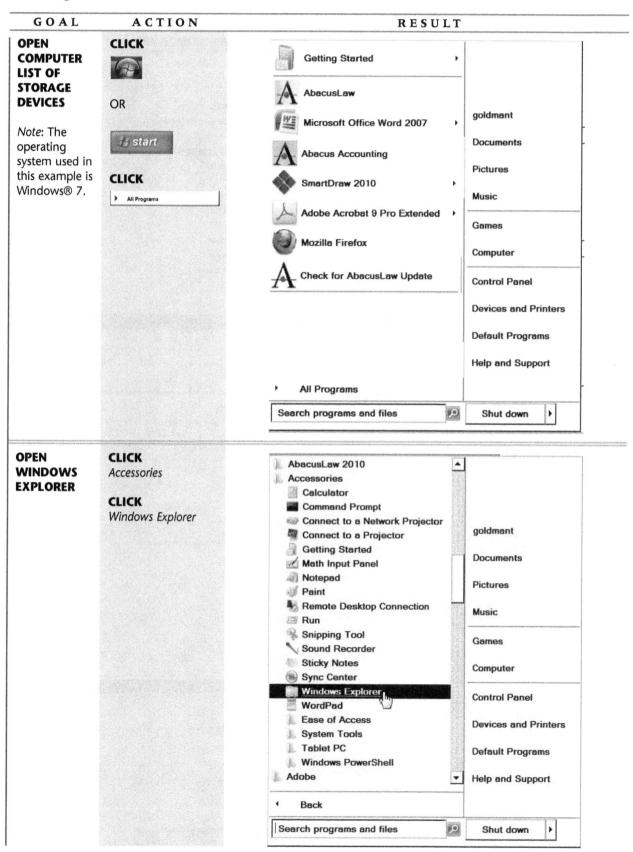
OPEN WINDOWS EXPLORER	**CLICK** *Accessories* **CLICK** *Windows Explorer*	

Creating Folders in the Docs Folder in AbacusLaw (*continued*)

GOAL	ACTION	RESULT
OPEN FOLDERS ON COMPUTER TO SHOW DOC FILES FOR MATTERS *Note*: The ⊞ sign changes to a ⊟sign when the folder is opened.	**CLICK** ⊞ *sign* by C: drive (or other drive on your computer) **CLICK** ⊞ *sign* by AbacusLaw folder **CLICK** ⊞ *sign* by Docs folder	
CREATE NEW FOLDER *Note*: Folders may be renamed by selecting Rename from the same right-click menu that was used to set up the new folder. Place cursor on the file name and right click, enter the new name, and click to close.	**PLACE** Cursor on *Docs* **RIGHT CLICK** *Docs folder* **CLICK** *New* **CLICK** *Folder*	

Creating Folders in the Docs Folder in AbacusLaw (*continued*)

GOAL	ACTION	RESULT
LABEL NEW FOLDER AS A SUBFOLDER	**ENTER** *1243* Or other new matter folder number	📁 Docs
		📁 1230
		📁 1235
		📁 1242
	CLICK To accept new label	📁 1243

Continue with the following tutorial.

HOW CAN I ADD A PICTURE TO A CONTACT (NAME)?

Many people link a picture to a name in their cell phone so that the picture appears when the number is called or a call is received from a specific person.

A picture may be linked to a name or contact in AbacusLaw so that it will appear when the Name Window is opened. By default, these pictures are stored in a subfolder of AbacusLaw called Pictures. The path is

C:\Abacus\Pictures\.

Pictures for contacts are stored in the subfolder Names.

C:\Abacus\Pictures\Names

In this tutorial you will use Windows Explorer and *drag and drop* a picture file from a folder on your computer to the AbacusLaw subfolder Pictures\Names. Before starting the tutorial, take a picture of yourself (or someone else) and save it on your computer in a sample pictures file such as C:\desktop\pictures\sample, or use an existing picture on your computer.

BEFORE YOU START

In this exercise a picture will be linked to an existing name and matter that you have created in AbacusLaw. You will need the matter ID and the name ID to complete this exercise.

Practice accessing names and matters by finding the IDs. For example, in this exercise we show Elisabeth Stein.

> **TIP**
>
> Write down the ID number before starting. It is necessary to link the picture to the name (contact).

The ID number for Elisabeth Stein is MYFIRM-95675.

In the following lesson you will find the picture you want to use on your computer using Windows Explorer, move the picture to the Abacus\Pictures\names folder, and rename the picture with the ID number.

Add a Picture to a Contact

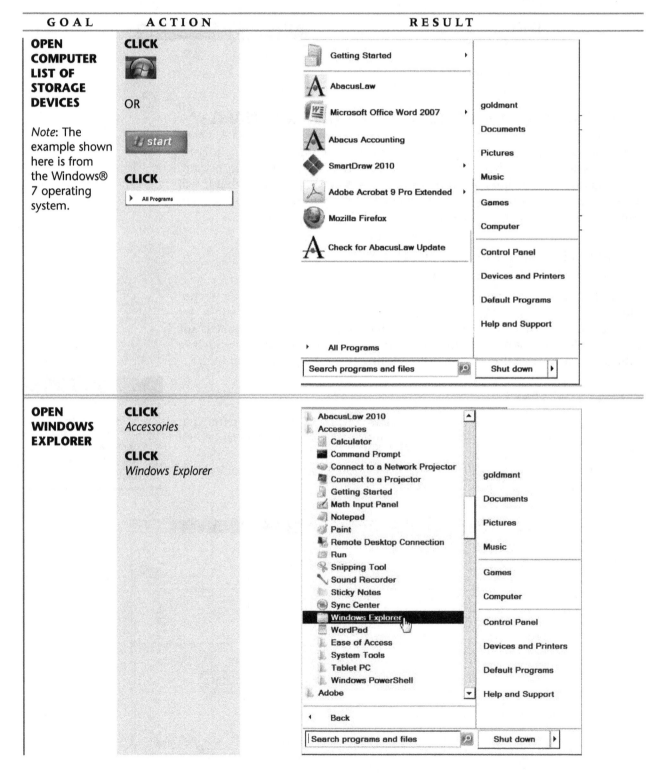

GOAL	ACTION	RESULT
OPEN COMPUTER LIST OF STORAGE DEVICES *Note*: The example shown here is from the Windows® 7 operating system.	**CLICK** OR *start* **CLICK** All Programs	
OPEN WINDOWS EXPLORER	**CLICK** *Accessories* **CLICK** *Windows Explorer*	

Add a Picture to a Contact (*continued*)

GOAL	ACTION	RESULT
LOCATE PICTURE ON YOUR COMPUTER USING WINDOWS EXPLORER *Note*: The example shown here is from the Windows® 7 operating system.	**Locate** Picture folder	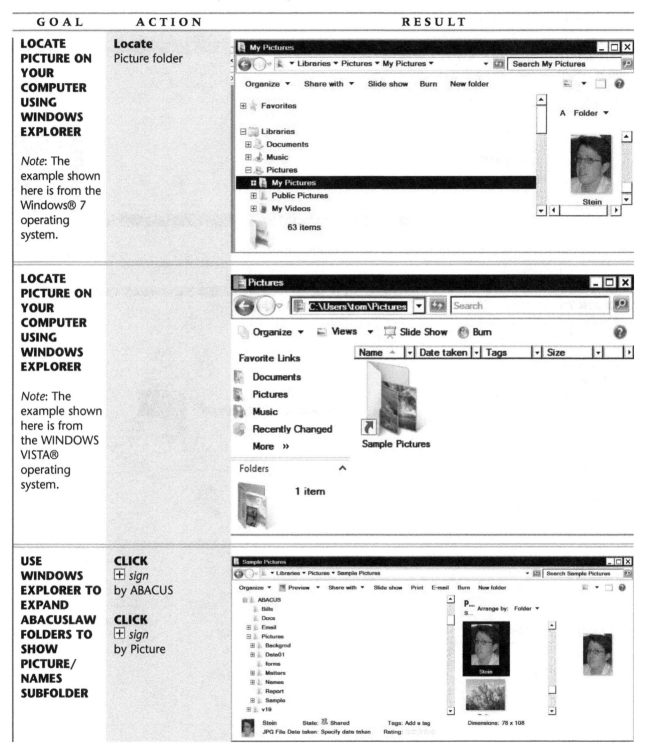
LOCATE PICTURE ON YOUR COMPUTER USING WINDOWS EXPLORER *Note*: The example shown here is from the WINDOWS VISTA® operating system.		
USE WINDOWS EXPLORER TO EXPAND ABACUSLAW FOLDERS TO SHOW PICTURE/ NAMES SUBFOLDER	**CLICK** ⊞ *sign* by ABACUS **CLICK** ⊞ *sign* by Picture	

Add a Picture to a Contact (*continued*)

GOAL	ACTION	RESULT
DRAG PICTURE TO ABACUSLAW\ PICTURE\ NAMES FOLDER	**CLICK and HOLD** *Left cursor button* on picture **DRAG** Cursor to names folder **RELEASE** Cursor	
OPEN NAMES FOLDER TO SHOW CONTENTS IN RIGHT PANEL. RENAME A FILE OR PICTURE. *Note*: The name's ID number appears on the individual Names window.	**DOUBLE CLICK** *Names folder* **CLICK** on picture **RIGHT CLICK** *(open menu)* **CLICK** *Rename* **ENTER** *Myfirm-95675* OR Other ID Number **CLICK** *Enter key* on keyboard **CLOSE** *Windows Explorer*	

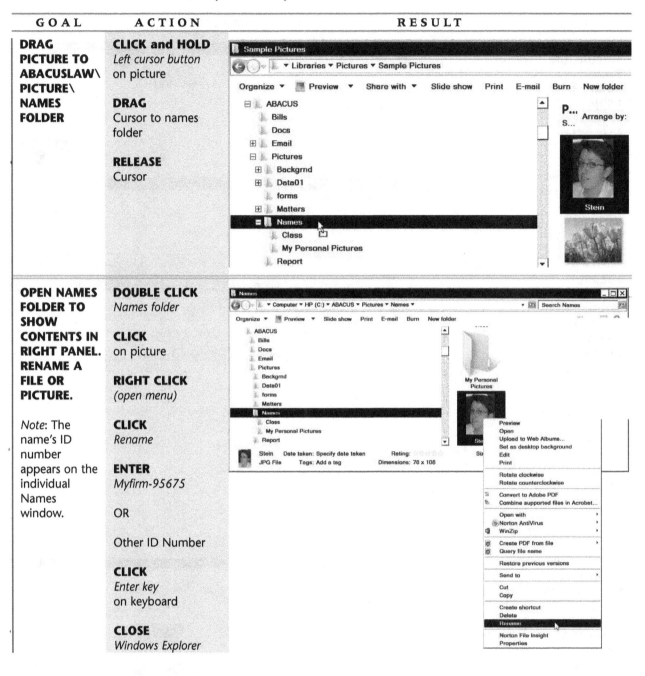

Add a Picture to a Contact (*continued*)

GOAL	ACTION	RESULT
START ABACUSLAW AND OPEN NAMES WINDOW WITH PICTURE	**CLICK** *AbacusLaw icon* **CLICK** *Contacts* **DOUBLE CLICK** *Elisabeth Stein* **CLICK** *X* on picture window to close	
REOPEN PICTURE USING WINDOW MENU *Note:* The Picture Window option is only available if there is a picture and the picture is not already open in the work space.	**CLICK** *Window menu* **SELECT** *Picture Window*	

Continue with the following tutorial.

HOW CAN I ADD A PICTURE TO A MATTER?

Pictures may be linked to matters in the same way as pictures were linked to names in the previous tutorial. The only difference is the folder where the pictures are stored—Abacus\Pictures\Matters and the number used to identify them—file/case #.

Names use the ID number, displayed in the Names window; matters use the file/case # displayed on the Matter window. In the case of Bates v Howard, the file/case # is 1240. This is a personal injury (PI) case. By default, whenever the case code is PI the picture of an ambulance appears until another picture is used.

In this tutorial you will add a picture to the matter picture file (C:\Abacus\Pictures\Matters) using the copy and paste method.

To demonstrate the concept, in this tutorial you will use an existing sample picture in the AbacusLaw folder.

Add a Picture to a Matter

GOAL	ACTION	RESULT
OPEN WINDOWS EXPLORER	**CLICK** OR start **CLICK** All Programs **CLICK** *Accessories* **CLICK** *Windows Explorer*	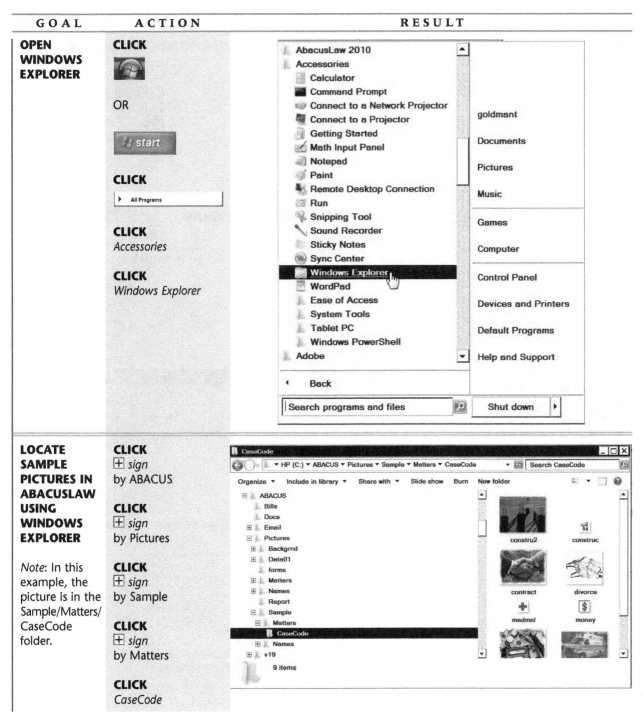
LOCATE SAMPLE PICTURES IN ABACUSLAW USING WINDOWS EXPLORER *Note*: In this example, the picture is in the Sample/Matters/CaseCode folder.	**CLICK** ⊞ *sign* by ABACUS **CLICK** ⊞ *sign* by Pictures **CLICK** ⊞ *sign* by Sample **CLICK** ⊞ *sign* by Matters **CLICK** *CaseCode*	

Add a Picture to a Matter (*continued*)

GOAL	ACTION	RESULT
COPY PICTURE	**PLACE** Cursor on picture **RIGHT CLICK** **CLICK** *Copy* in drop-down menu	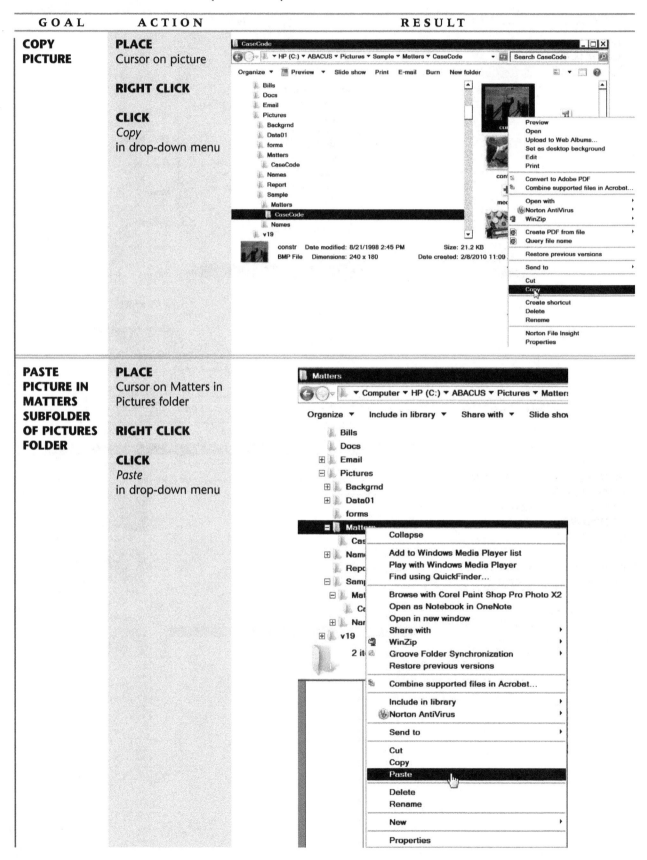
PASTE PICTURE IN MATTERS SUBFOLDER OF PICTURES FOLDER	**PLACE** Cursor on Matters in Pictures folder **RIGHT CLICK** **CLICK** *Paste* in drop-down menu	

Add a Picture to a Matter (*continued*)

GOAL	ACTION	RESULT
OPEN PICTURE IN RIGHT PANEL AND RENAME PICTURE TO MATTER FILE/CASE #	**DOUBLE CLICK** *Matters* in Pictures folder **PLACE** Cursor on picture **RIGHT CLICK** **CLICK** *Rename* on drop-down menu **ENTER** *1240* **PRESS** *Enter key* on keyboard	
OPEN ABACUSLAW AND CHECK PICTURE IN MATTER	**CLICK** **AbacusLaw** *Practice Manager icon* on desktop **CLICK** *Matters* **SELECT** *Bates v Howard*	

Exit AbacusLaw.

The Basics: Check Registers and Trust Accounts in Abacus Accounting

- Why Do I Need a Client Trust Account
- How Do I Set Up a Client Trust Account?
  - ▲ *Tutorial—Setting Up a Client Trust Account in Abacus Accounting*
- How Do I Make Payments from the Client Trust Account?
  - ▲ *Tutorial—Paying an Expense from the Client Trust Account*
- How Do I Transfer Earned Fees from a Client Trust Account?
  - ▲ *Tutorial—Pay Legal Fees from a Client Trust Account*

TRUST ACCOUNTS

Trust Deposits – Add

Client Number	MYFIRM-95675	Client Name	Elisabeth Stein
Matter Number	1241	Matter Description	Stein v Curtis
Trust Account	11020.00	Account Description	Cash - Trust Account I

Date 02-08-2010
Amount 1000.00

Description

General Information

Save   Close   Help

Matter Trust Activity

Matter Number	1241	Stein v Curtis	
Client Name	Elisabeth Stein		
Start Date	01-01-1900	End Date 02-08-2010	

Trust Balance Forward $0.00
Trust Ending Balance $835.00

△ Date	Deposits	Withdrawals	Account #	Payee	Description
02-08-2010	$1,000.00		11020.00	Trust Deposit	Fee and Cost Retainer
02-08-2010		$165.00	11020.00	CLERK of COURTt	Complaint Filing Fee

A/R Balance: $0.00   UnBilled Time: $0.00   UnBilled Costs: $0.00   Total Due: $0.00

Details   Print   Refresh   Close   Help

Print Demand Trust Checks

Please be sure of the Posting Date and make any necessary adjustments to the next check number to be assigned.

Account Number 11020.00 - Cash - Trust Account I

Check/Post Date 02-08-2010   Journal Number

Next Check Number 1

Check Horizontal Offset in Inches. Positive numbers move
the check date to the right, negative numbers to the left.   0

Check Vertical Offset in Inches. Positive numbers move the
check data down, negative numbers moves the data up.   0

☐ Post Only, Do Not Print a Check   Printer HP LaserJet 4250 PCL6

OK   Cancel   Help

Print Demand Trust Checks

Account Number	11020.00	Cash - Trust Account I	
Matter Number	1241	Stein v Curtis	Bal Before This Check $835.00

Check # AUTO
02-08-2010

Payee MASON, MARSHALL & BENJAMIN $ 735.00

Seven Hundred Thirty Five Dollars & 00/100   Dollars

Address

Memo

Description FEES BILLED

Print   Close   Help

Print Demand Trust Checks

Account Number	11020.00	Cash - Trust Account I	
Matter Number	1241	Stein v Curtis	Bal Before This Check $1,000.00

Check # AUTO
02-08-2010

Payee CLERK of COURT $ 165.00

One Hundred Sixty Five Dollars & 00/100   Dollars

Address

Memo

Description Complaint Filing Fee

Print   Close   Help

WHY DO I NEED A CLIENT TRUST ACCOUNT?

The ethics rules of the legal profession prohibit the commingling of attorney and client funds. Even money received from a client to be applied to future work, commonly called a retainer, is usually not that of the attorney until the work has been performed. Typically, retainers against fees and costs are maintained in a trust account. Depending on the amount involved and local ethical rules, it may need to be placed in an individual account or combined with other client funds—a common trust account. In some cases the funds are not enough to justify the time and cost of recording and reporting any interest earned on the account to the client. In these cases, the funds are usually required by local rules to be placed in an interest-bearing account with the interest going to a designated state agency, under the Interest on Lawyer Trust Account rules (IOLTA). For purposes of this tutorial, it is assumed there is a common trust fund, which may contain the funds of multiple clients, and there is no interest earned on the account.

HOW DO I SET UP A CLIENT TRUST ACCOUNT?

In most cases, the trust account is the same as a checking account, an account into which deposits may be made and checks written to pay expenses and fees.

Setting Up a Client Trust Account in Abacus Accounting

GOAL	ACTION	RESULT
START ABACUS ACCOUNTING	**CLICK** **A** Abacus Accounting *Abacus Accounting icon*	

Setting Up a Client Trust Account in Abacus Accounting (*continued*)

GOAL	ACTION	RESULT
MAKE A DEPOSIT INTO THE CLIENT TRUST ACCOUNT	**CLICK** *Trust Deposit icon* **CLICK** Matter Number *Up arrow* **SELECT** *Stein v Curtis matter* **CLICK** OK	
PREPARE A TRUST DEPOSIT FOR A MATTER *Note*: After saving information, a new blank form will appear.	**ENTER** Date **ENTER** *1000.00* in the Amount field **ENTER** *Fee and Cost Retainer* in the Description field **CLICK** Save **CLICK** Close	

Setting Up a Client Trust Account in Abacus Accounting (*continued*)

GOAL	ACTION	RESULT
REVIEW AND CONFIRM DATE BEFORE ADDING TO TRUST ACCOUNT	**SELECT** Listed item **REVIEW** For accuracy **CLICK** *Deposit Slip* **CLICK** *Print*	
POST AND ACKNOW-LEDGE DEPOSIT DATE WARNING	**CLICK** *Yes* **CLICK** *Yes*	

Trust Deposits

△ Client	Matter	Date	Amount	Account #	Description
MyFIRM 95625	1241	02-08-2010	$1,000.00	11020.00	Fee and Cost Retainer

Deposit Date: 02-08-2010

Total Deposits in Posting File: $1,000.00

Total Deposits Selected for Posting: $1,000.00

Select All | Deselect All | Help

Add | Details | Delete | Print | Deposit Slip | Post | Refresh | Close

Trust Deposits

Printing Deposit Slip

Please put a deposit slip into the proper printer, select that printer and double check the deposit date.

Number of Items on Deposit Slip: 1

Printer: HP LaserJet 4250 PCL6

Total Amount of Deposit: $1,000.00

Date of Deposit: 02-08-2010

Offsets
Vertical: 0
Horizontal: 0

Print | Cancel | Help

Abacus Accounting

Do you want to post the items on your deposit slip right now?

Yes | No

Abacus Accounting

Remember: The Deposit Date on your screen should be the ACTUAL DATE the payments are deposited into the bank account. Continue with posting?

☐ Do not show me this again.   Yes | No

Setting Up a Client Trust Account in Abacus Accounting (*continued*)

GOAL	ACTION	RESULT
PRINT DEPOSIT SLIP	**CLICK** *Print* on Output Destination Selection window	
REVIEW ACCOUNT	**CLICK** *Trust menu* **SELECT** *Matter Trust Activity*	
VIEW TRUST MATTER ACTIVITY	**CLICK** Matter Number / Up arrow **DOUBLE CLICK** *Stein v Curtis matter* **CLICK** *Print* **CLICK** *X* To close all windows	

Continue with the following tutorial.

HOW DO I MAKE PAYMENTS
FROM THE CLIENT TRUST ACCOUNT?

Payments for costs and expenses for a client may, subject to the retainer agreement, be paid directly from the trust account. Having a cancelled check is always a good backup documentation to show the propriety of the expenditure.

In the following tutorial, a check is issued to pay a filing fee where the payee, the clerk of courts, is not on the vendor list.

Paying an Expense from the Client Trust Account

GOAL	ACTION	RESULT
WRITE A CHECK FROM TRUST ACCOUNT TO PAY A FILING FEE	**CLICK** *Trust menu* **SELECT** *Trust Demand Check Writer* **CLICK** Matter Number *Up arrow* **DOUBLE CLICK** *Stein v Curtis matter*	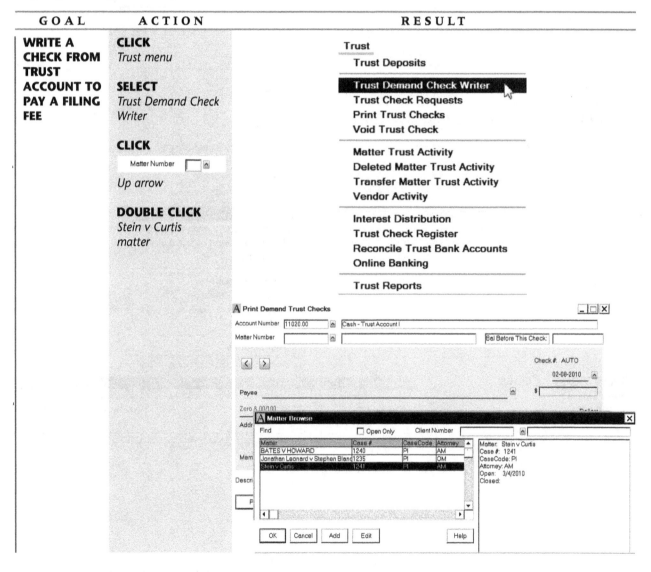

Paying an Expense from the Client Trust Account (*continued*)

GOAL	ACTION	RESULT
PREPARE CHECK FOR PRINTING	**ENTER** *CLERK of COURT* as Payee *165.00* as Amount *Complaint Filing Fee* as Description **CLICK** *Print*	
PRINT CHECK WHERE PAYEE (VENDOR) IS NOT IN DATABASE	**CLICK** *Yes*	
PRINT CHECK *Note*: This assumes the use of preprinted three-part checks, as used in many offices, with the actual check in the middle section.	**CLICK** *OK*	

Paying an Expense from the Client Trust Account (*continued*)

GOAL	ACTION	RESULT
REVIEW ACCOUNT	**CLICK** *Trust menu* **SELECT** *Matter Trust Activity*	Trust **Trust Deposits** **Trust Demand Check Writer** **Trust Check Requests** **Print Trust Checks** **Void Trust Check** **Matter Trust Activity** **Deleted Matter Trust Activity** **Transfer Matter Trust Activity** **Vendor Activity** **Interest Distribution** **Trust Check Register** **Reconcile Trust Bank Accounts** **Online Banking** **Trust Reports**
VIEW TRUST MATTER ACTIVITY	**CLICK** Matter Number *Up arrow* **SELECT** *Stein v Curtis matter* **CLICK** *OK* **CLICK** *Close*	Matter Trust Activity Matter Number 1241 Stein v Curtis Trust Balance Forward $0.00 Client Name Elisabeth Stein Trust Ending Balance $835.00 Start Date 01-01-1900 End Date 02-08-2010 Date / Deposits / Withdrawals / Account # / Payee / Description 02-08-2010 $1,000.00 11020.00 Trust Deposit Fee and Cost Retainer 02-08-2010 $165.00 11020.00 CLERK of COURTt Complaint Filing Fee A/R Balance: $0.00 UnBilled Time: $0.00 UnBilled Costs: $0.00 Total Due: $0.00 Details Print Refresh Close Help

Continue with the next tutorial before exiting Abacus Accounting.

HOW DO I TRANSFER EARNED FEES FROM A CLIENT TRUST ACCOUNT?

It bears repeating, that the rules of ethics of the legal profession prohibit a lawyer from commingling funds with a client's funds. When a fee has been earned, that portion of the funds on account in the trust account belongs to the attorney. At that point, leaving the funds in the trust account is technically commingling of the funds. Therefore, the earned portion should be removed from the trust fund and placed in the firm or attorney operating account. The best way is to issue a check, as if paying another expense, to the firm from the trust account and then depositing the check into the firm checking account. This creates a paper trail of dates, amounts, and accounts to prove the funds are not commingled. It can be argued that the time to remove the funds is after the client has been billed and a reasonable time to object has passed.

A trust check may be issued to the firm as shown in the previous tutorial.

Pay Legal Fees from a Client Trust Account

GOAL	ACTION	RESULT
WRITE A CHECK FROM TRUST ACCOUNT TO PAY A FILING FEE	**CLICK** *Trust menu* **SELECT** *Trust Demand Check Writer* **CLICK** Matter Number *Up arrow* **SELECT** *Stein v Curtis matter* **CLICK** *OK*	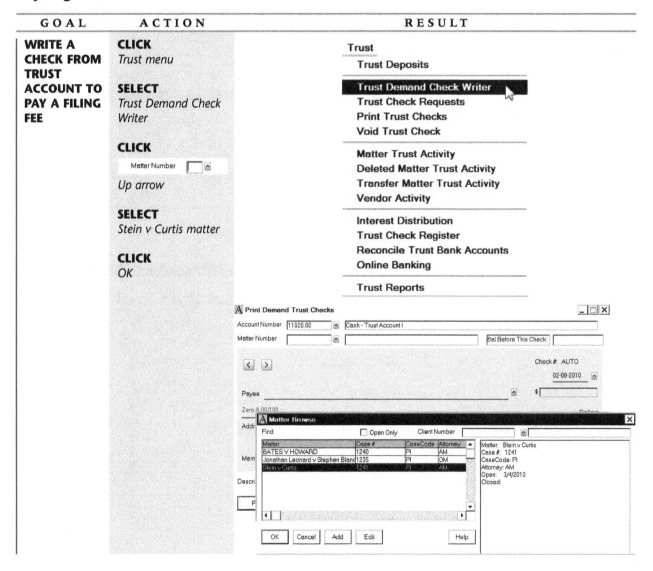

Pay Legal Fees from a Client Trust Account (*continued*)

GOAL	ACTION	RESULT
PREPARE CHECK FOR PRINTING	**ENTER** *MASON, MARSHALL & BENJAMIN* as Payee *735.00* as Amount *FEES BILLED* as Description **CLICK** *Print*	
PRINT CHECK	**CLICK** *Yes* in vendor notice **CLICK** *OK* in Print Demand Trust Checks window	

Pay Legal Fees from a Client Trust Account (*continued*)

GOAL	ACTION	RESULT
REVIEW BALANCE AFTER ACTIVITY	**CLICK** *Trust menu* **SELECT** *Matter Trust Activity* **CLICK** Matter Number ▢ ▲ *Up arrow* **SELECT** *Stein v Curtis matter* **CLICK** *Close*	Trust

Trust Deposits

Trust Demand Check Writer
Trust Check Requests
Print Trust Checks
Void Trust Check

Matter Trust Activity
Deleted Matter Trust Activity
Transfer Matter Trust Activity
Vendor Activity

Interest Distribution
Trust Check Register
Reconcile Trust Bank Accounts
Online Banking

Trust Reports

Matter Trust Activity   _ |□|X|

Matter Number 1241	▲ Stein v Curtis	Trust Balance Forward	$0.00
Client Name	Elisabeth Stein	Trust Ending Balance	$100.00
Start Date	01-01-1900 ▲ End Date 02-08-2010 ▲		

△ Date	Deposits	Withdrawals	Account #	Payee	Description
02-08-2010	$1,000.00		11020.00	Trust Deposit	Fee and Cost Retainer
02-08-2010		$165.00	11020.00	CLERK of COURTt	Complaint Filing Fee
02-08-2010		$735.00	11020.00	MASON, MARSHALL...	FEES BILLED

A/R Balance: $0.00   UnBilled Time: $0.00   UnBilled Costs: $0.00   Total Due: $0.00

| Details | Print | | Refresh | | Close | Help |

Exit Abacus Accounting.

Accounting: Payroll and Accounts Payable

- Tutorial Information Used
- How Do I Set Up the Firm Check Register?
  - ▲ *Tutorial—Deposit Fees into the Firm Checking Account*
- How Can I Use AbacusLaw to Prepare Payroll?
  - ▲ *Tutorial—Create an Employee Profile for Payroll*
- How Do I Process the Payroll and Print Paychecks?
  - ▲ *Tutorial—Process Payroll and Print Paychecks*
- How Do I Prepare a Payroll Summary Report?
  - ▲ *Tutorial—Prepare a Payroll Summary Report*
- How Do I Pay Recurring Bills?
  - ▲ *Tutorial—Add and Pay Recurring Vendor*
- How Do I Print My Checkbook Register?
  - ▲ *Tutorial—Print Checkbook Register*

PAYROLL

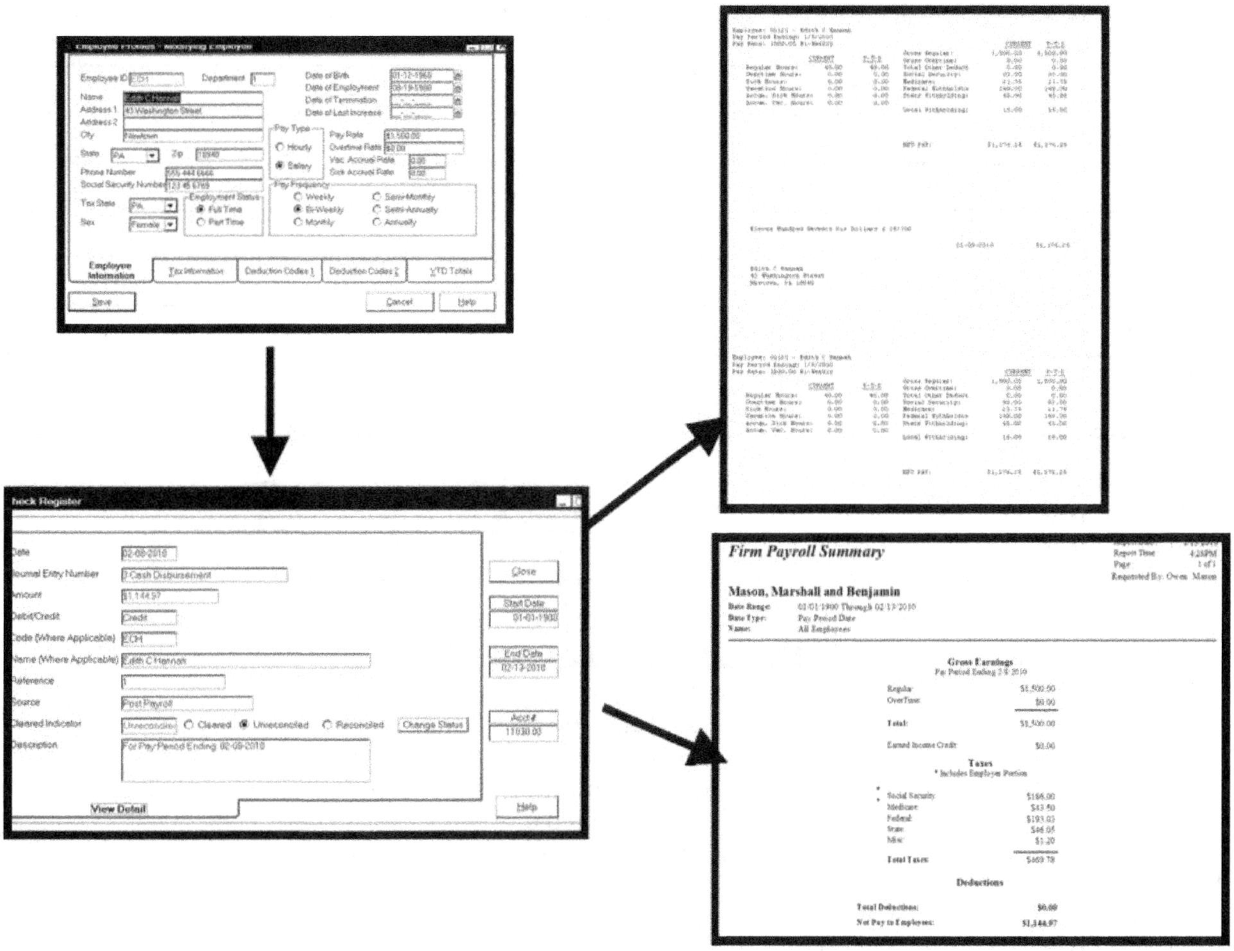
Employee ID
Department
Date of Birth
Date of Employment
Date of Termination
Date of Last Increase
Name
Address 1
Address 2
City
State
Zip
Phone Number
Social Security Number
Tax State
Sex
Pay Type
Hourly
Salary
Pay Rate
Overtime Rate
Vac. Accrual Rate
Sick Accrual Rate
Employment Status
Full Time
Part Time
Pay Frequency
Weekly
Bi-Weekly
Monthly
Semi-Monthly
Semi-Annually
Annually
Employee Information
Tax Information
Deduction Codes 1
Deduction Codes 2
YTD Totals
Save
Cancel
Help
heck Register
Date
02-09-2010
Journal Entry Number
Cash Disbursement
Amount
$1,144.97
Debit/Credit
Credit
Code (Where Applicable)
ECH
Name (Where Applicable)
Edith C Hannah
Reference
Source
Post Payroll
Cleared Indicator
Cleared
Unreconciled
Reconciled
Change Status
Description
For Pay Period Ending 02-09-2010
View Detail
Close
Start Date
01-01-1900
End Date
02-13-2010
Acct #
11030.00
Help
Firm Payroll Summary
Report Time
4:28PM
Page
1 of 1
Requested By: Owen Mason
Mason, Marshall and Benjamin
Date Range:
02/01/1900 Through 02/13/2010
Date Type:
Pay Period Date
Name:
All Employees
Gross Earnings
Pay Period Ending 2/8/2010
Regular
$1,500.00
OverTime
$0.00
Total:
$1,500.00
Earned Income Credit
$0.00
Taxes
* Includes Employer Portion
Social Security
$186.00
Medicare
$43.50
Federal
$193.03
State
$46.05
Misc
$1.20
Total Taxes
$469.78
Deductions
Total Deductions:
$0.00
Net Pay to Employees:
$1,144.97

TUTORIAL INFORMATION USED

The following tutorial information is used to illustrate the tutorials in this section. Substitute your personal information.

Fill in your information before starting the tutorials.

	TUTORIAL INFORMATION	YOUR INFORMATION
Employee ID	Mason, Marshall and Benjamin	
Address 1	43 Washington Street	
City	Newtown	
State	PA	
Zip	18940	
Phone Number	555 453 3134	
Social Security #	123-45-6790	
Sex	Female	
Date of Birth	1-12-1960	
Pay Rate	1500	
Last Name	Snowbank Telephone Service	
Label	Snowbank Telephone PO Box XYZ	
Zip	99740	
City	FT. YUKON	
State	AK	

HOW DO I SET UP THE FIRM CHECK REGISTER?

For purposes of this tutorial, it will be assumed that the only funds received by the firm are from a client. In the real world, the sole practitioner or the partners (firm owners) would have to put in some amount (capital contribution) to cover operating expenses until fees are generated and received. These funds would be entered in the accounting records of the firm reflecting the deposits into the firm checking account and shown in the owner's or partner's capital accounts, or reflected as coming from a loan payable in the future.

Fees come from clients for service already rendered. Funds from clients may also be received as retainers for services to be rendered in the future. In the previous tutorial we deposited client funds received as retainers into a client trust account. As fees are earned they should be transferred from the trust account to the firm checking account (operating account). Ethical rules prohibiting commingling of funds require a separation of client and firm funds. The best practice is to generate a check from the trust account, after the fees are earned and billed, and then deposit it into the firm operating account.

Deposit Fees into the Firm Checking Account

GOAL	ACTION	RESULT
START ABACUS ACCOUNTING	**CLICK** *Abacus Accounting icon* OR **CLICK** **Billing** *Billing icon on AbacusLaw Practice Manager toolbar*	
ENTER FUNDS RECEIVED FROM A CLIENT TO BE APPLIED TO FEES EARNED *Note*: Matter Number is the same as File/Case # in Matter window	**CLICK** *Payments icon* **CLICK** Matter Number *Up arrow* **SELECT** *Stein v Curtis* **CLICK** OK	

Deposit Fees into the Firm Checking Account (*continued*)

GOAL	ACTION	RESULT
ALLOCATE AMOUNT RECEIVED BETWEEN COSTS AND FEES	**ENTER** *735.00* as Payment Amount on General Info tab **ENTER** *FEES BILLED* (as Description) **CLICK** *Breakout tab* **ENTER** *735.00* in the Fees field as Payment Distribution amount **CLICK** *Fee Distribution tab*	
APPLY AMOUNT RECEIVED TO TIMEKEEPER WHO GENERATED FEES	**CLICK** *Up arrow* by Timekeeper 1 **SELECT** *AM* **ENTER** *735* in the Fee Amount 1 field **CLICK** *Save*	

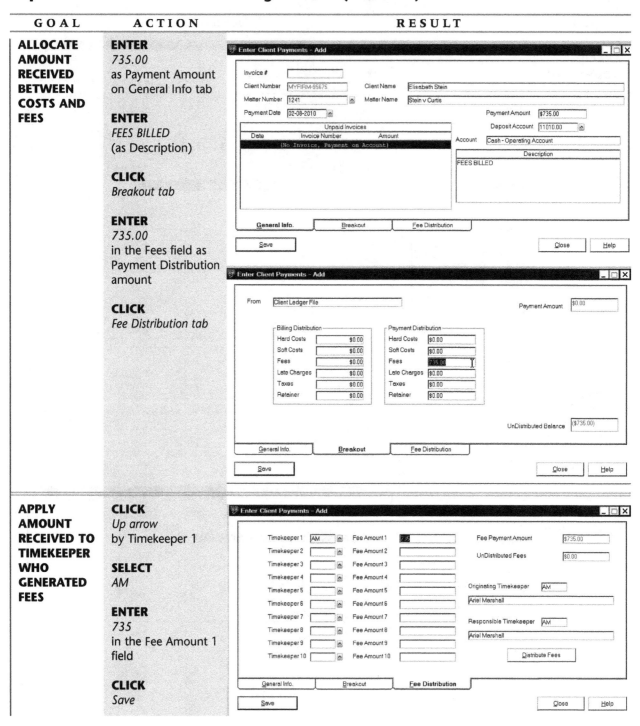

Deposit Fees into the Firm Checking Account (*continued*)

GOAL	ACTION	RESULT
PRINT A DEPOSIT TICKET TO BE USED TO MAKE DEPOSIT INTO CHECKING ACCOUNT	**CLICK** *Deposit Ticket*	*Enter Client Payments screen and Printing Deposit Slip screen*
POST (ENTER) ACTIVITY TO FIRM ACCOUNTING RECORDS AND CHECK REGISTER	**CLICK** *Yes*	*Printing Deposit Slips dialog: "Do you want to post the items on your deposit slip right now?"*
ACCURACY OF DEPOSIT WARNING ON DATES	**CLICK** *Yes*	*Abacus Accounting: Remember: The Deposit Date on your screen should be the ACTUAL DATE the payments are deposited into the bank account. Continue with posting?*

Continue to the next tutorial or exit the program.

HOW CAN I USE ABACUSLAW TO PREPARE PAYROLL?

With the possible exception of a sole practitioner with no employees, preparing and processing payroll is a weekly, biweekly, or monthly function. Tax compliance also requires quarterly and annual reports and payment of taxes withheld from employees and matched by employers to local, state, and federal government tax agencies. An annual report of earnings (W-2 form) must also be prepared and issued to employees to allow them to prepare their personal income tax returns.

Note:

Term	Number of pay periods per year
Weekly	52
Biweekly	26
Semimonthly	24
Monthly	12
Semiannually	2
Annually	1

SETTING UP AN EMPLOYEE IN THE PAYROLL

Information on the method of compensation, fringe benefits, and federal, state, and local regulations impacting the individual employee is required to set up an employee payroll record. The frequency of payment is based in part on firm preferences, but also on federal or state law that dictates the minimum frequency, generally not less than monthly.

During the hiring process, certain forms must be completed to satisfy federal regulations, including a form indicating marital status and number of dependants claimed. This information is required to determine the amount of mandatory withholdings. States, and some local jurisdictions, may also require that taxes be withheld from the employee and forwarded directly to the tax authorities by the employer.

As part of its update service, AbacusLaw provides current tax tables to help automate the process. Before processing payroll, update your copy of AbacusLaw. Update using the Help Menu Update option.

Create an Employee Profile for Payroll

GOAL	ACTION	RESULT
START ABACUS ACCOUNTING	**CLICK** *Abacus Accounting icon* OR **CLICK** **Billing** *Billing icon on AbacusLaw Practice Manager toolbar*	
ADD AN EMPLOYEE TO EMPLOYEE PROFILES LIST	**CLICK** *Payroll menu* **SELECT** *Employee Profile*	**Payroll** **Process Payroll** **Employee Payroll Activity** **Payroll Check Register** **Void Payroll Check** **Employee Profile** **Deduction Codes** **State Unemployment Taxes** **Payroll Reports**

Create an Employee Profile for Payroll (*continued*)

GOAL	ACTION	RESULT
CREATE EMPLOYEE PROFILE *Note*: Use the same employee ID for this person as a timekeeper ID and user ID.	**CLICK** *Add* on Employees Browse window	**A Employees Browse** Find Employee ID Name Add / Edit / Delete / Print OK Cancel Help **Employee Profiles – Adding a New Employee** Employee ID [ ] Department [0] Date of Birth [---] Date of Employment [---] Name [ ] Date of Termination [---] Address 1 [ ] Date of Last Increase [---] Address 2 [ ] City [ ] Pay Type: Pay Rate [$0.00] ○ Hourly Overtime Rate [$0.00] State [▼] Zip [ ] ● Salary Vac. Accrual Rate [0.00] Phone Number [ ] Sick Accrual Rate [0.00] Social Security Number [ ] Tax State [▼] Employment Status: Pay Frequency: ● Full Time ○ Weekly ○ Semi-Monthly Sex [Female ▼] ○ Part Time ● Bi-Weekly ○ Semi-Annually ○ Monthly ○ Annually Employee Information / Tax Information / Deduction Codes 1 / Deduction Codes 2 / YTD Totals Save Cancel Help
ENTER EMPLOYEE PAYROLL INFORMATION *Note*: State tax rates and information will be automatically entered based on the tax state information entered.	**ENTER** Employee information as shown here in Employee Profiles **ENTER** *1* for Department (any number from 1 to 10 can be entered)	**Employee Profiles – Adding a New Employee** Employee ID [ECH] Department [1] Date of Birth [01-12-1960] Date of Employment [08-19-1980] Name [Edith C Hannah] Date of Termination [---] Address 1 [43 Washington Street] Date of Last Increase [---] Address 2 [ ] City [Newtown] Pay Type: Pay Rate [$1,500.00] ○ Hourly Overtime Rate [$0.00] State [PA ▼] Zip [18940] ● Salary Vac. Accrual Rate [0.00] Phone Number [555 444 6666] Sick Accrual Rate [0.00] Social Security Number [123 45 6789] Tax State [PA ▼] Employment Status: Pay Frequency: ● Full Time ○ Weekly ○ Semi-Monthly Sex [Female ▼] ○ Part Time ● Bi-Weekly ○ Semi-Annually ○ Monthly ○ Annually Employee Information / Tax Information / Deduction Codes 1 / Deduction Codes 2 / YTD Totals Save Cancel Help

Create an Employee Profile for Payroll (*continued*)

GOAL	ACTION	RESULT
ENTER EMPLOYEE PAYROLL TAX INFORMATION	**CLICK** *Tax Information tab* **ENTER** Employee information as shown **CLICK** *Save* **CLICK** *Cancel* **CLICK** *Cancel*	

Employee Profiles – Adding a New Employee

Federal
Marital Status
Single / HOH

Exemptions 0
Additional Withholding
$0.00

EIC
○ Yes ● No

State
Tax Rate
Regular

Add'l Withholding
$0.00

Local Taxes
EIT Tax Rate %
1

OIT Tax Yearly $ Amt
50

PENNSYLVANIA STATE WITHHOLDING INSTRUCTIONS

FOR EIT %, enter the Earned Income Tax Percentage if applicable. For OIT %, enter the Occupational Privilege Tax Amount for the year for this employee, if applicable.

Employee Information | **Tax Information** | Deduction Codes 1 | Deduction Codes 2 | YTD Totals

Save | Cancel | Help

Exit the program.

HOW DO I PROCESS THE PAYROLL AND PRINT PAYCHECKS?

First an employee must be set up in the payroll system (database), and then payment for a specific work period calculated. The total number of hours for all employees must be entered to comply with federal and state regulations for calculating minimum wage laws that require payment for hours in excess of a maximum number for nonexempt employees.

Gross wages are reduced by required and voluntary deductions, including retirement plan contributions. A record of the gross wages and details of each deduction must also be provided with the payment of the net wages. All of the withheld amounts must also be recorded, paid to the required agencies, and accounted for by the employer.

Process Payroll and Print Paychecks

GOAL	ACTION	RESULT
START ABACUS ACCOUNTING	**CLICK** *Abacus Accounting icon* OR **CLICK** *Billing icon on AbacusLaw Practice Manager toolbar*	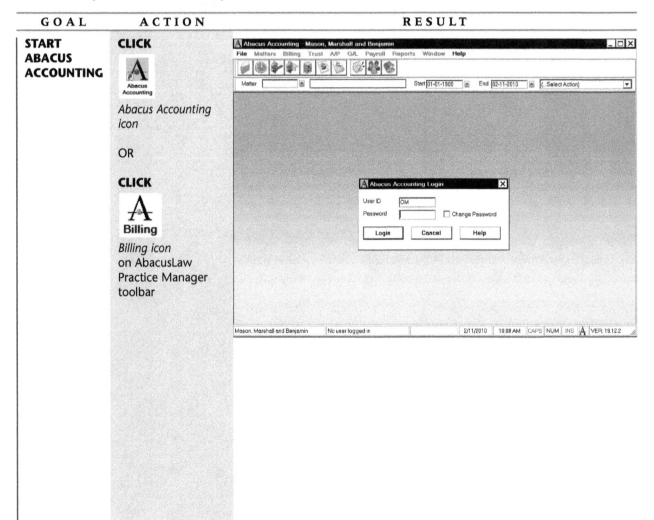

Process Payroll and Print Paychecks (*continued*)

GOAL	ACTION	RESULT
SELECT EMPLOYEE TO PROCESS PAYROLL CHECK	**CLICK** *Payroll menu* **SELECT** *Process Payroll* OR **CLICK** *Payroll icon* **CLICK** *Add*	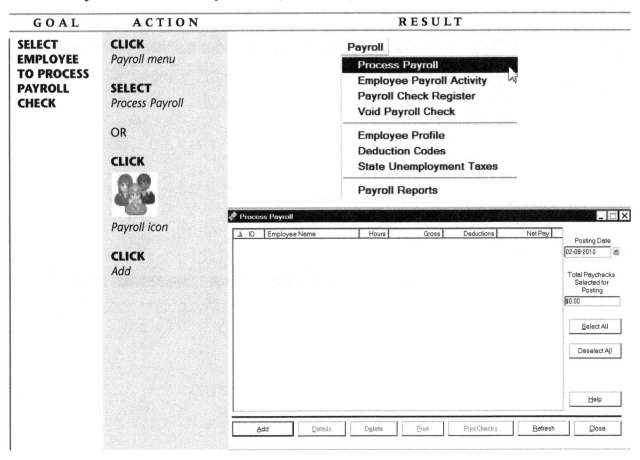

Process Payroll and Print Paychecks (*continued*)

GOAL	ACTION	RESULT
ADD EMPLOYEE TO PRINT CHECKS LIST	**CLICK** *Bi-Weekly* **ENTER** *40* as Default Work Hours **CLICK** *Select All* **CLICK** *OK* **CLICK** *Select All* **CLICK** *Print Checks*	

Process Payroll - Add

▲ ID	Name	Department	Pay Freq	Pay Type
ECH	Edith C Hannah	1	Bi Weekly	Salary

Pay Frequency
Pay Period Ending Date 02-08-2010

○ Weekly   ○ Semi-Monthly
● Bi-Weekly   ○ Semi-Annually
○ Monthly   ○ Annually

Employee Type
● All
○ Full Time
○ Part Time

Pay Type
● All   ○ Salary   ○ Hourly
☐ Show Teminated Employees
Default Work Hours   40.00

☐ Bonus Payroll Run   Ok   Select All   Deselect All   Refresh   Cancel   Help

Process Payroll

▲ ID	Employee Name	Hours	Gross	Deductions	Net Pay
ECH	Edith C Hannah	40.00	$1,500.00	$355.03	$1,144.97

Posting Date
02-08-2010

Total Paychecks Selected for Posting
$0.00

Select All

Deselect All

Help

Add   Details   Delete   Print   Print Checks   Refresh   Close

Process Payroll and Print Paychecks (*continued*)

GOAL	ACTION	RESULT
	CLICK *Print* **CLICK** *OK*	

Output Destination Selection

Select Printer: HP LaserJet 4250 PCL6 on Ne05

Paper Size: Letter

Number of Copies: 1

Orientation
- Portrait
- Landscape

Paper Bins
PLEASE NOTE: If clicking this dropdown box causes an error, it will be necessary to use another printer driver for your printer in order to use bin selection from within DLS.

Paper Bin: (Windows Default)

Print   Cancel

Process Payroll

ID | Employee Name
ECH | Edith C Hannah

Posting Date: 02-08-2010

Total Paychecks Selected for Posting: $1,144.97

Select All
Deselect All
Help

Add   Details   Delete   Print   Print Checks   Refresh   Close

Process Payroll

Please be sure of the Posting Date and make any necessary adjustments to the next check number to be assigned.

Account Number: 11030.00

Next Check Number: 1

GL Posting Date: 02-08-2010

Journal Number:

Account balance after these checks have been posted: ($1,144.97)

Total of the checks selected for printing: $1,144.97

Do Not Print   Printer: Adobe PDF

Check Horizontal Offset in Inches. Positive numbers move the check data to the right, negative numbers to the left. 0

Check Vertical Offset in Inches. Positive numbers move the check data down, negative numbers moves the data up. 0

OK   Cancel   Help

Process Payroll and Print Paychecks (*continued*)

GOAL	ACTION	RESULT
REVIEW PAYROLL CHECK AND STATEMENT OF EARNINGS *Note*: The image shows the three-part laser check with the check in the middle. You can set up the printing to accommodate top or bottom print as well.	**REVIEW** For accuracy	

Employee: ECH - Edith C Hannah
Pay Period Ending: 2/8/2010
Pay Rate: 1500.00 Bi-Weekly

	CURRENT	Y-T-D		CURRENT	Y-T-D
			Gross Regular:	1,500.00	1,500.00
			Gross Overtime:	0.00	0.00
Regular Hours:	40.00	40.00	Total Other Deduct	0.00	0.00
Overtime Hours:	0.00	0.00	Social Security:	93.00	93.00
Sick Hours:	0.00	0.00	Medicare:	21.75	21.75
Vacation Hours:	0.00	0.00	Federal Withholdin	193.03	193.03
Accum. Sick Hours:	0.00	0.00	State Withholding:	46.05	46.05
Accum. Vac. Hours:	0.00	0.00			
			Misc. Withholding:	1.20	1.20
			NET PAY:	$1,144.97	$1,144.97

Eleven Hundred Forty Four Dollars & 97/100

02-08-2010 $1,144.97

Edith C Hannah
43 Washington Street
Newtown, PA 18940

Employee: ECH - Edith C Hannah
Pay Period Ending: 2/8/2010
Pay Rate: 1500.00 Bi-Weekly

	CURRENT	Y-T-D		CURRENT	Y-T-D
			Gross Regular:	1,500.00	1,500.00
			Gross Overtime:	0.00	0.00
Regular Hours:	40.00	40.00	Total Other Deduct	0.00	0.00
Overtime Hours:	0.00	0.00	Social Security:	93.00	93.00
Sick Hours:	0.00	0.00	Medicare:	21.75	21.75
Vacation Hours:	0.00	0.00	Federal Withholdin	193.03	193.03
Accum. Sick Hours:	0.00	0.00	State Withholding:	46.05	46.05
Accum. Vac. Hours:	0.00	0.00			
			Misc. Withholding:	1.20	1.20
			NET PAY:	$1,144.97	$1,144.97

Process Payroll and Print Paychecks (*continued*)

GOAL	ACTION	RESULT
REVIEW WITHHELD AMOUNTS *Note*: This information is necessary to determine the amount that must be paid, such as payroll taxes, to federal, state, and local tax authorities. Employers must match certain items, such as social security.	**SELECT** *Edith C. Hannah* **CLICK** *Details* in the Process Payroll window **CLICK** *Close* **CLICK** *Close* in Process Payroll window	

Continue to the following tutorial or exit.

HOW DO I PREPARE A PAYROLL SUMMARY REPORT?

Amounts withheld from the employees and the employer's contributions must be regularly deposited with the local, state, and federal tax collectors or depository agencies. The timing is based in part on the total amount—the greater the total, the more frequent the required deposits or payments.

A payroll summary report may be prepared for any period showing the amount withheld and the matching share of the employer, such as the matching amount for social security and Medicare.

Prepare a Payroll Summary Report

GOAL	ACTION	RESULT
START ABACUS ACCOUNTING	**CLICK** *Abacus Accounting icon* OR **CLICK** *Billing icon in AbacusLaw*	

Prepare a Payroll Summary Report (*continued*)

GOAL	ACTION	RESULT
CREATE FIRM PAYROLL SUMMARY REPORT	**CLICK** *Reports menu* **SELECT** *Payroll* **SELECT** *Firm Payroll Summary* **ENTER** Start Date and End Date for payroll period **CLICK** *Preview*	

Reports
- 1099 and 1096
- Accounts Payable
- Accounts Receivable
- Audit Trail
- Billing
- General Ledger
- Matter
- **Payroll**
- Productivity
- Trust

Report Groups
Setup

Payroll Reports

Employee Payroll Summary
Employee Profile Printouts
Employer's 940 Tax Return
Employer's 941 Tax Return
Firm Payroll Summary
Payroll Deduction Listing
Payroll Register
Payroll Tax Report
Qtrly Unemployment Compensation Report
W-2 Wage and Tax Statement
W-3 Transmittal

Report Criteria

Date Range

Start Date 01-01-1900   End Date 02-08-2010

Date Type

◉ by Pay Period Date   ○ by G/L Posting Date

Destination
◉ Print Preview
○ Printer
○ File
○ Email
○ Report Group

Preview
Close
Help

Employee
◉ All
○ Employee Code

Firm Payroll Summary

Report Date :	2/8/2010
Report Time :	4:48PM
Page :	1 of 1
Requested By:	Owen Mason

Mason, Marshall and Benjamin

Date Range:	01/01/1900 Through 02/08/2010
Date Type:	Pay Period Date
Name:	All Employees

Gross Earnings
Pay Period Ending 2/8/2010

Regular:	$1,500.00
OverTime:	$0.00
Total:	$1,500.00
Earned Income Credit:	$0.00

Taxes
* Includes Employer Portion

Social Security:	$186.00
Medicare:	$43.50
Federal:	$193.03
State:	$46.05
Misc:	$1.20
Total Taxes:	$469.78

Deductions

Total Deductions:	$0.00
Net Pay to Employees:	$1,144.97

Exit Abacus Accounting.

HOW DO I PAY RECURRING BILLS?

Checks may be written to pay bills using either a one-step method or a two-step method. The two-step method allows payments for multiple categories of expenses to be included on one check, such as the breakdown of expenses covered by the payment of a firm credit card bill used for various expenses (copier costs, travel, supplies, and postage). The two-step method for payables requires each expense to be entered first into a payable account, and then a check written that may combine the multiple expense categories. The result is the same—a check is written and the bill paid.

The one-step demand check writer can only be used for a single account, such as telephone expense.

There are many recurring bills for a law firm—rent, telephone, copier rental, and Internet services—for which the one-step demand check writer will work.

Each of these recurring expenses is paid to a vendor. Vendors for whom recurring payments are made are set up in the Practice Manager in the same way other names and contacts are added. The difference is the class code is vendor.

T I P

Obtain all vendor federal ID numbers before issuing payments.

Add and Pay Recurring Vendor

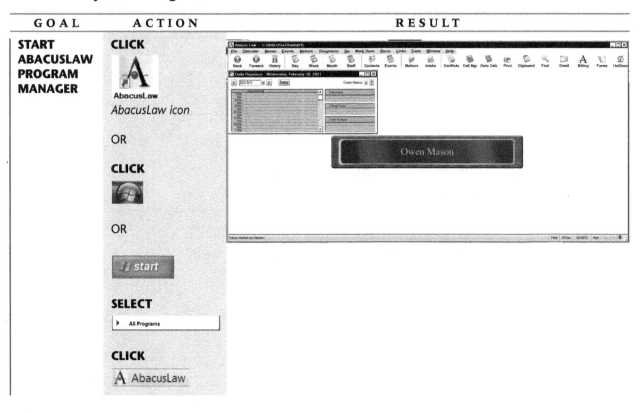

GOAL	ACTION	RESULT
START ABACUSLAW PROGRAM MANAGER	**CLICK** *AbacusLaw icon* OR **CLICK** OR **start** **SELECT** All Programs **CLICK** A AbacusLaw	

Add and Pay Recurring Vendor (*continued*)

GOAL	ACTION	RESULT
COMPLETE NAME WINDOW FOR A VENDOR	**CLICK** *Names menu* **SELECT** *Add a new Name* **ENTER** Vendor information as shown **CLICK** Class[ ] *Up arrow* **SELECT** *Vendor* **CLICK** *Save*	
ENTER VENDOR IN ABACUS ACCOUNTING	**CLICK** *Yes*	

Add and Pay Recurring Vendor (*continued*)

GOAL	ACTION	RESULT
EDIT VENDOR ACCOUNTING INFORMATION *Note*: A federal Form 1099 is required to be issued to anyone paid more than a minimum amount; this is set by federal law.	**CHECK** *Year End 1099* **ENTER** *000-111-1111* for Federal ID Number **CLICK** *Up arrow* by Default Expense Account Number **SELECT** *Telephone Expense* **CLICK** *OK* **CLICK** *OK*	
OPEN DEMAND CHECK WRITER	**CLICK** **A** **Billing** *Billing icon* to open Accounting **CLICK** *Check register icon* on Abacus Accounting toolbar **CLICK** *Demand Check Writer* in Checkbook menu	

Add and Pay Recurring Vendor (*continued*)

GOAL	ACTION	RESULT
PREPARE CHECK TO PAY VENDOR USING DEMAND CHECK WRITER	**CLICK** Payee *Up arrow* **SELECT** *Snowbank Telephone* in the Vendors Browse window **CLICK** *OK* **ENTER** *125* for Amount **ENTER** *Monthly Service* as Description **CLICK** *Print*	
CHECK WRITER PRINTING NOTICE	**CLICK** *OK*	

Add and Pay Recurring Vendor (*continued*)

GOAL	ACTION	RESULT
OPEN CHECK REGISTER AFTER TRANSACTION ADDED	**CLICK** *Check register icon on Abacus Accounting toolbar* **SELECT** *Checkbook Register*	
REVIEW PAYMENT DETAILS	**CLICK** *Details* on check register after selecting transaction OR **DOUBLE CLICK** On *transaction* **REVIEW** Payment details **CLICK** *Close* **CLICK** *Close*	

Continue with the following tutorial.

HOW DO I PRINT MY CHECKBOOK REGISTER?

The checkbook register may be printed from within the check register window as shown in the following tutorial.

Print Checkbook Register

GOAL	ACTION	RESULT
OPEN CHECK REGISTER	**CLICK** *Checkbook icon* **CLICK** *Checkbook Register in drop-down menu*	**Check Register** Account Number 11010.00 — Account Description Cash - Operating Account — Beginning Balance $0.00 Start Date 01-01-1900 — End Date 02-08-2010 — Ending Balance $610.00 Date / Check # / Clrd / Payee / Deposit ($) / Payment ($) / Balance 02-08-2010 Clnt Pymt No Payments posted from Payments Rec... 735.00 $735.00 02-08-2010 1 No Snowbank Telephone Service 125.00 $610.00 Details Print Refresh Close Help
PRINT CHECKBOOK REGISTER	**CLICK** *Print*	*Checkbook Register* **Mason, Marshall and Benjamin** Dates Included: From 01-01-1900 to 02-08-2010 Checkbook Account Number 11010.00 Checkbook Account Name: Cash - Operating Account Date / Check No. / Transaction / Payee / Description / Debit Balance Forward 02/08/2010 Clnt Pymt Payments posted from Payments Received Client Payment(s) posted on 2/8/2010 $735.00 02/08/2010 1 Snowbank Telephone Service $735.00

Exit the program.

Court Rules Calendars

(More Stuff You Can Do without Being a Computer Expert)

- What Are Calendar Rules?
- How Do I Create a Calendar Rule?
    - ▲ *Tutorial—Create a New Rule for a Two-Year Statute of Limitations*
- How Do I Link a Rule to a Matter?
    - ▲ *Tutorial—Adding a Rule to a Matter (Case)*
- How Do I Change Rules?
    - ▲ *Tutorial—Editing a Rule*

SETUP RULES

ADD RULES TO EVENTS

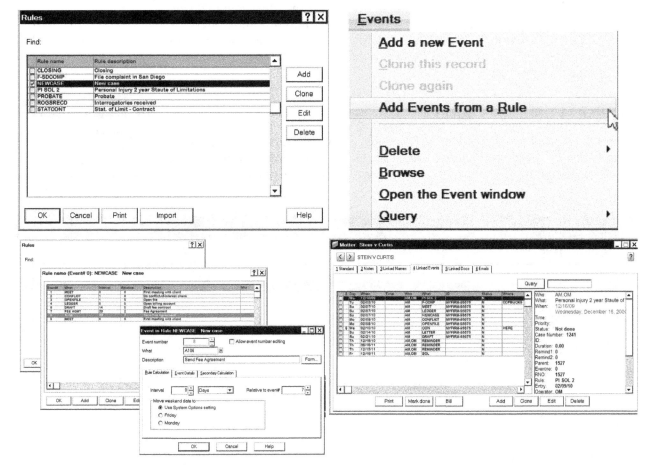

WHAT ARE CALENDAR RULES?

In every case or matter there are calendar events. These events or dates may be reminders to the legal staff to take some action or critical deadlines for filing documents with the court, such as the requirement to give notice before a hearing or file a complaint before the statute of limitations expires. The dates of these events are related (or relative) to some other event date. For example, the statute of limitation is a date in the future calculated from the date of some occurrence such as the date of the accident or breach of the contract. In an accident with a two-year statute of limitation, the relative statute of limitations date is two calendar years after the accident.

AbacusLaw calendar rules or rules, for short, provide an automated process of entering these event dates in the Practice Manager and set up reminders.

The following example shows the rules for reminders for a new case and rules for reminders for a breach of contract matter, with a one-year statute of limitations.

NEW CASE REMINDER RULES

In the new case reminder rules, each activity, or WHAT, is calculated *forward* from event #1 meet, such as the conflict check to be done within one day of event #1 or the drafting of the fee contract within 14 days of event #1.

T I P

Rules may be created for reminders both before and after any event on the list.

Rule name (Event# 0): NEWCASE   New case   ? X

Event#	What	Interval	Relative	Description	Who
1	MEET	0	0	First meeting with client	
2	CONFLICT	1	0	Do conflict-of-interest check	
3	OPENFILE	1	0	Open file	
4	LEDGER	0	0	Open billing account	
5	LETTER	7	0	Confirmation letter	
6	DRAFT	14	0	Draft fee contract	

| OK | Add | Clone | Edit | Delete | Options | Print | Help |

NEW CASE REMINDER RULES

ONE-YEAR STATUTE OF LIMITATION FOR CONTRACT BREACH

In the one-year statute of limitations rule, every reminder is calculated *back-wards* from the statute date event #1, such as one day, seven days, one month, three months, and six months before the statute of limitation date.

Relative refers to the event # to which the item is related.

Rule name (Event# 0): STATCONT Stat. of Limit – Contract	?	X

Event#	What	Interval	Relative	Description	Who
1	STATUTE	1Y	0	1 year statute of limitations	
2	REMINDER	-6M	1	6 months to statute deadline	
3	REMINDER	-3M	1	3 months to statute deadline	
4	REMINDER	-1M	1	1 month to statute deadline	
5	REMINDER	-7	1	7 days to statute deadline	
6	REMINDER	-1	1	1 day to statute deadline	

OK	Add	Clone	Edit	Delete	Options	Print	Help

ONE-YEAR STATUTE OF LIMITATION FOR CONTRACT BREACH

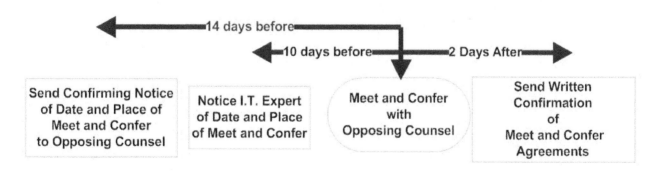

HOW DO I CREATE A CALENDAR RULE?

In most states the statute of limitations for a personal injury is one or two years from the date of the accident; however, it may vary according to jurisdiction and type of injury. For this tutorial we will create a two-year statute of limitation personal injury rule and add it to a matter.

Create a New Rule for a Two-Year Statute of Limitations

GOAL	ACTION	RESULT
START UP ABACUSLAW PRACTICE MANAGER	**CLICK** **AbacusLaw** *AbacusLaw icon*	
CREATE AND ADD A NEW RULE TO THE RULES LIST	**CLICK** *File menu* **SELECT** *Setup* **SELECT** *Rules...*	

Create a New Rule for a Two-Year Statute of Limitations (*continued*)

GOAL	ACTION	RESULT
ADD A NEW RULE **ACKNOW-LEDGE THAT ANY NEW WHAT CODE WILL BE ADDED TO LIST OF VALID WHAT CODES**	**CLICK** *Add* **CLICK** *OK*	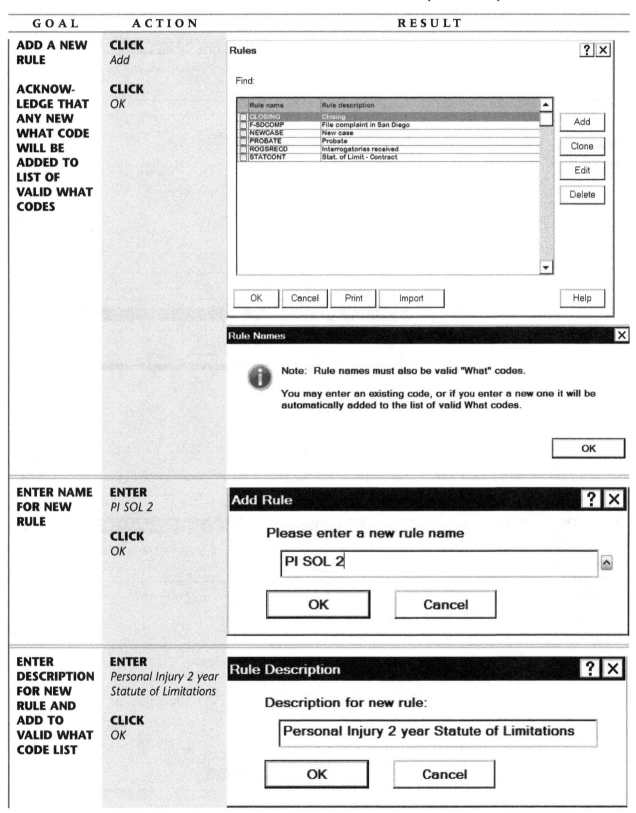
ENTER NAME FOR NEW RULE	**ENTER** *PI SOL 2* **CLICK** *OK*	
ENTER DESCRIPTION FOR NEW RULE AND ADD TO VALID WHAT CODE LIST	**ENTER** *Personal Injury 2 year Statute of Limitations* **CLICK** *OK*	

The RESULT column contains the following dialog boxes:

Rules — Find: — Rule name / Rule description list:
- CLOSING — Closing
- F-SDCOMP — File complaint in San Diego
- NEWCASE — New case
- PROBATE — Probate
- ROGSRECD — Interrogatories received
- STATCONT — Stat. of Limit - Contract

Buttons: Add, Clone, Edit, Delete, OK, Cancel, Print, Import, Help

Rule Names

Note: Rule names must also be valid "What" codes.

You may enter an existing code, or if you enter a new one it will be automatically added to the list of valid What codes.

OK

Add Rule

Please enter a new rule name

PI SOL 2

OK   Cancel

Rule Description

Description for new rule:

Personal Injury 2 year Statute of Limitations

OK   Cancel

Create a New Rule for a Two-Year Statute of Limitations (*continued*)

GOAL	ACTION	RESULT
ENTER THE NEW WHAT CODE FROM LIST OF CURRENT VALID WHAT CODES FOR STATUTE OF LIMITATION	**CLICK** *Up arrow* **SELECT** *SOL* from Valid WHAT Entries window **CLICK** *OK*	Event in Rule PI SOL 2 Personal Injury 2 year Statute of Limitations Event number 1 ☐ Allow event number editing What _____ Description _____ Form... *Rule Calculation	Event Details	Secondary Calculation* Interval 0 Days Relative to event# 0 Move weekend date to ◉ Use System Options setting ○ Friday ○ Monday [OK] [Cancel] [Help] **Valid WHAT Entries** ? ✕ Find: WHAT — Description — Link SOL — Statute of limitations SOP — Service of Process SPD — Soft Costs Paid STATCONT — Stat. of Limit - Contract TASK — Miscellaneous task TAX — Sales Taxes Billed TAXES — Determine if taxes are due TE — Travel Expenses TEL — Telephone TITLE — Check title TPD — Sales Taxes Paid TRIAL — Trial TRIAL-SD — Trial in San Diego Superior TRS — Trust Retainer [Add] [Edit] [Delete] [Print] [Color] [Link] [OK] [Cancel] [Help]
ENTER THE DESCRIPTION FOR THE NEW EVENT AND TIME PERIOD TO BE USED IN CALCULATING LINKED EVENT	**ENTER** *2 Year Statute of Limitations* **SELECT** 0 *2* AND **SELECT** *Years*	Event in Rule PI SOL 2 Personal Injury 2 year Statute of Limitations _ □ ✕ Event number 1 ☐ Allow event number editing What SOL Description 2 Year Statute of Limitations Form... *Rule Calculation	Event Details	Secondary Calculation* ◉ No calculation ○ Use earlier date ○ Use later date Interval 2 Days Relative to event# 0 Days Court days Weeks Months Quarters Years [OK] [Cancel] [Help]

Create a New Rule for a Two-Year Statute of Limitations (*continued*)

GOAL	ACTION	RESULT
ENTER WHO WILL HAVE EVENTS ADDED TO CALENDAR	**CLICK** *Event Details tab* **CLICK** Who — *Up arrow* **CHECK** *AM* and *OM* to add as responsible WHO **CLICK** *OK*	
	CLICK Type — *Up arrow* **SELECT** *Reminder* **CLICK** *OK*	

Create a New Rule for a Two-Year Statute of Limitations (*continued*)

GOAL	ACTION	RESULT
	CLICK Priority [ ] *Up arrow* **SELECT** *1* **CLICK** *OK* **CLICK** *OK*	

Create a New Rule for a Two-Year Statute of Limitations (*continued*)

GOAL	ACTION	RESULT
ADD EVENT 2—REMINDER OF ONE YEAR TO STATUTE OF LIMITATIONS	**CLICK** *Add* on Rule Name window **CLICK** [What] *Up arrow* **SELECT** *Reminder* **ENTER** *1 Year TO Statute of Limitations* in the Description field **SELECT** [0] Use arrows to set interval to *−1* **Select** *Years* **SELECT** [0] Use arrows to set Relative to event# *1*	

The result panel shows:

Event in Rule PI SOL 2 Personal Injury 2 year Statute of Limitations

- Event number: 2   ☐ Allow event number editing
- What: REMINDER
- Description: 1 Year TO Statutue of Limitations   [Form...]

Tabs: Rule Calculation | Event Details | Secondary Calculation

- Interval: -1 Years   Relative to event#: 1
- Move weekend date to
  - ◉ Use System Options setting
  - ○ Friday
  - ○ Monday

[OK] [Cancel] [Help]

Create a New Rule for a Two-Year Statute of Limitations (*continued*)

GOAL	ACTION	RESULT
ENTER WHO AND ENTER FOR NEW EVENT 2	**CLICK** *Event Details tab* **CLICK** Who ⬆ *Up arrow* **CHECK** *AM, OM* **CLICK** Type ⬆ *Up arrow* **SELECT** *R* **CLICK** Priority ⬆ *Up arrow* **SELECT** *1* **CLICK** *OK*	Event in Rule PI SOL 2 Personal Injury 2 year Statute of Limitations _ □ ✕ Event number ___2___ ☐ Allow event number editing What REMINDER ⬆ Description 1 Year TO Statutue of Limitations Form... Rule Calculation | Event Details | Secondary Calculation Who AM,OM ⬆ Priority 1 ⬆ Type R ⬆ Time ___ Hours 0.00 OK Cancel Help

Create a New Rule for a Two-Year Statute of Limitations (*continued*)

GOAL	ACTION	RESULT
ADD EVENT 3 REMINDER OF SIX MONTHS TO STATUTE OF LIMITATIONS	**CLICK** *Add* in Rule Name window **CLICK** What [____] Up arrow **SELECT** *Reminder* **ENTER** *6 Months TO Statute of Limitations* in the Description field **SELECT** [0] Use arrows to set interval to −6 **Select** *Months* **SELECT** [0] Use arrows to set Relative to event# to *1*	Event in Rule PI SOL 2 Personal Injury 2 year Statute of Limitations [_][□][X] Event number [3] Allow event number editing What [REMINDER] Description [6 Months TO Statute of Limitations] [Form...] _Rule Calculation_	Event Details	Secondary Calculation Interval [-6] [Months ▼] Relative to event# [1] Move weekend date to ⦿ Use System Options setting ○ Friday ○ Monday [OK] [Cancel] [Help]

Create a New Rule for a Two-Year Statute of Limitations (*continued*)

GOAL	ACTION	RESULT
	CLICK *Event Details tab* **CLICK** Who [____] *Up arrow* **CHECK** AM, OM **CLICK** Type [____] *Up arrow* **SELECT** R **CLICK** Priority [____] *Up arrow* **SELECT** 1 **CLICK** OK **CLICK** OK	**Event in Rule PI SOL 2 Personal Injury 2 year Statute of Limitations** _ □ ✕ Event number [3] ☐ Allow event number editing What REMINDER Description 6 Months TO Statute of Limitations Form... _Rule Calculation_	_Event Details_	_Secondary Calculation_ Who [AM,OM] Priority [1] Type [R] Time [____] Hours [0.00] [OK] [Cancel] [Help]
ADD EVENT 4 REMINDER OF ONE DAY TO STATUTE OF LIMITATIONS	**ENTER** *EVENT 4 Rule Calculation* Using previous examples, set Interval to –1 days.	**Event in Rule PI SOL 2 Personal Injury 2 year Statute of Limitations** _ □ ✕ Event number [4] ☐ Allow event number editing What REMINDER Description 1 DAY TO STATUTE OF LIMTATOINS Form... _Rule Calculation_	_Event Details_	_Secondary Calculation_ Interval [-1] [Days ▾] Relative to event# [1] ┌ Move weekend date to ───── ● Use System Options setting ○ Friday ○ Monday [OK] [Cancel] [Help]

Create a New Rule for a Two-Year Statute of Limitations (*continued*)

GOAL	ACTION	RESULT
	ENTER Event 4 details using previous examples	**Event in Rule PI SOL 2 Personal Injury 2 year Statute of Limitations** _ □ ✕ Event number 4 ☐ Allow event number editing What REMINDER Description 1 DAY TO STATUTE OF LIMTATOINS Form... Rule Calculation	Event Details	Secondary Calculation Who AM,OM Priority 1 Type R Time Hours 0.00 OK Cancel Help
REVIEW NEW RULE	**REVIEW** For accuracy **CLICK** *OK*	**Rule name (Event# 0): PI SOL 2 Personal Injury 2 year Statute of Limitations** ? ✕ | Event#	What	Interval	Relative	Description	Who
---	---	---	---	---	---
0	SOL	2Y	0	2 Year Statute of Limitations	
2	REMINDER	-1Y	1	1 Year TO Statute of Limitations	
3	REMINDER	-6M	1	6 Months to Statute of Limitations	
4	REMINDER	-1D	1	1 DAY TO STATUTE OF LIMTATOINS	AM,O	 OK Add Clone Edit Delete Options Print Help
ENTER NEW RULE IN RULES LIST	**CLICK** *OK*	**Rules** ? ✕ Find: 	Rule name	Rule description
---	---
☐ CLOSING	Closing
☐ F-SDCOMP	File complaint in San Diego
☐ NEWCASE	New case
☐ PI SOL 2	Personal Injury 2 year Statute of Limitations
☐ PROBATE	Probate
☐ ROGSRECD	Interrogatories received
☐ STATCONT	Stat. of Limit - Contract	 Add Clone Edit Delete OK Cancel Print Import Help

HOW DO I LINK A RULE TO A MATTER?

Rules contain events that are added to the list of linked events in a matter. The events are also added to the calendars of the people and places listed as the WHO when an event is added to a rule or the rules are edited. The graphic shows the addition of a two-year statute of limitation rule that contains a number of reminders before the statute of limitation expires for a personal injury claim in the specific jurisdiction. Each of the events is also linked to appear on the calendars of the responsible party's calendars.

Adding a Rule to a Matter (Case)

GOAL	ACTION	RESULT
START UP ABACUSLAW PRACTICE MANAGER	**CLICK** AbacusLaw *AbacusLaw icon*	

Adding a Rule to a Matter (Case) (*continued*)

GOAL	ACTION	RESULT
ADD A RULE TO A CURRENT MATTER (CASE)	**CLICK** *Events menu* **SELECT** *Add Events from a Rule* **SELECT** *PI SOL 2* from the Rules window **CLICK** *OK*	Events Add a new Event Clone this record Clone again Add Events from a Rule Delete ▶ Browse Open the Event window Query ▶ Adding a new Event Add Clone Delete Wednesday, December 16, 2009. 55 days past Who OM Owen Mason What PI SOL 2 Personal Injury 2 year Statute of Limitations When 12/16/09 at for 0.00 hours Where << Less Creating Events from Rule: PI SOL 2 You are scheduling an event that is associated with a Rule. Do you want the related events scheduled? Yes No Priority Type Status N ders - 0 0 None WHEN OM
SELECT MATTER TO WHICH RULE EVENTS ARE TO BE ADDED	**CLICK** *<< More* to open bottom of Event window **CLICK** Matter Up arrow **SELECT** *Stein v Curtis matter* from Matters Browse window **CLICK** When Up arrow **ENTER** *12/16/09* **CLICK** *Save*	Adding a new Event Add Clone Delete Save Cancel . No Date. Who OM Owen Mason What PI SOL 2 Personal Injury 2 year Statute of Limitations When 12/16/09 at for 0.00 hours Where << Less Name Priority Type Matter Stein v Curtis Status N 1241 Reminders - 0 0 Private Alarm None Bill Form Query Index WHEN OM Matters Browse Find: Query Matter / Case # / Casecode / BILL_REC / CRT BATES V HOWARD 1240 PI .T. First Matter 1234 PI .F. OFI Jonathan Leonard v Stephen Blanco 1235 PI .T. Stein v Curtis 1241 PI .T. **Stein v Curtis** AM 1241 Case Type: PI Court: Court Case Number: Opened: 03/04/10 Closed: / / OK Cancel Add Actions Index

Adding a Rule to a Matter (Case) (*continued*)

GOAL	ACTION	RESULT
WARNING BEFORE CREATING EVENTS	**CLICK** *Yes*	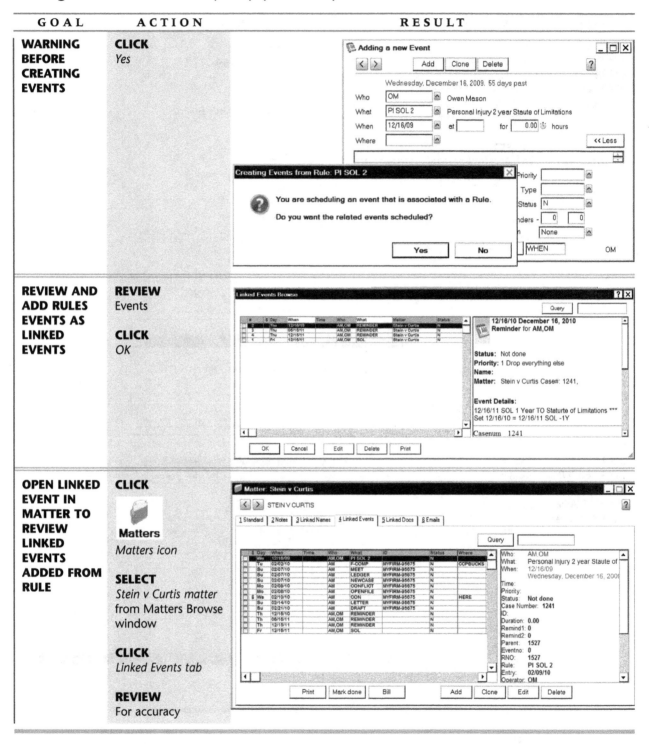
REVIEW AND ADD RULES EVENTS AS LINKED EVENTS	**REVIEW** Events **CLICK** OK	
OPEN LINKED EVENT IN MATTER TO REVIEW LINKED EVENTS ADDED FROM RULE	**CLICK** Matters icon *Matters icon* **SELECT** *Stein v Curtis matter from Matters Browse window* **CLICK** *Linked Events tab* **REVIEW** For accuracy	

HOW DO I CHANGE RULES?

Existing rules may be edited to change the basic relationships of events, the responsible persons on whose calendar the reminders should appear, or other elements. A rule may be changed by using the Edit function. Until you are comfortable with making changes, or if you just want to use a current rule as a model, it is suggested you use the Clone function. This will allow you to make the desired changes and preserve the original rule. In the clone process you will be prompted to enter a new name for the new rule.

In this tutorial, the new case rule will be used as a template. Instead of editing the original, it will be cloned, and then edited and saved with a new description, New Matter.

The changes reflect a desire to send a fee agreement as soon as the conflict check is completed and the time for doing it shortened. With the new fee agreement communication by letter, there is no longer a need for the seven-day confirmation letter to the client.

Editing a Rule

GOAL	ACTION	RESULT
START UP ABACUSLAW PRACTICE MANAGER	**CLICK** *AbacusLaw icon*	
OPEN RULES	**CLICK** *File menu* **SELECT** *Setup* **SELECT** *Rules...*	
CLONE AND EDIT EXISTING RULE	**CHECK** *NEWCASE* in Rules window **CLICK** *Clone* **CLICK** *Yes*	

Editing a Rule (*continued*)

GOAL	ACTION	RESULT
ENTER A NEW NAME AND DESCRIPTION FOR NEW RULE	**ENTER** *New Matr* as new rule name **CLICK** *OK* **ENTER** *New matter* as description **CLICK** *OK*	
ADD A NEW EVENT	**CLICK** *Add*	
SET UP A NEW EVENT 7. ENTER A WHAT CODE AND SET THE INTERVAL OF TIME AND THE DEPENDENT (RELATIVE) EVENT NUMBER	**CLICK** What *Up arrow* **SELECT** *FEE AGMT* **SELECT** *2 Days* for Interval **CLICK** 0 Arrow to set Relative to event# **Select** *2* **CLICK** *OK*	

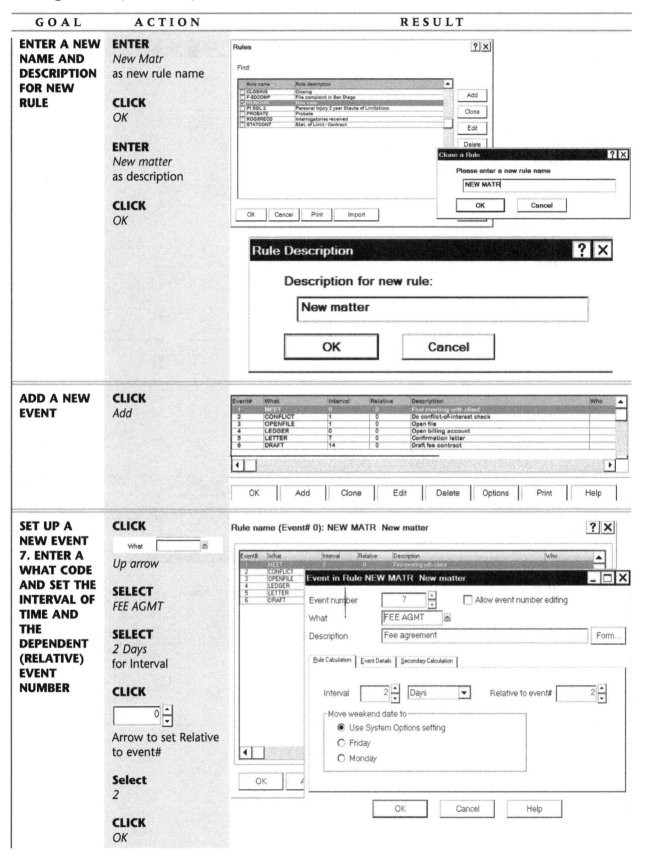

Editing a Rule (*continued*)

GOAL	ACTION	RESULT
SET UP A NEW EVENT EDIT DESCRIPTION AND SET INTERVAL AND RELATED EVENT	**CLICK** *Add* **CLICK** What ▢ *Up arrow* **SELECT** *A106* **ENTER** *Communicate (with client) send fee agreement* as Description **ENTER** *0 Days* as Interval **ENTER** *7* as Relative to event# **CLICK** *OK*	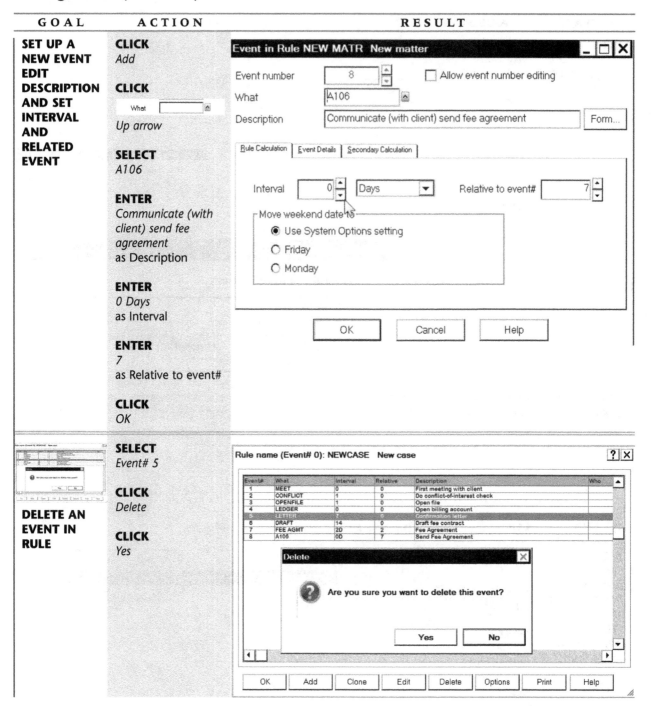
DELETE AN EVENT IN RULE	**SELECT** *Event# 5* **CLICK** *Delete* **CLICK** *Yes*	

Editing a Rule (*continued*)

GOAL	ACTION	RESULT
REVIEW NEW RULE	**REVIEW** For accuracy **CLICK** *OK* **CLICK** *OK*	

Exit AbacusLaw.

SECTION

10

Forms, Templates, and More Stuff

- What Are AbacusLawForms?
  - ▲ *Tutorial—Filling a Form from the AbacusLaw Forms Library*
- How Can I Create and Edit Document Templates?
  - ▲ *Tutorial—Generating and Saving Document Templates in Practice Manager*
- How Can I Retrieve a Document from Linked Docs in a Matter?
  - ▲ *Tutorial—Retrieving a Document from Linked Docs in a Matter*
- How Can I Create a Document from a Linked Event?
  - ▲ *Tutorial—Opening a Form from a Linked Event*
- How Can I Change the Document Template Blanks?
  - ▲ *Tutorial—Change the Merge Fields (Blanks) in a Document Template*
- How Can I Create My Own Document Template?
  - ▲ *Tutorial—Create a Document Template for Use as an AbacusLawForms Form*

Home   Insert   Page Layout   References   Mailings   Review   View   Add-Ins   Acrobat

Envelopes   Labels   Start Mail Merge ▾   Select Recipients ▾   Edit Recipient List   Highlight Merge Fields   Address Block   Greeting Line   Insert Merge Field ▾   Rules ▾   Match Fields   Update Labels   Preview Results   Find Recipient   Auto Check for Errors   Finish & Merge ▾   Merge to Adobe PDF

Create   Start Mail Merge   Write & Insert Fields   Preview Results   Finish   Acrobat

«MyFirm_Label1»

«MyFirm_Label2»
«MyFirm_Label3»
«MyFirm_Label4»
«MyFirm_City», «MyFirm_State» «MyFirm_Zip»
Fax «MyFirm_FaxPhone» Tel «MyFirm_WorkPhone»

April 15, 1998

«Contact_Address»

RE: «File_Matter»

Dear «Contact_Dear»:

This letter is to confirm our settlement offer in the above referenced matter made during our meeting of «Event_When».

Sincerely,

«Firm»

«File_Attorney»

WHAT ARE ABACUSLAWFORMS?

AbacusLawForms are documents created by Abacus for use in AbacusLaw that have blank spaces (fields) into which information from Matters, Names, and Events in AbacusLaw may be inserted.

Document templates are letters, memos, court forms, and other documents you create using your word processor, such as Corel® WordPerfect® or Microsoft Word, that have blank spaces (fields) that may be automatically filled out using information from information in AbacusLaw. A sample set of document templates created with a word processor and a sample set of AbacusLawForms court forms have been supplied with your program. Additional AbacusLawForms court forms for different jurisdictions may be purchased to add to the list.

In the following tutorials you will fill out a sample AbacusLawForms, Welcome to AbacusLaw Form, and a sample document template letter with information from one of the matters you created in an earlier tutorial. You will make changes to the form and document template, adding items using your word processor to make other changes, and saving a new document template.

A sample AbacusLawForms is shown below. The pages show the source of the information used to complete the forms, and the completed form using sample information from the tutorial examples.

NOTE

Forms are filled out from information in a matter. Information can only be entered if there is related information stored with the selected matter. For example, the court information was not set up in the Stein matter and the result is the blanks in the completed filled-in form.

FORM SHOWING SOURCES OF INFORMATION AND RELATED CODES

AbacusForms

WELCOME TO ABACUS FORMS

This form shows you how your current user settings affect the output of Abacus data to commonly used fields in forms. If you do not see data in any of the following fields, follow the instructions in each section to include that data and configure your system to work with forms. Note that if the Matter field name is not long enough, you can add a note with the full caption and a Note Type of CAPTION and that will be used instead.

Current Abacus User: Owen Mason

Selected Matter (Case Caption):

Assigned Attorney

Name: All People

Bar#:

Email:

Assigned Attorney information is pulled from the WHO code for the Attorney assigned to a matter. If the above fields are blank or incorrect, confirm that the correct attorney is assigned to the matter you are using to generate this form by going to Matters/Find, find the matter, then change the Attorney field there. If your Bar# or Email are incorrect or missing go to File/Setup/User Preferences and input the correct values there.

My Firm Information:

Firm Name: Mason, Marshall, and Benjamin

(Your firm name is pulled from your AbacusLaw firm registration.)

Address 1:

Address 2:

City Newtown   State Pennsylvania   Zip 00000

Office Phone (555)111-2222

Office Fax ( ) -

Your firm's address and phone/fax information is pulled from the Name record that you have designated as the MyFirm record. To assign a MyFirm name record, click on File/Setup/MyFirm... and choose your firm's Name record or click Add to fill a new Name record with your firm's information; the address lines will fill from label 3 and label 4. The Firm Name comes from the Registered Name as input in File/Register.

- 1 -

AbacusForms

Your firm's Address 1 information should appear in the second address field under the Label field on the default Abacus name record. Adjust your existing MyFirm name record if it is not displaying correctly in this form.

Default Court:

Court Name:

Branch:

Street Address:

Mailing Address:

City: State: Zip:

The Default Court information is pulled from the default court you selected in your Forms Library settings or from the court you have selected for the matter you used to generate a form. To access your Default Court settings, open Forms Library (F8), click the gear icon in the Forms Library toolbar, and select a court from the courts database using the Default Court listbox.

If your default court does not appear in the Courts database, click the Court Maintenance button, then click Add and complete the Court information form.

- 2 -

FORM SHOWING FILLED-IN INFORMATION

Filling a Form from the AbacusLaw Forms Library

GOAL	ACTION	RESULT
START UP ABACUSLAW PRACTICE MANAGER	**CLICK** AbacusLaw *AbacusLaw icon*	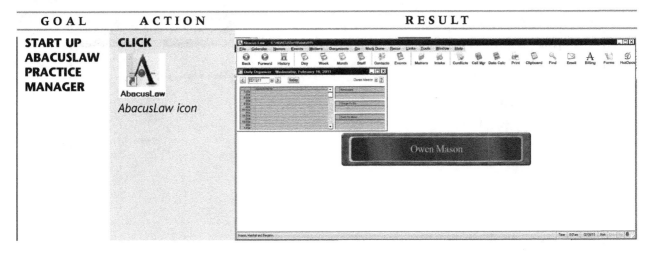

Filling a Form from the AbacusLaw Forms Library (*continued*)

GOAL	ACTION	RESULT
OPEN FORMS LIBRARY *Note*: The Forms Library may also be opened from file menu/ setup/forms library.	**CLICK** **Forms** *Forms icon* on AbacusLaw Practice Manager toolbar	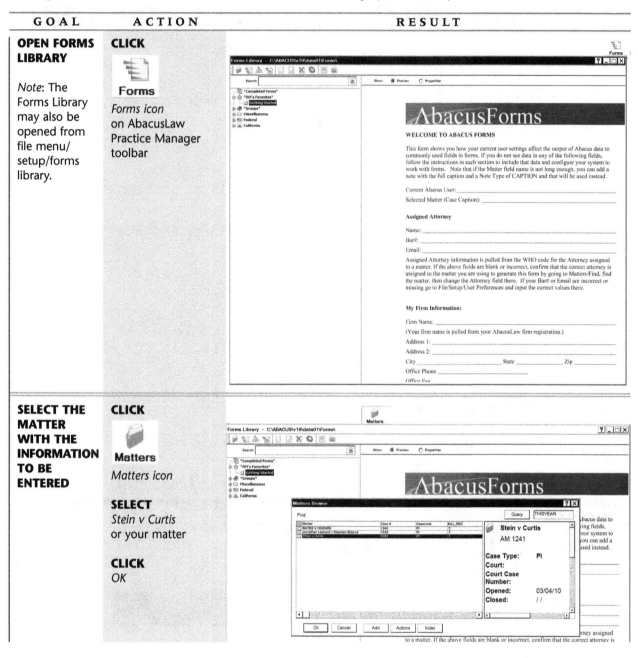
SELECT THE MATTER WITH THE INFORMATION TO BE ENTERED	**CLICK** **Matters** *Matters icon* **SELECT** *Stein v Curtis* or your matter **CLICK** *OK*	

Filling a Form from the AbacusLaw Forms Library (*continued*)

GOAL	ACTION	RESULT
SELECT FORM TO BE FILLED *Note*: If a matter has been selected you may automatically fill the form by double clicking on the form. For purposes of the tutorial *do not double click this time*.	**CLICK** *Getting Started*	
FILL FORM WITH INFORMATION FROM THE SELECTED MATTER *Note*: The Fill Forms icon in the Forms Library is *not* the same as the Forms icon in the Practice Manager toolbar.	**CLICK** **Forms** *Fill Form icon* in Form Library **CLICK** *OK* on AbacusLaw Forms Info screen	

Filling a Form from the AbacusLaw Forms Library (*continued*)

GOAL	ACTION	RESULT
FILL FORM INSTRUCTIONS	**CLICK** *OK*	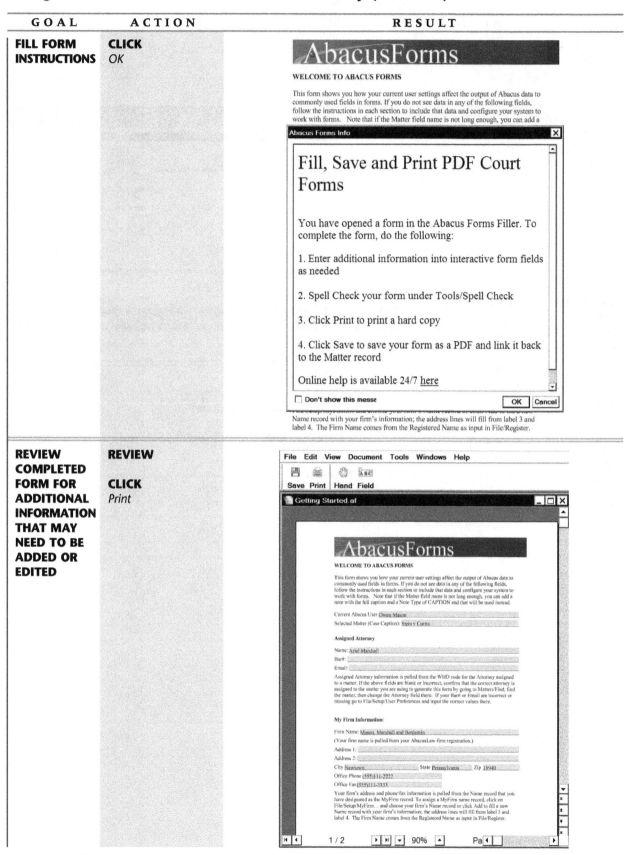
REVIEW COMPLETED FORM FOR ADDITIONAL INFORMATION THAT MAY NEED TO BE ADDED OR EDITED	**REVIEW** **CLICK** *Print*	

Filling a Form from the AbacusLaw Forms Library (*continued*)

GOAL	ACTION	RESULT

SAVE FORM IN ABACUSLAW DOCS FOLDER
 	
Note: Use Windows Explorer to find the folder with the matter number (File/Case #) in the Docs folder in AbacusLaw on your computer. See the previous section for details on using Path locations.
	CLICK
	🖫
	Save
	Save icon
	
	SELECT
	Path to ABACUS/Docs/1241
	
	CLICK
	Save
		Abacus Forms: Save new document — ☒
		
		◀ ▶ · ⬇ · ▾ Computer ▾ HP (C:) ▾ ABACUS ▾ Docs ▾ 1241 ▾ 🔍 Search 1241
		
		Organize ▾ New folder
		
		⊟ 📗 ABACUS
		  📗 Bills
		⊟ 📗 Docs
		  📗 1241
		⊞ 📗 Email
		⊟ 📗 Pictures
		  ⊞ 📗 Backgrnd
		  ⊞ 📗 Data01
		  📗 forms
		  ⊞ 📗 Matters
		  ⊞ 📗 Names
		  📗 Report
		  ⊞ 📗 Sample
		  📗 SETUP
		⊞ 📗 v19
		
		Name ▴
		
		No items match your search.
		
		File name: 1241_GETTINGSTARTED_02-09-10.pdf
		Save as type: Saved Documents
		
		Hide Folders Save Cancel

CONFIRM DETAILS OF REVISED DOCUMENT TEMPLATE AND PATH TO WHERE FILE IS STORED	**REVIEW** Information **CLICK** *OK*	**Document Details** ? ☒ Full path C:\ABACUS\Docs\1241\1241_GETTINGSTARTED_02- Short name 1241_GETTINGSTA Linked Name Curtis, Sigmund ID: MYFIRM-95676 Matter Stein v Curtis Case #: 1241 Type [ ] Date 02/09/10 Where [ ] Author [ ] Box # [ ] Status [ ] From Form... C:\ABACUS\v19\data01\Forms\Library\Getting Started.c Notes [ ] OK Cancel Next Prev. Open Help

Filling a Form from the AbacusLaw Forms Library (*continued*)

GOAL	ACTION	RESULT
USE THE LINKED DOCUMENTS TAB IN THE MATTER TO VIEW THE DOCUMENT, OPEN DOCUMENT, AND REVIEW FOR ACCURACY	**OPEN** *Stein v Curtis matter* **CLICK** *Linked Docs tab* **SELECT** *Linked document* **CLICK** *Open*	

Exit AbacusLaw.

HOW CAN I CREATE AND EDIT DOCUMENT TEMPLATES?

The blank areas that may be filled in with information from AbacusLaw Matters, Name, and Events are represented in document templates by the << >> symbols. These symbols tell the program to look for the information in AbacusLaw and substitute it for the valid information that appears. For example, <<MyFirm_Label1>> tells AbacusLaw to look for the *MyFirm information label 1* in the Record for MY Firm (remember the firm information that was checked in the beginning of the tutorial in Section 2).

In this tutorial, you will use a form document template to create a letter, open a folder for the related matter, save the document, and link the document to the matter.

Documents for matters may be saved in the Docs folder in AbacusLaw on your computer. They may also be saved in other folders, but for ease of use, we will demonstrate the method using the Docs folder.

> **N O T E**
>
> The *Docs folder* is different from the *Forms folder* used to store the document template files.

«MyFirm_Label1»
«MyFirm_Label2»
«MyFirm_City», «MyFirm_State», «MyFirm_Zip»
«MyFirm_WorkPhone»

February 9, 2010
«Client_Address»
RE: Employment of «Firm»

Dear CLIENT:

Thank you for selecting «Firm» to represent you with respect to «File_Matter».
This letter will confirm our recent discussion regarding the scope and terms of this engagement.
«Firm» has agreed to represent you in the case of «File_Matter».
I will personally supervise this case.
Sincerely,
«Firm»

«File_Attorney»

Mason, Marshall and Benjamin
2 South State Street
Newtown, Pennsylvania, 18940
(555)111-2222

February 9, 2010
Jonathon Leonard
152 Timber Ridge Road
Newtown, PA 18940
RE: Employment of Mason, Marshall and Benjamin

Dear CLIENT:

Thank you for selecting Mason, Marshall and Benjamin to represent you with respect to Jonathon Leonard v Stephen Blanca.
This letter will confirm our recent discussion regarding the scope and terms of this engagement.
Mason, Marshall and Benjamin has agreed to represent you in the case of Jonathan Leonard v Stephen Blanca.
I will personally supervise this case.
Sincerely,
Mason, Marshall and Benjamin

Owen Mason

Generating and Saving Document Templates in Practice Manager

GOAL	ACTION	RESULT
START ABACUSLAW PRACTICE MANAGER	**CLICK** *AbacusLaw icon*	
OPEN A LINKED NAME IN A MATTER	**CLICK** **Matters** *Matters icon* **SELECT** *Jonathon Leonard v Stephen Blanca* or your personal matter **CLICK** *Linked Names tab* **SELECT** *Leonard, Jonathon* OR Your personal name selection	
START FORM GENERATION PROCESS *Note*: If you set up a different word processor, such as WordPerfect®, that will appear instead of Microsoft Word.	**CLICK** *Print icon* on AbacusLaw toolbar **SELECT** *Form generation* **CLICK** *MS Word*	

Generating and Saving Document Templates in Practice Manager (*continued*)

GOAL	ACTION	RESULT
SELECT AND OPEN FORM LETTER FROM ABACUSLAW-FORMS AND MERGE INFORMATION INTO SELECTED DOCUMENT TEMPLATE FROM ABACUSLAW	**DOUBLE CLICK** *Forms* **DOUBLE CLICK** *setlet.dot*	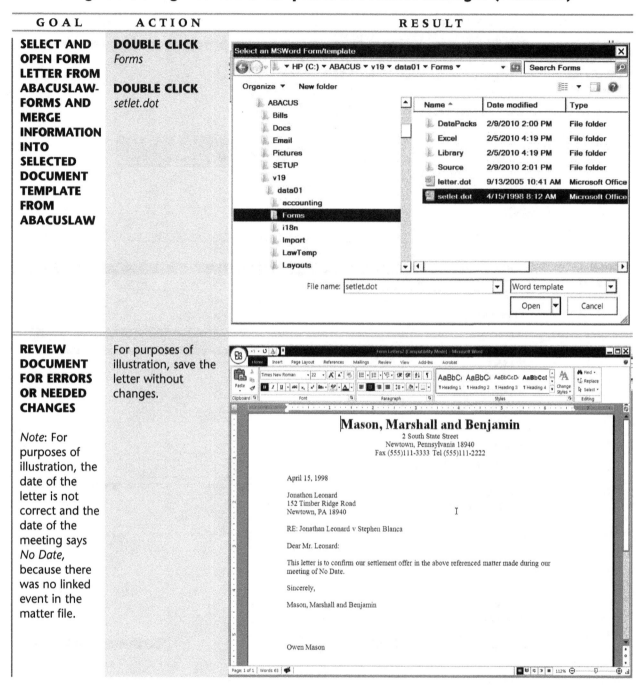
REVIEW DOCUMENT FOR ERRORS OR NEEDED CHANGES *Note*: For purposes of illustration, the date of the letter is not correct and the date of the meeting says *No Date*, because there was no linked event in the matter file.	For purposes of illustration, save the letter without changes.	

Generating and Saving Document Templates in Practice Manager (*continued*)

GOAL	ACTION	RESULT
OPEN A FOLDER FOR DOCUMENTS FOR THE MATTER AND SAVE THE DOCUMENT IN THE ABACUSLAW DOCS FOLDER *Note*: Use Windows Explorer to find the folder with the *matter number* in the Docs folder in AbacusLaw on your computer. *Note*: The date of the letter is not correct.	**CLICK** *Save As* in Word processor **RIGHT CLICK** on *ABACUS\Docs* **CLICK** *New* **CLICK** *Folder* **ENTER** *1235* as matter ID number **CLICK** *Folder* **ENTER** *Settlement letter* as Name of document **CLICK** *OK*	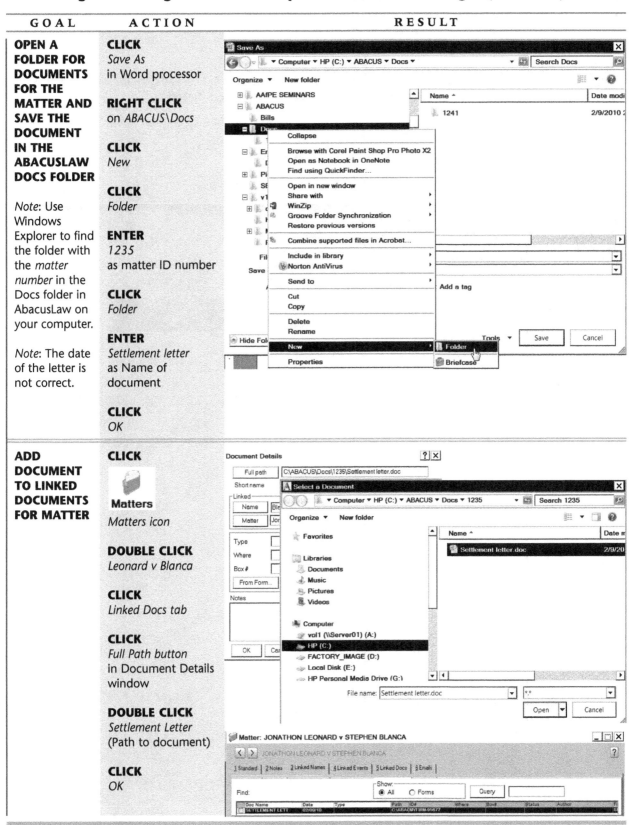
ADD DOCUMENT TO LINKED DOCUMENTS FOR MATTER	**CLICK** **Matters** *Matters icon* **DOUBLE CLICK** *Leonard v Blanca* **CLICK** *Linked Docs tab* **CLICK** *Full Path button* in Document Details window **DOUBLE CLICK** *Settlement Letter* (Path to document) **CLICK** *OK*	

Exit AbacusLaw.

HOW CAN I RETRIEVE A DOCUMENT FROM LINKED DOCS IN A MATTER?

One of the biggest time savers in AbacusLaw is the ability to set up *linked documents* to a matter. The linked documents can be stored anywhere on a computer, a server, or a removable storage drive. If the correct path is entered when linking a document to a matter, it can be retrieved and opened directly from the *Matter linked docs window*.

Retrieving a Document from Linked Docs in a Matter

GOAL	ACTION	RESULT
START ABACUSLAW PRACTICE MANAGER	**CLICK** AbacusLaw *AbacusLaw icon*	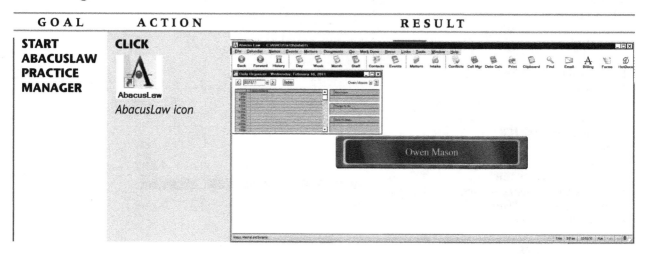

Retrieving a Document from Linked Docs in a Matter (*continued*)

GOAL	ACTION	RESULT
OPEN A LINKED DOC IN A MATTER	**CLICK** **Matters** *Matters icon* **SELECT** *Jonathon Leonard v Stephen Blanca* OR Your personal matter **CLICK** *Linked Docs tab* **DOUBLE CLICK** On the document **EDIT DATE TO** *February 15, 2010* **EDIT NO DATE TO** *February 15, 2010* **CLICK** *Save* in Word Processor **DOUBLE CLICK** on Document to open Revise Doc	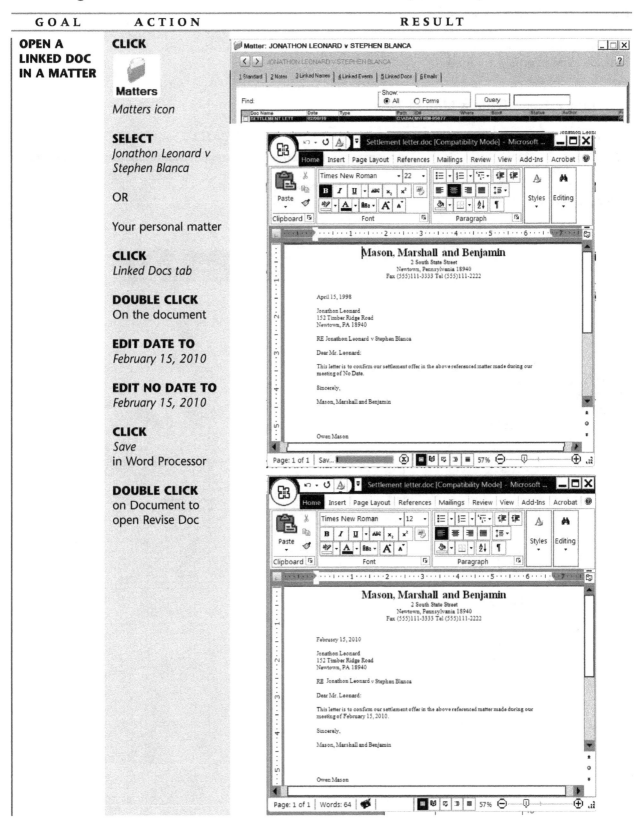

Exit AbacusLaw.

HOW CAN I CREATE A DOCUMENT FROM A LINKED EVENT?

Reminder notes or letters can be created using the date and party information in the linked events for a matter.

Opening a Form from a Linked Event

GOAL	ACTION	RESULT
START ABACUSLAW PRACTICE MANAGER	**CLICK** *AbacusLaw icon*	
ADD DATE FROM A LINKED EVENT	**CLICK** *Matters* **SELECT** *Stein v Curtis* **CLICK** *Linked Names* **SELECT** *Elisabeth Stein* **CLICK** *Linked Event* **SELECT** *Meet* **CLICK** *Print menu* **SELECT** *Form generation* **SELECT** *MS Word*	

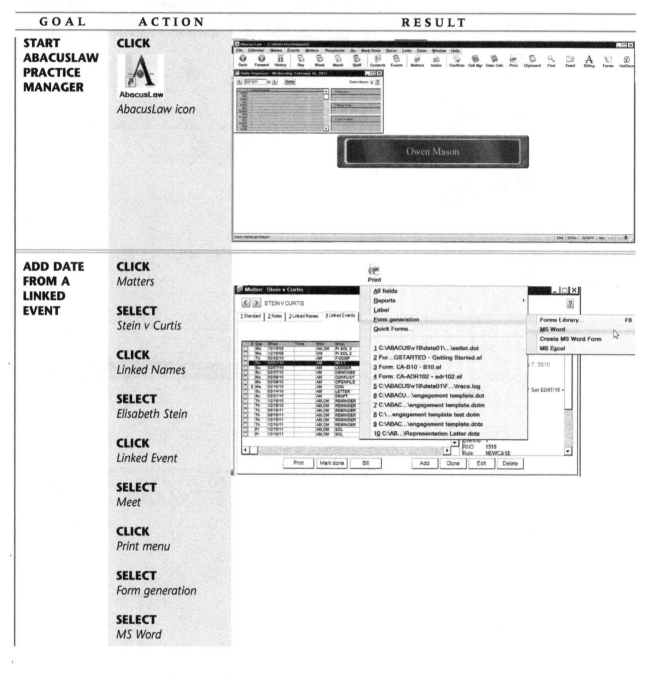

Opening a Form from a Linked Event (*continued*)

GOAL	ACTION	RESULT
GENERATE FORM LETTER WITH DATE OF MEETING	**CLICK** *Forms folder* in AbacusLaw folder **CLICK** *setlet* **CLICK** *Open*	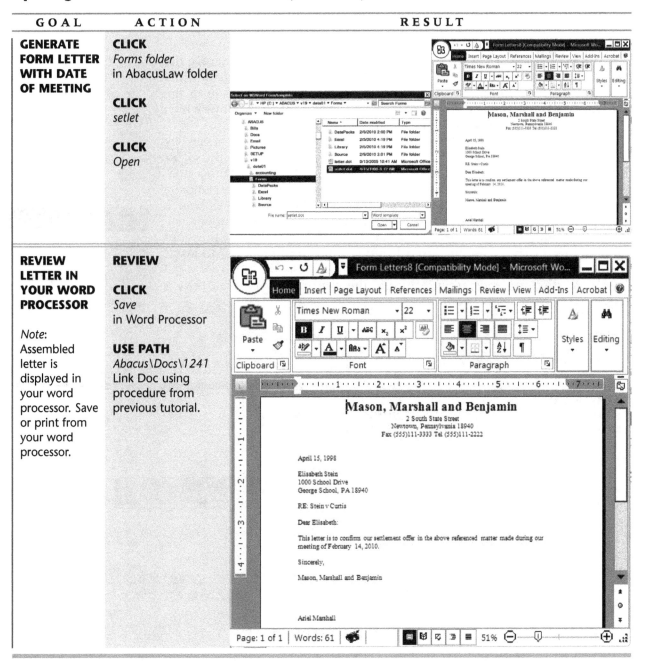
REVIEW LETTER IN YOUR WORD PROCESSOR *Note:* Assembled letter is displayed in your word processor. Save or print from your word processor.	**REVIEW** **CLICK** *Save* in Word Processor **USE PATH** *Abacus\Docs\1241* Link Doc using procedure from previous tutorial.	

HOW CAN I CHANGE THE DOCUMENT TEMPLATE BLANKS?

Any document template created using your word processor may be saved as a document template. The word processor can be used to create and save the document template. When an existing document template is opened, using the Create MS Word Form option, it opens in your word processor, in the tutorial, MS Word. It is displayed in MS Word in the Mailing window, which contains the mail merge tools of the word processor.

You can switch between the template view and the complete form view by clicking on the Preview Results icon in the toolbar. Anything within the << >> is an AbacusLaw entry; everything else was created with the word processor.

With AbacusLaw you can change or add blanks to the document template as long as there is a related link to the information. When you add a blank, a list of available codes for the information will appear from a drop-down list.

In this tutorial you will open an existing template, setlet.dot, use the word processor to rewrite it, use the insert feature of the word processor to insert the current date, and add new AbacusLaw entry blanks.

To use the form generation feature in the print menu you *must* have a matter or name window open.

> **TIP**
>
> Use the Preview Results button on the MS Word menu to switch view after each change.

Change the Merge Fields (Blanks) in a Document Template

GOAL	ACTION	RESULT
START ABACUSLAW PRACTICE MANAGER	**CLICK** **A** *AbacusLaw* *AbacusLaw icon*	
OPEN A MATTER AND OPEN FORM GENERATOR *Note*: Form generator is only available if the matter or name window is open.	**CLICK** *Matters* *Matters icon* **DOUBLE CLICK** *Bates v Howard* **CLICK** *Print icon* **SELECT** *Forms generation* **SELECT** *Create MS Word Form*	

Change the Merge Fields (Blanks) in a Document Template (*continued*)

GOAL	ACTION	RESULT
SELECT EXISTING DOCUMENT TEMPLATE	**SELECT** *setlet.dot* in ABACUS/v19/data01/ Forms folder **CLICK** *Open*	
USE MERGE PREVIEW TO SEE CODES AND REPLACED WORDS	**CLICK** *Preview* on menu bar	

Change the Merge Fields (Blanks) in a Document Template (*continued*)

GOAL	ACTION	RESULT
ADD NEW WORDS AND MERGE FIELD *Note*: A list of merge codes is available in a drop-down menu by clicking Insert Merge Fields.	**ENTER** *Retention of << Firm>>* after RE: in document **CLICK** *Preview Results*	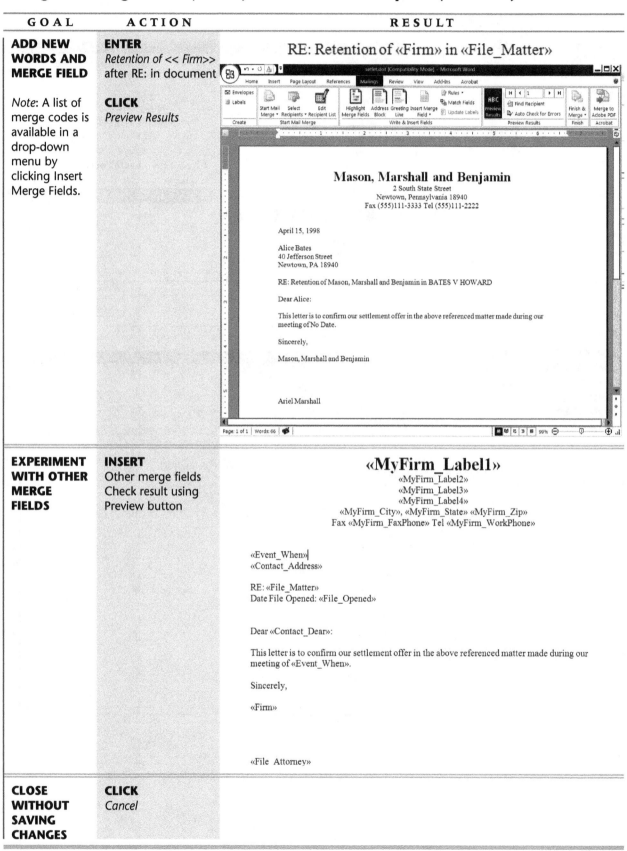
EXPERIMENT WITH OTHER MERGE FIELDS	**INSERT** Other merge fields Check result using Preview button	
CLOSE WITHOUT SAVING CHANGES	**CLICK** *Cancel*	

HOW CAN I CREATE MY OWN DOCUMENT TEMPLATE?

If you can ENTER a document in a word processor, you can create a document template and use that document template as an AbacusLawForms form. The following tutorial uses Microsoft Word (MS Word). Corel® WordPerfect® will also create the same documents and templates for use with AbacusLaw.

In this tutorial you will create a new document template using your word processor and save it as a Microsoft Word template, then use it as an AbacusLawForms form to create a letter using information in a matter in AbacusLaw.

In this tutorial you will use the Microsoft select text function. To select text, place your cursor before the first letter or number of the word or address (ꟾFIRM INFO).

Then, press and hold the left mouse button as you drag the mouse over the letters and numbers to be selected, (FIRM INFOꟾ) and then release the mouse button. The selected text should be highlighted.

With the text selected, click a menu choice on the menu bar. In this exercise, you will click the *Insert Merge Field*.

	T I P

Microsoft Word has a merge document Preview choice on the menu bar. Use this to check the fields inserted each time to verify it is what you wanted inserted.

Save template with same file name. You can always open and edit the file and resave using a different name in the future.

Create a Document Template for Use as an AbacusLawForms Form

GOAL	ACTION	RESULT
USE YOUR WORD PROCESSOR TO WRITE THE CONTENT OF THE LETTER	**CLICK**  Microsoft Office Word 2007 **ENTER** Letter as shown	**FIRM INFO** FIRM ADDRESS FIRM CITY, FIRM STATE, FIRM ZIP FIRM PHONE TODAY'S DATE CLIENT NAME AND ADDRESS RE: Employment of FIRM Dear client: Thank you for selecting FIRM to represent you with respect to MATTER. This letter will confirm our recent discussion regarding the scope and terms of this engagement. FIRM has agreed to represent you in the case of MATTER. I will personally supervise this case. Sincerely, FIRM RESPONSIBLE ATTORNEY

Create a Document Template for Use as an AbacusLawForms Form (*continued*)

GOAL	ACTION	RESULT
SAVE TEMPLATE FOR USE AS ABACUSLAW-FORMS FORM	**CLICK** *Office button* **CLICK** *Save As* **CLICK** *Word Template* **SAVE** In ABACUS\v19\data01\ Forms folder with template name *Engagement Template*	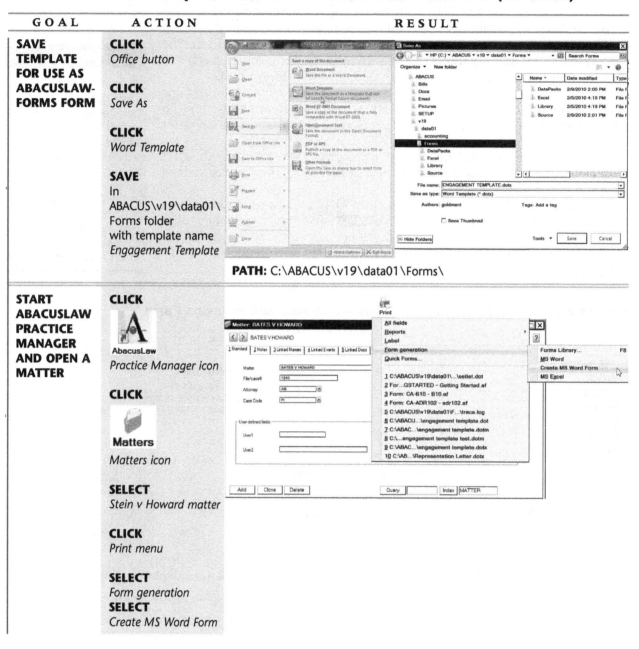 **PATH:** C:\ABACUS\v19\data01\Forms\
START ABACUSLAW PRACTICE MANAGER AND OPEN A MATTER	**CLICK** *Practice Manager icon* **CLICK** *Matters icon* **SELECT** *Stein v Howard matter* **CLICK** *Print menu* **SELECT** *Form generation* **SELECT** *Create MS Word Form*	

Create a Document Template for Use as an AbacusLawForms Form (*continued*)

GOAL	ACTION	RESULT
SELECT DOCUMENT TEMPLATE FROM FORMS FOLDER	**SELECT** *Engagement Template.dotx* **CLICK** *Open*	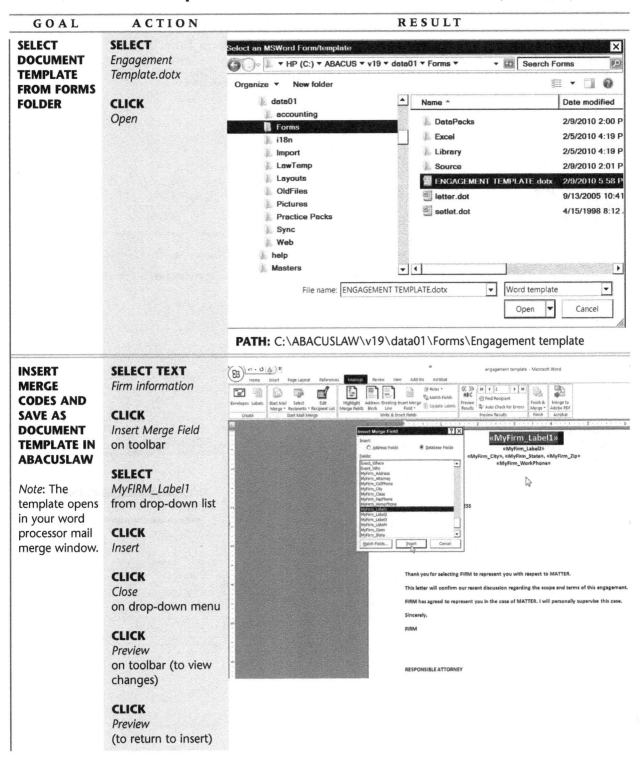
INSERT MERGE CODES AND SAVE AS DOCUMENT TEMPLATE IN ABACUSLAW *Note:* The template opens in your word processor mail merge window.	**SELECT TEXT** *Firm information* **CLICK** *Insert Merge Field* on toolbar **SELECT** *MyFIRM_Label1* from drop-down list **CLICK** *Insert* **CLICK** *Close* on drop-down menu **CLICK** *Preview* on toolbar (to view changes) **CLICK** *Preview* (to return to insert)	

Create a Document Template for Use as an AbacusLawForms Form (*continued*)

GOAL	ACTION	RESULT
INSERT ALL OF THE DESIRED FIELDS *Note*: Client_Address will insert entire client name and address from a matter window. Contact_ Address will insert a name and address for a contact name from a names window.	**SELECT TEXT and INSERT MERGE FIELDS** For remaining items in document	«MyFirm_Label1» «MyFirm_Label2» «MyFirm_City», «MyFirm_State», «MyFirm_Zip» «MyFirm_WorkPhone» TODAY'S DATE «Client_Address» RE: Employment of «Firm» Dear «Client_Dear»: Thank you for selecting «Firm» to represent you with respect to «File_Matter». This letter will confirm our recent discussion regarding the scope and terms of this engagement. «Firm» has agreed to represent you in the case of «File_Matter». I will personally supervise this case. Sincerely, «Firm» «File_Attorney»
USE WORD PROCESSOR FUNCTION TO INSERT CURRENT DATE WHEN LETTER PRODUCED	**SELECT TEXT** Today's date **CLICK** *Insert* in Word menu **CLICK** *Date format* **CHECK** *Update automatically* **CLICK** *OK*	

Create a Document Template for Use as an AbacusLawForms Form (*continued*)

GOAL	ACTION	RESULT
SAVE REVISED DOCUMENT TEMPLATE FOR USE AS ABACUSLAW-FORMS FORM	**CLICK** *Office button* **CLICK** *Save As* **CLICK** *Word Template* **SAVE AS** *Engagement Template* in AbacusLaw forms folder	

Create a Document Template for Use as an AbacusLawForms Form (*continued*)

GOAL	ACTION	RESULT
PRINT FILLED-OUT DOCUMENT	**CLICK** *Finish & Merge* on toolbar **CHECK** *Current Record* in Merge to Printer menu **CLICK** *OK* **CLICK** *OK* on Printer menu **CLOSE** Word processor	*Finish & Merge* «MyFirm_Label1» «MyFirm_Label2» «MyFirm_City», «MyFirm_State», «MyFirm_Zip» «MyFirm_WorkPhone» January 25, 2010 «Client_Address» RE: Employment of «Firm» Dear «Client_Dear»: Merge to Printer Print records ○ All ● Current record ○ From: ___ To: ___ OK Cancel Thank you for selecting «Firm» ...Matter». This letter will confirm our rece... rms of this engagement. «Firm» has agreed to represen... personally supervise this case. Sincerely, «Firm» «File_Attorney»
OPEN ABACUSLAW PRACTICE MANAGER AND USE THE MICROSOFT WORD FORM ENGAGEMENT DOCUMENT TEMPLATE TO GENERATE THE ENGAGEMENT LETTER	**CLICK** *AbacusLaw Practice Manager icon* **CLICK** *Matters icon* **CLICK** *Form generation* **CLICK** *MS Word* **SELECT** *Engagement Template* **CLICK** *Open*	Print All fields Reports Label Form generation → Forms Library... F8 Quick Forms... → MS Word 1 C:\ABACUS\v19\data01\...\setlet.dot → Create MS Word Form 2 For...GSTARTED - Getting Started.af → MS Excel 3 Form: CA-B10 - B10.af 4 Form: CA-ADR102 - adr102.af 5 C:\ABACUS\v19\data01\F...\trace.log 6 C:\ABACU...\engagement template.dot 7 C:\ABAC...\engagement template.dotm 8 C:\...engagement template test.dotm 9 C:\ABAC...\engagement template.dotx 10 C:\AB...\Representation Letter.dotx Matter: BATES V HOWARD BATES V HOWARD 1 Standard 2 Notes 3 Linked Names 4 Linked Events 5 Linked Docs Matter: BATES V HOWARD File/case#: 1340 Attorney: AM Case Code: PI User-defined fields User1: ___ User2: ___ Add Clone Delete Query ___ Index MATTER Select an MSWord Form/template HP (C:) ▸ ABACUS ▸ v19 ▸ data01 ▸ Forms ▸ Search Forms Organize ▾ New folder data01	Name ^	Date modified accounting	DataPacks	2/9/2010 2:00 P Forms	Excel	2/5/2010 4:19 P i18n	Library	2/5/2010 4:19 P Import	Source	2/9/2010 2:01 P LawTemp	ENGAGEMENT TEMPLATE.dotx	2/9/2010 5:58 P Layouts	letter.dot	9/13/2005 10:41 OldFiles	setlet.dot	4/15/1998 8:12 Pictures Practice Packs Sync Web help Masters File name: ENGAGEMENT TEMPLATE.dotx Word template Open Cancel

Create a Document Template for Use as an AbacusLawForms Form (*continued*)

GOAL	ACTION	RESULT
PRINT LETTER AND SAVE IN ABACUSLAW DOCS FOLDER FOR MATTER	**CLICK** *Print* on MS Word button menu **CLICK** *Save As* **ENTER** File name (Save in ABACUS\Docs\) **CLICK** *Save*	**Mason, Marshall and Benjamin** 2 South State Street Newtown, Pennsylvania, 18940 (555)111-2222 February 9, 2010 Jonathon Leonard 152 Timber Ridge Road Newtown, PA 18940 RE: Employment of Mason, Marshall and Benjamin Dear CLIENT: Thank you for selecting Mason, Marshall and Benjamin to represent you with respect to Jonathon Leonard v Stephen Blanca. This letter will confirm our recent discussion regarding the scope and terms of this engagement. Mason, Marshall and Benjamin has agreed to represent you in the case of Jonathon Leonard v Stephen Blanca. I will personally supervise this case. Sincerely, Mason, Marshall and Benjamin Owen Mason

AbacusLaw Product Options

SPECIALTY VERSIONS

AbacusLaw has specialty versions for many practice areas (such as Family Law, Personal Injury, Immigration, Estate Planning, and more). They function with the most current version of AbacusLaw and work side by side with each other to manage multiple practice areas within one firm.

Example: The AbacusLaw Personal Injury Specialty version automates routine tasks in the PI case phases to ensure your case is proactively moving forward. Features include customized name and matter screens, designed to give you the necessary information relevant to each type of contact you have.

The matter screen gives you a concise dashboard of everything happening in your case, including the case phase, court information, client information, accident information, insurance information, defendant's information, and your settlement control center.

FORMS

AbacusLaw is an official provider of California Judicial Council forms, as well as many other jurisdictions. All forms from AbacusLaw are preconfigured so you can automatically fill them from your AbacusLaw database.

Example: Choose the form(s) for your matter and AbacusLaw will populate those fields with a single mouse click. Enter in any additional information and then save to PDF, print, or e-file your documents. Forms stay linked to the matter record for fast and easy retrieval.

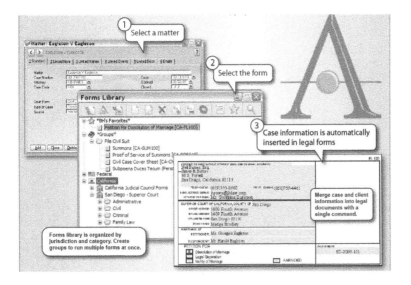

RULES

AbacusLaw court rules are specific to particular jurisdictions. All related deadlines and activities will be automatically calculated and incorporated into your AbacusLaw calendar.

Example: Just select the rule you want and AbacusLaw automatically calculates your deadlines.

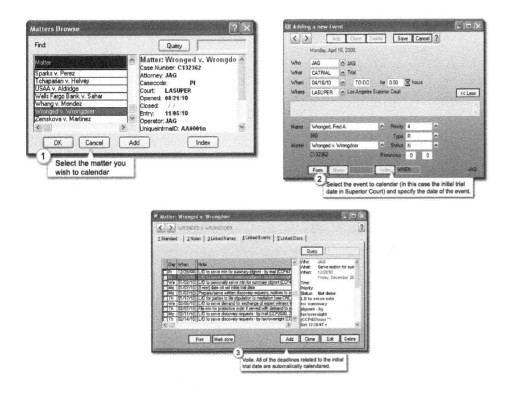

HOW TO ORDER ABACUSLAW

You can continue using AbacusLaw once your demo or academic version trial period expires by purchasing the full version. All information will be preserved. To order, call toll free 800-726-3339 or visit www.AbacusLaw.com to request your complimentary quote.

Frequently Asked Questions

SOFTWARE INSTALLATION

Installing or setting up software on a computer is a relatively simple process. In many cases it is automatic, requiring minimal user effort. A few of the issues that you may find are discussed here.

FIREWALL ISSUES

A firewall is a program designed to limit access to a computer or server on a network. In some installations a firewall limits access from outside sources such as Internet downloads, e-mail from unknown sources, or personal computers not authorized for access. This limitation may include access from the companion Web site or from a software vendor Web site. In some locations your ability to *send* files may also be restricted by a firewall.

Permission to override these limitations must come from the network administrator. If you are working in a law office, corporate facility, or governmental agency, check with the network administrator before starting the tutorials in the text.

RESTRICTED COMPUTER USE

Many schools, libraries, and public locations restrict the users' ability to download and install software programs on their computers. In many locations, anything that might be saved on the computer such as a data file is deleted when the computer is turned off or restarted.

If you use this type of computer access, be sure you have appropriate media for saving your work, such as a USB memory device, floppy disk, or memory card. Many newer computers only provide the ability to use USB devices. Check the computer to determine what can be saved and the type of storage devices allowable.

In some educational settings, the software may have already been installed to allow you to use the program. Generally, you can save your personal data files onto external memory devices. However, in some locations the software may be a network version that will not allow independent use of separate memory. Always check with your instructor before starting work to avoid disappointment when you cannot save your work product.

ANTIVIRUS SOFTWARE ISSUES

Antivirus software is designed to prevent malicious software code (the virus) from entering your computer system or to isolate it from running on your computer. One of the ways these programs work is to look for programs that are self-executing or have the power to install them. The software applications will typically have as the extension *.exe* or *.com*. When you install one of the demo programs used with this text your virus software may try to block these programs and ask for your confirmation that you do wish to install them. Other programs as part of the installation want to write entries into the registry of the operating software you are using. The registry is like a command center for computer operations. As a result, the antivirus program blocks writing needed entries, in some cases without advising users it is doing this. You will know if this happens because the software will not work properly. If you are sure the software to be installed is from a reliable and trusted source, turn your antivirus software *off* when installing the program and turn it back *on* after you finish with the installation.

Remember: Antivirus software is only of value if it is kept up-to-date. Be sure to update the antivirus software regularly—there are new viruses created every day.

DOWNLOADING

The process of downloading software is fairly simple: Go to a trusted source and click a download button. The software will either automatically download and install itself, or it will ask you where you want to save the program on your computer and then ask you to install it after it is downloaded.

Preliminary issues:

- Will the computer you are using allow downloading of software?
- Is it a restricted computer?
- Is there a firewall?
- Is it a trusted site?

Assuming there are no preliminary issues, determine if your computer has the needed resources. For example, downloading the trial version of Microsoft Office 2007 requires a minimum set of resources.

Some programs, like the Microsoft® downloads, may require validation of the existence of authorized or properly licensed software on the computer (see the following validation screen from Microsoft®) or may require the use a specific Web browser such as Windows® Internet Explorer®.

If you are using a download manager, after the program download is saved on your computer you will need to launch the program (install it). This may be done using the launch button on the download manager or finding where the program was saved and double left clicking the mouse button when it is on the icon to the left of the program name. Clicking on the program name may bring up the rename option and not launch the program as desired.

The time it takes to download a program depends on the size of the program and the speed of the Internet connection. It is essential that the Internet connection be kept open until the download is complete. With a large program and slow-speed connections it is not unusual to lose the connection and have to start over.

AUTOMATIC INSTALLATION

Many programs supplied on a CD will automatically launch and install the program once it is inserted in the computer's CD drive.

MANUAL INSTALLATION

Some software will not automatically launch and install itself. The user must find the necessary file to install the software manually. The file to install the software is usually labeled setup.exe, or install.exe, or in some cases launch.exe.

To find the file, insert the CD into the computer CD drive.

- Click on the Start icon
- Then click the Run selection

From the Run interface screen, select Browse and look for the files on the CD using the CD drive letter designation for your computer.

You may need to look in one of the folders to find the correct program. Look for the program name Setup, Install, or Launch with the extension of .exe (which means execute) or .com.

With the desired program name in the open window, click on OK.

ACTIVATION

You can activate your demo or academic trial version of AbacusLaw from the File menu Register option.

TRANSFERRING THE PROGRAM

AbacusLaw may be transferred for use on another computer. Before transferring, make a backup of your data or it will not be available for use in the new installation. Deactivate the program on the current computer by using the Register option on the AbacusLaw file menu and selecting Transfer. Remember your customer ID and firm name; you will need it to activate the program on the new computer. After installation, use the Restore Backup option to reinstall your backed up data files.

NETWORK INSTALLATION

Installing AbacusLaw on a network is a two-step process: installing the program on the server and then installing AbacusLaw on the workstations. For example, in an office with a sole practitioner and a secretary, the program would be installed on the network server and then on the workstations of the attorney and the secretary.

AbacusLaw Message Slips should be installed on a network to allow users to send messages to each other over the network.

Details of the network installation can be found in the AbacusLaw Installation and Setup Guide or at www.AbacusLaw.com

APPENDIX C

Video Training

home > Training > Quick Training

AbacusLaw Quick Training

The AbacusLaw Quick Training modules show you how to perform everyday tasks to help you get the most out of your software. These lessons are available online, can be reviewed in any order and revisited at any time. It's a quick and easy way to learn AbacusLaw, and a convenient method to train new hires. Unlimited access to this training is available to users with current customer care agreements.

  I like being able to access Abacus Quick Training on my own schedule. If I get interrupted, I can go back to where I left off. The information is very helpful and easy to follow."

Stephanie Byrd, Legal Secretary Lebanon, TN

START QUICK
TRAINING

AbacusLaw Quick Training

Select Contents: Training Menu ▼

Navigation

Fundamentals Training   [Syllabus]

Overview - Start Here   11 Minutes
How AbacusLaw will benefit your law office

Using Calendars   11 Minutes
Using the AbacusLaw calendars

Linking Information   9 Minutes
Linking information to names and matters

Using Forms   11 Minutes
Creating and using forms

Using Queries   10 Minutes
Using queries to find what you need

Printing   8 Minutes
Printing what you need

Advanced Training   [Syllabus]

Customizing Screens   10 Minutes
Personalize AbacusLaw Screens

Using MessageSlips   11 Minutes
Send and receive instant messages

Working with Reports   11 Minutes
Using and editing AbacusLaw Reports

Using Rules   12 Minutes
Using rules to calendar events

AbacusLaw Accounting Management Training

Time & Billing	Daily/Weekly Activities	Printing Bills & Reports
Introduction	Daily/Weekly Activities in AM	List of Steps
Setting up Codes	Bringing Forward Billing Balances	Printing Prebills
Linking Names and Matters	Entering Softs Costs	Correct Prebills
Billing Notes and Linked Events	Viewing the Matter Billing Activity	Printing Actual Bills
AM Setup: Company Preferences	Using the A/P Demand Check Writer	Posting Actual Bills
Workstation Options	Setting up Vendors	Printing Trust Checks
Editing Time Tickets	Entering Client Payments	Posting Client Payments from Trust
User Manager	Using Trust	Printing an Accounts Receivable Report
New Matter Defaults	Using the Trust Demand Check Writer	Printing Productivity Reports
Individual Matter Settings	Voiding Trust Checks	Unposting of Bills
Timekeeper Codes with Rates	Trust Check Register	
Help		

Quick training is available at http://www.abacuslaw.com/goldmantraining/

Shortcuts

Print (Ctrl + P)	Print your document. Displays the Print dialog to select the printer, number of copies, and other properties before printing.
Print Preview	See how your printed document will look.
Export as Graphic	Export drawings in a number of common graphics formats, such as JPEG, EMF, and many others.
E-Mail	Open a new e-mail message in your default e-mail program and automatically attach the current AbacusLaw document.
Publish to Web	Share files and publish your AbacusLaw documents as Web pages.
Spelling	Change the way AbacusLaw checks the spelling in your documents.
Libraries	Open, create, or automatically build symbol libraries.
AbacusLaw Options	Set the properties (such as line linking and shape linking) of your document and general AbacusLaw options.
Select New Template	Go back to the Document browser to select a different template.
File Conversion Wizard	Automatically convert files from other programs into AbacusLaw files.
Close Document (Ctrl + W)	Close this document. Does not close other open AbacusLaw documents.
Close AbacusLaw (Alt + F4)	Quit the entire program.

Case Study Material

SAMPLE DATA FOR DEMONSTRATION PURPOSES

LAW OFFICE INFORMATION

Law Office of Mason, Marshall and Benjamin
138 North Street
Newtown, PA 18940
Office Phone 555 111-2222

PERSONAL INFORMATION

Owen Mason, Esquire
138 South Main Street
Newtown, PA and 18940
Social Security Number 123-45-6789
Office Phone 555 111-2222
Home Phone 555 345-3333
Date of Birth 08-19-1980

Mrs. Edith C. Hannah
43 Washington Avenue
Newtown, PA 18940
Social Security Number 123-45-6790
Home Phone 555 453-3134
Date of Birth 1-12-1960

Ariel Marshall, Esquire
621 Merion Road
Old Station, Your State and Zip
Social Security Number 123-45-6792
Office Phone 555 222-2224
Home Phone 555 432-5673
Date of Birth 7-26-1978

Emily Gordon
2916 Boulevard Avenue
Forest Park, Your State and Zip
Social Security Number 123-45-6793
Home Phone 555 468-3335
Date of Birth 1-28-1994

Caitlin Gordon
76 Medford Road
Lawnview, Your State and Zip
Social Security Number 999-11-0000
Home Phone 555-444-8888
Date of Birth 1-28-1994

Ethan Benjamin
12 Schan Drive
Richboro, Your State and Zip
Social
Security Number 555-22-7890
Home Phone 555 987-6543
Date of Birth 6-23-1995

Billing Rates
Owen Mason, attorney $250/hour
Edith Hannah, paralegal $75
Ariel Marshall, attorney $200/hour
Emily Gordon, litigation paralegal $90/hour
Caitlin Gordon, paralegal $65/hour
Ethan Benjamin, attorney $150/hour

YOUR HOURLY RATE, $20 HOUR

Contingent Fee Cases

Thirty (30) percent of the net recovery if settled before trial, forty (40) percent if settled after trial commences, plus all out-of-pocket expenses.

COMPREHENSIVE CASE STUDY

The comprehensive case study is based on actual facts as reported in a National Transportation Safety Board (NTSB) Report. Content has been edited and reproduced in the words of the report to provide as much authenticity as possible. Figures are reproduced from the same report. Some liberty has been taken with the identity of the parties, and no names used represent or are actual parties involved in the tragic accident reported. The use of an actual incident is to allow you to perform basic legal and factual research that will present actual information that would be found in a real case on which you may in the future work.

Multi-vehicle Collision
Interstate 90
Hampshire–Marengo Toll Plaza
Near Hampshire, Illinois
October 1, 2003

ABSTRACT

On October 1, 2003, a multi-vehicle accident occurred on the approach to an Interstate 90 toll plaza near Hampshire, Illinois. At about 2:57 P.M., a 1995 Freightliner tractor-trailer chassis and cargo container combination unit was traveling eastbound on the interstate, approaching the Hampshire–Marengo toll plaza at milepost (MP) 41.6, when it struck the rear of a 1999 Goshen

GC2 25-passenger specialty bus. As both vehicles moved forward, the specialty bus struck the rear of a 2000 Chevrolet Silverado 1500 pickup truck, which was pushed into the rear of a 1998 Ford conventional tractor-box-trailer. As its cargo container and chassis began to overturn, the Freightliner also struck the upper portion of the pickup truck's in-bed camper and the rear left side of the Ford trailer. The Freightliner and the specialty bus continued forward and came to rest in the median. The pickup truck was then struck by another eastbound vehicle, a 2000 Kenworth tractor with Polar tank trailer. Eight specialty bus passengers were fatally injured, and 12 passengers sustained minor-to-serious injuries. The bus driver, the pickup truck driver, and the Freightliner driver received minor injuries. The Ford driver and co-driver and the Kenworth driver were not injured.

INTERVIEW NOTES

OUR CLIENT

Jonathan Leonard
152 Timber Ridge Road
Newtown, Pa 18940
Phone 555 432-1098
Social Security Number 111-22-3333

> Note to file: I agreed to a contingent fee for the personal injury case. Usual rates unless he brings in other passengers as clients, then reduced to 20%. Note: Someone needs to check if that reduction is allowed under our state law and ethics rules.
> O.M.

PASSENGERS

Refer to seat numbers on National Transportation Safety Board (NTSB) seating chart.

1A	Alice Bates 40 Jefferson Street, Newtown, PA 18940
1B	Betty Charles
1C	Clara Donald
1D	Donna Edwards
2A	Amy Francs
2B	Allan Gordon
2C	Clarisa Howard
2D	Doris Issacs
3A	Agnes Jones
3B	Beth Kaye
3C	Callie Leonard
3D	Delia Masons
4A	Ariel Nathan
4B	Barbara Osgood
4C	vacant
4D	vacant

5A   Ashley Peters

5B   Bently Quist

5C   Colleen Roberts

5D   vacant

6A   vacant

6B   Beula Victors

6C   vacant

6D   Davia Thompson

6E   Elisabeth Stein 1000 School Drive, George School, PA 18940

OTHER DRIVERS AND PARTIES

Chevrolet Silverado
    Robert Howard

Freightliner Tractor-Trailer
    Stephen Blanca
    110 North River Trail
    Titusville, NJ 08680
    Day 609 555 9999
    EVE 609 555 8888

Kenworth Tractor-Trailer
    Glen Davids

Ford Tractor-Box-Trailer
    Sigmund Curtis
    5 Swamp Road
    Penns Park, Pa 18943

Sample Data Used in Tutorials by Section

SECTION 2 INFORMATION USED IN TUTORIAL

	TUTORIAL INFORMATION	YOUR INFORMATION
Firm Name	Mason, Marshall and Benjamin	
Attorney	Owen Mason	
ID	OM	
E-Mail	mason@masonmarshallandbenjamin.com	
Attorney	Ariel Marshall	
ID	AM	
Address	138 North Street	
City	Newtown	
State	PA	
Zip	18940	
Day Phone	555 111 2222	
Eve Phone	555 111 3333	
Printer		
Reports	HP LASERJET 4250	
Labels	SMARTLABEL PRINTER	
Envelopes	HP LASERJET 4050	
Word Processor		
Executable	C:\programfiles\microsoft office\winword	

SECTION 3 INFORMATION USED IN TUTORIAL

	TUTORIAL INFORMATION	YOUR INFORMATION
Client Name	Jonathon Leonard	
Address	152 Timber Ridge Road	
City	Newtown	
State	PA	
Zip	18940	
Phone		
Matter	Jonathon Leonard vs. Stephen Blanca	
Court	Court of Common Pleas of Bucks County, Pennsylvania	
Court ID	CCP-BUCKS	
Mailing Address	Court Street	
Mailing Zip	18901	
Mailing City	DOYLESTOWN	
Mailing State	PA	
Court Phone	215 5555555	
E-Mail	www.bucks.gov/courts	
Matter	Bates v Howard	
Client	Alice Bates	
Label	40 Jefferson Court Newtown Pa 18940	
Client	Martin Bates	
Label	40 Jefferson Court Newtown Pa 18940	
Matter Plaintiff v. Defendant	Stein v Curtis	
Attorney	AM	
Last Name	Stein	
First Name	Elisabeth	
Dear	Elisabeth	
Addressee	Elisabeth Stein	

	TUTORIAL INFORMATION	YOUR INFORMATION
Street Address 1	1000 School Drive	
Zip	18940	
City	George School	
State	PA	
Zip	18940	
Responsible Attorney	AM	
Other Driver 1		
Last Name	Curtis	
First Name	Sigmund	
Dear		
Addressee	Sigmund Curtis	
Street Address 1	5 Swamp Road	
Zip	18943	
City	Penns Park	
State	PA	
Where	CCPBUCKS Court of Common Pleas Bucks County	
Court ID	US DIST_EDPA	
Jurisdiction ID	United States District Court Eastern District of Pennsylvania	
Mailing Address	601 Market Street, Room 2609	
Mailing Zip	19106-1797	
Mailing City	Philadelphia	
State	Pa	
URL	http://www.paed.uscourts.gov/	
Phone	215 597-7704	
Fax	215 597-6390	

SECTION 4 INFORMATION USED IN TUTORIAL

	TUTORIAL INFORMATION	YOUR INFORMATION
Firm Name	Mason, Marshall and Benjamin	
Attorney	Owen Mason	
ID	OM	
Attorney	Ariel Marshall	
ID	AM	
Attorney	Ethan Benjamin	
ID	EB	
Address	138 North Street	
City	Newtown	
State	PA	
Zip	18940	
Day Phone	555 111 2222	
Fed Tax ID	23 000 0001	

SECTION 8 INFORMATION USED IN TUTORIAL

	TUTORIAL INFORMATION	YOUR INFORMATION
Employee ID	Mason, Marshall and Benjamin	
Address 1	43 Washington Street	
City	Newtown	
State	PA	
Zip	18940	
Phone Number	555 453 3134	
Social Security #	123-45-6790	
Sex	Female	
Date of Birth	1-12-1960	
Pay Rate	1500	
Last Name	Snowbank Telephone Service	
Label	Snowbank Telephone PO Box XYZ	
Zip	99740	
City	FT. YUKON	
State	AK	

STUDENT USERS

The following are suggested for academic users.

MATTER	CLIENT	YOUR MATTER (Your Course Name)	YOUR CLIENT (Your Professor)
Introduction to _____	Professor_____		
Legal Research	Professor_____		
Civil Litigation	Professor_____		
Family Law	Professor_____		
Technology in the Law Office	Professor_____		
Torts	Professor_____		
Contracts	Professor_____		

Glossary

AbacusLaw forms library   A collection of AbacusLawForms.

AbacusLaw message slip   Instant messaging system in AbacusLaw.

AbacusLawForms   Documents created by Abacus for use in AbacusLaw that have blank spaces (fields) into which information from matters, names, and events in AbacusLaw may be inserted.

Activate   Online transfer of the customer ID and firm name from the computer on which the software will be used.

Assigned attorney   The attorney responsible for the case and everyone who works on it.

Backup   Saving the data files.

Bill to   The client or other party, such as an insurance company or corporation, who is paying the legal fees.

Bill to link   A link between the AbacusLaw matter and Abacus Accounting for the party to whom bills are sent.

Capital contribution   Amounts paid in by the owners of the business or firm.

Case codes   The types of law practiced by your firm.

Case management   Maintaining all the information about a case or matter.

Class codes   The role of the person, such as attorney, adjuster, or applicant.

Clone   A function allowing another form or item to be duplicated and modified while preserving the original item.

Code description   Descriptions for the codes.

Codes   Abbreviations used in classifying information in matters, names, and events windows in the AbacusLaw database.

Common trust fund   An account that may contain the funds of multiple clients.

Conflict check report   Report showing a comparison of names to determine if they appear in a list of clients, attorneys, or others with whom there may be a conflict of interest.

Conflict checks Comparing names against a list to determine conflict of interest.

Conflict of interest Representing one client that will be directly adverse to the interest of another client, the attorney, or another third party not a client.

Contact An individual name and related information about that person or company.

Contact management Creating and maintaining a list of names and related information.

Context sensitive help Help on the item currently being used.

Contingency fee A case on which a fee is only collected if successful and the fee is typically based on a percentage.

Customer ID A number provided by Abacus to licensed users required to activate and register AbacusLaw.

Database A collection of information organized by types of information.

Demand check writer Abacus Accounting check writing module.

Demo mode In Abacus, a limitation on the functionality of certain features.

Docs folder A folder on the computer for storing documents related to a matter.

Document management Maintaining a comprehensive listing of all documents in a case or matter for easy access and reference.

Document templates Letters, memos, court forms, and other documents created using a word processor such as Corel® WordPerfect® or Microsoft Word, that have blank spaces (fields) that may be automatically filled out using information in AbacusLaw.

Drag and drop A computer function using the mouse to select and move an item to another location on the computer.

Ethics rules Rules of conduct for members of the legal profession, the violation of which may, for an attorney, result in the loss of the right to practice law.

Event Anything you add to a calendar.

Fields Individual pieces of information, typically a vertical column in a database.

File/case number The number used to identify a specific matter.

Files Specific documents and computer information; a single data document.

Firm name The name as provided to Abacus as the registered name at the time of purchase or pre-registration.

Folders A location on a computer containing subfolders and files.

Forms folder A folder on the computer for storing templates and forms.

Free time calendar Shows any periods of time when staff members or places and equipment are not scheduled.

Intake form A form with fields for specific information about the person and case that will be automatically entered into a matter or name window.

Interest on lawyer trust account rules (IOLTA) An interest-bearing account used when the individual amounts per client are too small to justify the cost of setting up and maintaining a separate account for the client, with the interest going to a designated state agency.

Linked documents Documents with a path, in a matter, that may be used to access or retrieve a document.

Names ID number The identifying number or letters for an individual name or contact in AbacusLaw.

Name window The screen that is used to add, edit, delete, and view information about the people in the names or contacts database.

Network installation One or more computers connected to a network server.

Operating account An account used by a firm to deposit fees and from which bills are paid.

Organizer A daily calendar.

Path The location to a specific item on a computer identifying the storage device designation, the folder, any subfolders, and the file name.

Payee One to whom a check or other negotiable instrument is payable.

Populate A menu option in Court setup used to determine if a court has already been defined by Abacus.

Post bills To add bills to the accounting records.

Prebill A preliminary bill used to verify accuracy and allow timekeepers and managers to make adjustments before the final bill is prepared and submitted to the client.

Query Search terms used to find information in the database.

Rates schedule A schedule of the hourly rates charged for different types of work or clients.

Record In a database, information about one specific person or item.

Recurring expenses Charges for goods and service paid on a regular basis.

Report Data from the database in an organized presentation.

Rules (calendar) An automated process of entering event dates and generating reminders.

Seniority level The order in which timekeeper information is presented in reports.

Server Any computer on a network that contains data or applications shared by users of the network on their client (workstation) computers.

Single-user program Authorized for installation on one computer.

Speed bar A menu on the desktop for selecting a specific matter to be worked on within a specific time range.

Table In a database, a collection of information about one item or subject matter, usually organized in rows and columns.

Task-based billing codes   Established by the American Bar Association and used to organize time entries by category to meet the American Bar Association billing standards.

Task-based code   Categories used to organize time.

Templates   See document template.

Time ticket   A record of time spent on an activity.

Time ticket codes   Codes (abbreviations) used to identify an activity.

Timekeeper   Anyone who keeps time records.

Timekeeper code   An abbreviation and description identifying the individual timekeeper, usually that person's initials.

Transfer   The process of unregistering the use of AbacusLaw on one computer and registering and activating it on a new computer.

Trust account   Account for funds belonging to a client or other person.

User   A person with a license to use the program and make entries and generate reports.

Valid entries   Those items that have been added to a list that the program will recognize.

What codes   Specific activities, usually related to billing.

Where codes   The location where an event will be held.

Who code   Shortcut for the program to locate related information about a person, thing, or place that has or may have a calendar.

Windows Explorer   Microsoft® tool for seeing the contents of computers, folders, and files.

Workstation   A computer connected to a network that is used for access consisting of a monitor, input device, and computer.